REDEFINING FINANCIAL SERVICES

REDEFINING

FINANCIAL

SERVICES

The new renaissance in value propositions

Joseph A. DiVanna

© Joseph A. DiVanna 2002

First published 2002 by
PALGRAVE MACMILLAN
Houndmills, Basingstoke, Hampshire RG21 6XS and
175 Fifth Avenue, New York, N.Y. 10010
Companies and representatives throughout the world

PALGRAVE MACMILLAN is the global academic imprint of the Palgrave Macmillan division of St. Martin's Press, LLC and of Palgrave Macmillan Ltd. Macmillan® is a registered trademark in the United States, United Kingdom and other countries. Palgrave is a registered trademark in the European Union and other countries.

ISBN 0–333–99552–X hardcover

This book is printed on paper suitable for recycling and made from fully managed and sustained forest sources.

A catalogue record for this book is available from the British Library.

A catalog record for this book is available from the Library of Congress.

10 9 8 7 6 5 4 3 2 1
11 10 09 08 07 06 05 04 03 02

Editing and origination by Aardvark Editorial, Mendham, Suffolk

Printed and bound in Great Britain by
Creative Print & Design (Wales), Ebbw Vale

To my parents, who gave me the tools, to my wife Isabel,
who gave me a push, and to Glenn Mangurian, whose courage
to face insurmountable hurdles continues to amaze and inspire me

CONTENTS

LIST OF FIGURES

PREFACE

The phrase 'financial services' is very new in the lexicon, having been coined by Harry Freeman at American Express in 1979; however, intermediaries performing financial services have existed for a very long time. At the present time, financial services companies have one thing in common: the new face of competition. The evolution of technology and the rise in computer literacy are redefining the nature of money and transforming the financial services industry. In this book we ask the questions: When is a bank a bank, and do banks still add value? The Internet has been heralded as a mechanism that is revolutionizing the financial services industry. However, the Internet and the business capabilities that are possible are not magic; they are simply a means to an end, not an end in itself. Technology continues to alter the way in which financial services conduct business and deliver services. Still, financial services firms who intend to survive over the next fifty years must have one main purpose: generating value for customers.

This book examines the value propositions of financial intermediaries, from their formation in thirteenth-century Florence to the current global market trends, providing a glimpse into the future of banking, and presenting a compilation of ideas, concepts and solutions from traditional firms to new market entrants around the world. We introduce the concept of value proposition in Part I, as well as a brief example of successful value propositions in history.

In Part II, The Future of Banking Services, we seek to explain what is changing in the offerings of financial services and in the financial services industry itself. Focus will be given to the activity of consumers, technology, economic forces, new market entrants and collaboration between businesses. It is our purpose to examine how these factors, coupled with globalization, taxation and the Internet, are reshaping the very nature of how financial services compete in the new economy. Additionally, we will explore the ways in which companies have been creating new value propositions over the past decade and the impact of the lack of a value proposition to other companies in our case studies. Some of the ideas presented here were partially published by IBM's *Building and Edge* magazine.

Part III focuses on where the changes in the financial services industry are happening. Global Viewpoints will offer an appraisal of contemporary elements such as globalization and the various definitions that the term has in today's world. It is the purpose of this section to put forward an alternative to the idea that all services are created equally and technology will be the only mechanism for market differentiation. Rather, it is our opinion that monitoring global trends, or, more importantly, observing how organizations are meeting the challenges of global, regional and local competition, provides a mosaic of solutions, product ideas and service offerings that reveal the complex fabric of product offerings that financial services companies must develop in order to compete. This section poses the question: Is globalization a question or an answer?

Part IV, The Future of Payment Systems, examines how financial services offerings are changing and will change over the next decades. We shall present technology, telecommunications, infrastructure and a host of delivery mechanisms as the cornerstone to competing in the new competitive landscape of financial services. The continued evolution of technology, social adoption or 'appetite', and organizations' ability to absorb change are the next wave of challenges for financial services firms operating to a global agenda. This section presents a variety of technological trends facing financial services firms and provides an insight into interpreting these market forces into a comprehensive set of strategies. The section labours at the question: What should financial services firms be doing to prepare for the future? A few of the chapters in this section were featured in IBM's *Building and Edge* magazine.

Part V, eMarketplaces: the New Frontier for Services, concentrates on why the financial services industry is changing. The introduction of eMarketplaces is an area overlooked by financial services firms because of its early stage of business maturity. The demand for global connectedness is creating areas of opportunity that traditional banks are unable to adapt to and capitalize on. These eMarketplaces provide a host of new value-added services which redefine the nature of financial services and present fertile ground for experimentation, product development, brand recognition and relationship-building between customers, partners and niche market players. This section introduces the need for financial services firms to develop a clear value proposition and craft new services that offer value-added transactions with new areas of revenue opportunities. Companies are asked to consider the question of redefining not only what they sell and how they sell it but to contemplate restructuring the organization for value, moving away from traditional hierarchical structures. Additionally, this section launches the idea of a double-sided value proposition in eMarket-places: the customer side and the shareholder side.

As a conclusion, we provide insight into how to develop a twenty-first-century action agenda to compete in the ever-changing global market-place. From direct observation, trend interpretation and analysis, the reader considers the development of an agenda for action as a continuous process, not as a simple planning technique. The intent is to alert individuals in the financial services industry to consider an array of factors that are often overlooked in developing strategic initiatives, but are now the nexus between competitive advantage and organizational shortcomings.

JOSEPH A. DIVANNA

Acknowledgements

First of all, I wish to acknowledge Richard Buckminster Fuller, whose lecture at Hood College in 1978 changed my perspective on everything, causing me to question and investigate how things work and challenge why they came to be.

I wish to thank my numerous colleagues at CSC Index who exemplify Fuller's dream of doing more with less by questioning why things work the way they do and searching for new answers. I would especially like to acknowledge Jim Champy, David Sutherland, Judi Rosen, Saj Nicole Joni, Steve Stanton, Richard Pawson, John Thompson, Al Levkis, Nick Vitalari, Karen Crennan, Karen Rancourt and David Robinson for their insight, mentoring and patience in challenging my ideas and encouraging me to embrace the white sheet of paper as the first step in business process design. I am especially grateful to Jay Rogers, a friend, sounding board and longtime thought partner, who introduced me to the human side of business at CSC Index.

Developing a point of view that spans so many geographic markets could not have been possible without the fellowship and exchange of ideas between many individuals in the financial services industry. I would like to acknowledge Mark Sievewright, John Stone, Jim Eckenrode, Fred Albright and many other colleagues of the Tower Group Research and Advisory Services for their knowledge, wisdom and insight into how the future of financial services will function. Bridging the gap between technology research and reality, I would like to thank Roy Frangione and Jeff Bartman from the IBM Corporation for facilitating many intense debates on how technology affects society. Additional thanks to Ralph Richards, independent consultant with UBS and First Boston, for providing insight into the European marketplace and Daragh O'Byrne from Kindle Banking Systems for his diligence in reading the original manuscript.

As for writing this text, a special thanks to Sir Peter Cochrane, whose kind words of encouragement urged me to write this book. I would like to give special recognition to Professor Patrick Bateson, Provost of King's

College, Cambridge, whose kindness and friendship made the continuation of my research into the ways of medieval craftsmen possible. I am forever grateful to my publishing editor Stephen Rutt for his willingness to take the ideas found in my lectures and formulate them into this text. It should also be noted this book could not have been developed without the inter-action, dialogue and exchange of ideas of the countless people who have attended my lectures.

Finally and most importantly, an enormous thank you to my wife Isabel for her tireless hard work at reading, editing and assisting in the construc-tion of the manuscript.

PART I

Introduction to Value Propositions

Man's technological potential is not only greater than we imagine, but greater than we can imagine.[1]

Since the birth of modern banking in thirteenth-century Italy, the role of the financial intermediary has continuously adapted to the changes in social attitudes regarding the exchange of value between parties. Encapsulated in transactions such as usury, investments, insurance, foreign exchange and commercial lending, this adaptation rapidly followed the evolution of technology, usually as a mechanism to supplement the process of intermediating. In each century, the definition of financial services was clear: the role of banking was to broker a transaction as a third party with an implied trust that provided a safe haven for the resulting exchange of value. The banking, insurance, capital markets and other financial sectors represent firms that span the entire spectrum of technology adopters from early implementers to laggards.

Traditionally, technology has then been employed by financial institutions to lower operating cost and, more recently, to offer new services. Now technology has advanced to the point where it can fundamentally change not only the role of the financial intermediary, but the social contract of trust in an exchange of value. Digital certification technology enables an expressed trust between parties that was previously enjoyed by the basic value proposition supplied by a bank. However, unlike previous implementations of technology, the current combination of computer and telecommunication technology known as the 'Internet effect' or 'disinter-mediation' reduces the need for an intermediary, which traditionally has been the primary function of financial institutions.[2]

Coupled with the Internet effect, the continued invention of digital currency with its expressed level of trust in its certification of value raises the question of whether traditional banks still add value in the new economy. This combination of trust-enabling technologies is at the early stages of development and implementation. One can extrapolate the broad use of these technologies to an end point which surmises that, over time, a technologically expressed trust may circumvent the need for an implied trust. The first impact of the Internet is an examination of a bank's funda-mental value proposition, the shift from an implicit to an explicit trust. Is it more risky to purchase shares of stock directly from a company, or just more costly? If the movement of the underlying share price is taken as a given, the cost of purchase is proportional to the perceived value in the marketplace. Therefore, it can be said that the value of the intermediary rests in the establishment, development and facilitation of the market, and not in the brokering of a transaction.

Will an expressed level of trust replace the implied trust that financial institutions have enjoyed as incumbents in a mature marketplace? The history of business provides numerous examples of how the perception of trust in a particular technology changes as the mechanism and use of the technology matures. The early commercialization of electricity by Thomas Edison is an illustration of a new, unproven, immature technology with indefinable potential that was misunderstood and even distrusted by the average consumer at its inception. As a new market entrant into an estab-lished gas utility market, Edison needed to create a value proposition that would unseat the incumbent industry. He therefore divided the problem of commercializing electricity by addressing ten facets of building an implied and expressed trust in the technology as the focus of how to bring the product to market. Edison's plan was simple: change the rules, shift the focus and educate the consumer to facilitate the abandoning of the entrenched natural gas infrastructure for his new suite of technologies based on electricity.

In order to jettison the rules and the focus, a fundamental shift from the male gender to the female gender as the principal decision maker at that time needed to occur. During the latter part of the nineteenth century and early twentieth century, men developed a curiosity about how things worked. This was especially true in the area of scientific technology and other gadgetry where this rising interest was spawning a generation of technocrats. In a contemporary example to which anyone can relate, the same market behaviour happened with the rise of PCs, shifting the primary buyer from data-processing people to ordinary individuals. The average person became knowledgeable enough to purchase the device and the industry specialist or data-processing people resisted and, in some cases, resented unsophisticated users evolving into primary technology acquirers. Edison circumvented the uphill push of electric technology by changing the target audience and catering to women.

The ten facets that Edison addressed were:

■ *Perceived advantage:* electric light was brighter than gas flame;

■ *Compatibility:* the installation used existing gas lines to run wires, thereby optimizing the idea to use existing infrastructure;

■ *Perceived simplicity:* the sales pitch was on the operation of the light which focused on the light switch, not the infrastructure and fuse box;

■ *Divisibility:* where would you like one? The offer was to install one light per house, to start typically in the living room, and let the technology sell itself over time;

■ *Communicability:* Edison used gas industry terms to describe the components of the new technology so as not to alienate individuals;

■ *Reversibility:* Edison waited to see the reaction if a customer wanted to reverse their decision;

■ *Relative costliness:* electricity was six times more expensive than gas, but housewives did not have to clean the soot off walls and ceilings;

■ *Reliability:* in Edison's time, this was not a significant consumer concern;

■ *Credibility:* his credibility was associated with his other inventions and his popularity;

■ *Failure consequence:* the failure of the new technology was no worse than that of the old technology. If the electric light failed, you would be in the dark; if the gaslight failed, an explosion could result in your death.

These were the basis of Edison's value proposition against the incumbent gas technology and were used as the baseline for the use of electricity, not only for his own benefit, but also for the birth of the new industry. Edison's ability to see beyond the technology to its long-term value proposition to customers is best said by Francis Robbins Upton, president of Edison Pioneers:

> It was largely Mr. Edison's work to make real and distinct the conception of electricity as something which could be sold commercially. This conception is now so widely known as to seem almost self-evident.[3]

The case of Edison's electricity is representative of the successful search for a new value proposition. The reader should not lose interest, we are about to reach the point that concerns us here: at the present time, financial services companies are in the position of being just as revolutionary as Edison was in the past. The incumbent industry, banks, brokerages, insurance companies, fund management, and capital markets are now presented with a question: What is the value proposition for financial services organizations in the new connected business environment?

Establishing a clear value proposition is not easy among the everclosing convergence of technologies and organizations' ability to provide services. Redefining what constitutes a transaction, and, more importantly, establishing the appropriate intermediary to facilitate a transaction, complicates the process of outlining a sustainable value proposition. This seemingly chaotic state brings to the forefront another question: What is the nature of the future role that financial services companies will play in the international business and consumer markets? This lack of definition in the marketplace continues to confuse and sometimes frustrate financial services clients, retail consumers and corporations engaged in business-to-business exchanges. Therefore, it can be expected that the next few years will yield a continued redesignation of the role of the transaction intermediary and, more importantly, the underlying value proposition offered by financial services companies. Put simply, the opportunity for financial institutions is to look beyond the traditional role of the intermediary and explore value propositions, such as those of Edison's, that shape an emerging new industry.

During the last two decades of the twentieth century, financial services firms invested heavily in technology as the primary means of market distinction and product differentiation. As the price versus performance ratio of computer and telephony manufacturing continues to drive down the cost of technology, opportunities for new market entrants continue to present a viable avenue for niche players to acquire customers in all industries. Acknowledging that the application of technology is a key ingredient to a new value proposition, and considering that almost any organization can rapidly purchase technology and duplicate a financial product offering, calls into question the overall value of technology in the value equation. This is not to say that the application of technology should not be a vital part of the value equation for financial services organizations; it is, however, reason to consider technology in the broader context of how a firm defines the value proposition. The value proposition for electricity demonstrated that the application of the technology to the process of everyday life was the foundation of a fundamental rethinking of the average lifestyle or life within the home. Just as important, the attributes and characteristics of the technology were used to develop the brand identity of an electric society. Hence technology is simply a mechanism that organizations employ to demonstrate value, not the determination of value itself. Consequently, during the strategic thinking process, technology is regarded as a commodity and one imagines that technology can do anything. However, this book endeavours to present the opinion that a value proposition must stand alone on the perceived value of the service or product, not on the instrument by which it is delivered. This raises yet another question: If the use of technology's potential is equal between competitors, what is the real or perceived value proposition that financial services firms bring to society and what will shape the new product and service offerings?

A quick search of the Internet for value proposition returns a variety of definitions that corporations and financial services firms have to offer. These definitions fall into two distinct categories: those who believe that simply reducing cost is a value proposition, and those who understand that the addition of value reaches beyond cost reduction to include revenue enhancement, improved quality of product, higher levels of service and organizational satisfaction, the sum of which offers the customer a better feeling about the purchase, not simply a cheaper price.

In that sense, another question comes to mind: Do traditional banking functions have a strong value proposition as technology continues to refine the intermediary processes of exchanging value between parties? The continued convergence of technology fosters the easy and convenient exchange between business and consumers, exacerbating the question: Does society still need traditional banks and banking functions? Are new market entrants in the financial services marketplace providing additional value, or are they simply displacing higher cost operations with fundamentally unchanged processes coupled with lower overheads? In reality, financial services institutions are playing a familiar game, using technology as a new label on the old wine bottle of banking services.

A factor that complicates the redefinition and establishment of a sustainable value proposition to consumers and shareholders is that financial services organizations have inherited a legacy of organizational structures that may be considered detrimental to their aim of establishing a value proposition. The paradox for financial firms defining a new value proposition is that, put simply, in the services industry people are their biggest asset and the structure in which they are organized may be a liability. A cursory analysis of new market entrants reveals that the ability to move quickly into a marketplace, and, more importantly, their ability to adapt rapidly to changes in market conditions, are directly attributable to the organizational structure and the leadership of the senior management team. Therefore, knowing that a radical redefinition of the marketplace is ongoing and a fundamental rethinking of financial products and services is taking place, financial services firms are left with the question: What will be the resulting changes in the business processes within the institution and their underlying organizational structures?

This book endeavours to examine the evolution of banking functions to the emerging value propositions in the new era of financial services. This assessment will place issues such as the adaptation to social change, the definition of services, the impact on the business processes to facilitate these services, and the evolution of organizational design into the broad context of the establishment of a new value proposition for financial services. The analysis reviews these contributing factors to provide insight into the structure of the new banking organization and the establishment of a twenty-first-century financial services agenda. Using a historical perspective coupled with contemporary examples of how organizations are combating this fundamental shift in the industry, the objective of each section is to provide an exploration of the four domains of knowledge (see Figure 0.1).

At the heart of things we know are the events that are observable in the industry and within any financial services company, that is, things that provide grounding, a common understanding that acts as the underpinning in the industry's knowledge. For example: a financial services firm provides a mechanism for savings, credit, investment, bill payment and a suite of products designed to facilitate transactions. One may have a detailed knowledge of the process of any single product line but rarely an in-depth knowledge of the idiosyncratic characteristics of every product and service that the institution offers. As a legacy of post-industrialized, or assembly line, thinking regarding the composition of business processes, the average person within a financial services firm has reached a level of specialization that makes him or her expert in one or a few processes, with

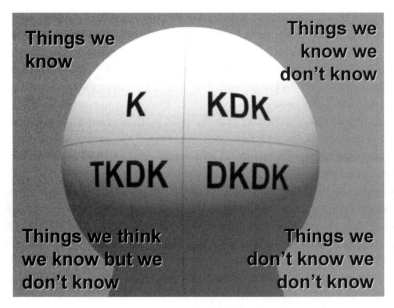

Figure 0.1   The four domains of knowledge

a cursory knowledge of the rest. Generally, the level of understanding of things we know can be expressed as having knowledge about a collection of topics that is said to be a kilometre deep and a metre wide.

The core of things we think we know but don't know is the trends of technology, aspects of organizational structure, consumer attitudes, political volatility and social behaviours in which one may have a general understanding but the dynamic nature of the market makes it impossible to be up to date in every aspect of every variable. For example: a doctor may know how to perform heart surgery but not be up to date on the latest technique; a computer programmer may be a seasoned veteran but not know the latest tool, plug-in or language. This aspect of knowledge that reflects the fluidity of information can be expressed as being a centimetre deep and a kilometre wide.

At the hub of things we know we don't know are things that we have identified to be beyond our general understanding or area of specialization. For example: consumer behaviour, the rate of technology adoption, external political factors, cultural variations and other areas of specialization that we can identify but do not know the process, information or aspect of the activity. One can be a mortgage broker and realize that one knows little about how to perform brain surgery or place an international letter of credit.

Things we don't know we don't know explores the area of experimentation, prediction, and placing the industry concerns, issues, and problems in a perspective that separates content from the context of a larger geo-political, socio-economic agenda. Simply, things which have happened or are happening to which a person may not have direct exposure or experience but may be indirectly informed. For example: how fingerprint-scanning technologies verify that the user is alive by sensing the temperature of fingers at specified points.

The premise of *Redefining Financial Services* is that the long-term value propositions lie in the area of things we don't know we don't know, and, like businesses adapting to the advent of new technologies in previous centuries, the financial services industry is poised to embrace the twenty-first century with the potential to redefine the relationship between individuals and the exchange of value. Thus the object of this book is to explore the four domains of knowledge by examining the past eight centuries of banking, and to offer a perspective on the future of financial services and stimulate the reflection that encourages the definition of new ways to provide value to consumers and business by questioning the way things are done today.

PART II

The Future of
Banking Services

In their book *Reengineering the Corporation*, Michael Hammer and James Champy noted a phenomenon of business behaviour labelled the 'lack of inductive thinking', repeated time and again by financial services firms as they embrace the Internet and other new advances in technologies. In their words:

> The fundamental error that most companies commit when they look at technology is to view it through the lens of their existing processes. They ask, 'How can we use these new technological capabilities to enhance or streamline or improve what we are already doing?' Instead, they should be asking 'How can we use technology to allow us to do things that we are not already doing?'[1]

Acknowledging this phenomenon, financial services firms are continually amazed that new market entrants are rapidly becoming viable contenders in consumer banking.

Consumers' lifestyles, technology evolution, economic forces, new market entrants and the need for businesses to collaborate are changing the product offerings of financial services firms. These factors, coupled with globalization, taxation and the effect of the Internet, are not only reshaping the very nature of how financial services compete in the new economy, but also the way in which these institutions realize profits. For many firms, a legacy rooted in traditional banking often frustrates the organization's ability to fashion products that meet the current desires of customers. This product latency is often attributed to a shortfall in employee understanding of technology, and an inability to alter well-entrenched business processes and incumbent bureaucracies that offer a stable structure in which to work. These components of business have traditionally provided the means in which a financial services firm could operate profitably and reflect the primary element of the value proposition presented by banks that appealed to customers and, more importantly, to their money. Stability, structure, security, and safety best describe the inherent value proposition of twentieth-century banks. However, a safe intermediary that stores money until it is needed to transact business, providing a fiduciary conduit to markets beyond the immediate geography of where one does business, is no longer a guaranteed proposition for sustaining long-term value. As Davies said:

> Technical improvements in the media of exchange have been made for more than a millennium. Mostly they have been of a minor nature, but exceptionally there have been two major changes: the first, at the end of the Middle Ages when the printing of paper money began to supplement the minting of coins; and the second occurred in our own time when electronic money transfer was invented. The former stimulated the rise of banking, while the latter is opening the way towards universal and instantaneous money transfer in the global village of the twenty-first century.[2]

It can be argued that the nature of money and, more importantly, the relationship between money and society has not changed since the time of the Middle Ages. Professor Lietaer, Research Fellow at the Center for Sustainable Resource Development of the College of Natural Resources, University of California, Berkeley, contends that the nature of money is undergoing a fundamental transformation as a result of mutually reinforcing trends in three areas: the international monetary system, geopolitics, and information technology. The first is a result of a transformation of the international monetary system that can be attributed to the awareness that 'Big Money' is now divorced from the side of governments, serving multiple masters and becoming increasingly unpredictable. The erratic behaviour is a product of a lack of an international standard of value, exacerbated by the persistent swing of the US dollar. The second is the effect of the ending of the Cold War on world governments and globalization. In this sense, the new economy is seen as driven by corporations and non-governmental organizations acting through deals and lobbies, whereas previous generations of governments mobilized armies and enacted treaties. The third is the continued evolution of information technology and the effect of communications technologies. Previously, banks were profit centres as a product of their seemingly monopolistic entrée to consumers. Technology has magnified the fact that money is simply an agreement of value between two parties and its transfer can be negotiated using just technology as the intermediary conduit. The digital representation of money now includes credit cards, smart cards, eCash, electronic purses, and Internet payment systems, and even frequent flyer miles programmes and other corporate loyalty schemes which allow customers to buy other linked services, such as limousine transportation, hotel accommodation and in some cases redemption in retail stores. It can be argued, therefore, that when a firm such as the British company Boots the Chemist issues a loyalty scheme which is redeemable in merchandize or other value commodity, it is technically minting a form of value or currency that is backed by the full faith and credit of the originating firm.

Lietaer's forecast of an emerging global bartered currency should not be taken lightly, as it describes a clear opportunity for financial services firms to develop new products to facilitate this new exchange of value as it matures. With a global bartered currency, firms will strike alliances and other business initiatives that will rival government-backed currency, primarily due to the fluidity of the bartered currency. Non-banking firms will offer this service at a low cost simply because it provides another access channel to market. Already the Internet is facilitating various forms of barter exchanges aimed at highly specialized market niches. For example, the International Reciprocal Trade Association has established The Universal Currency, which is a central accounting centre for corporate barter companies and trade exchanges throughout the world. It allows each trade company to expand their members' ability to sell into new markets and purchase needed items unavailable within their system.[3] Other bartering systems are emerging in Europe, such as the Euro Barter Business with exchanges in Belgium, Germany, Great Britain, Romania, Slovenia, Turkey and the United States, swapping one commodity for another without the necessary use of cash. It is therefore an exchange of goods and/or services for other goods and/or services.[4]

However, barter exchanges are not entirely new as a viable business, as demonstrated by Australia's BarterCard Trading Program established in 1991, with current membership of over 30,000 businesses worldwide. BarterCard's value proposition is simply acting as a third-party record keeper using an accounting/credit unit called the Trade Dollar to record the value of transactions.[5] Not limited to goods and services, Ireland's Contranet derives its value proposition by trading in commodities such as

unused storage capacity and the sale of excess inventory. As a trade
exchange, Contranet works just like a commercial bank. Each client is a
business who uses a Contranet cheque book to facilitate payments and
receives monthly statements detailing all transactions and balances.[6] These
types of exchange mostly concentrate on materials and/or goods unlike the
BarterTalent found on BarteritOnline, which offers 'a brokerage exchange
of professional abilities of free agents with the specific project needs of
member businesses and entrepreneurs'.[7] Likewise, BarteritOnline brokers
equity trades for goods and services by 'bringing together equity-rich firms
and vendors who have products and services they are willing to supply in
exchange for stock options, as full or partial payment'.[8] The opportunity for
financial services organizations is to leverage their technology infrastructure
in order to integrate bartered currencies and other value exchange services
into a menu of existing corporate and consumer offerings, linking barters
with loyalty schemas and other incentive programmes for merchants.

The biggest challenge that financial services firms face today is the
lack of a clear value proposition, especially because the role of an
intermediary is being redefined and customers have reservations about
the associated rising fees, charges and services. The future of financial
services can be encapsulated in the following questions: When is a bank
a bank? Does modern society still require their services?, and, more
importantly, if the basic activity of a bank is to facilitate transactions,
why do many institutions levy additional service fees on transactions
required as a course of normal business and not part of the underlying
value propositions?

Catherine England poses the question of whether the economic functions that a bank provides to society justify the need for continued subsi-
dies or oversight in the banking sector:

> More important, attempts to protect banks through federal deposit insurance,
> discount window loans, and government-directed closure systems have largely
> removed U.S. banks from the realm of market discipline.[9]

Previous generations of financial services firms have laboured under the
concept that a bank is a stand-alone entity servicing a specific market
requirement, without considering that the integration of additional related
services fosters the need to think along the lines of a digital value chain,
not simply reapplying technology to the same old processes but fundamentally rethinking how to derive value.[10] As members of a digital value
chain, firms should be examining the incremental value they add to a
transaction and pose the question: What is the relationship of that

value to the cost of processing the transaction, and when will it be commoditized to a value in which our firm can no longer compete? If there is little perceived market differentiation on the value added, it can be easily replicated, and a competitive analysis can predict when the value proposition for each process step in the service will become value-less to the firm that provides the service. Providing a clear, distinctive value-added service will be an essential ingredient to competing as the traditional functions of financial services intermediaries become commoditized by technology.

Traditionally, businesses exist for the principal purpose of finding and serving customers, satisfying a desire or a need. Profit results from fairly pricing the delivered satisfaction and controlling cost. Many financial services organizations have misinterpreted the concept of a value proposition as being merely a low-cost provider, and have failed to understand that a value proposition is the synergistic relationship between market-driven pricing, quality, timeliness, availability and any factor deemed valuable by the customer, and the cost of providing those valued factors and the incremental profit that can be achieved in excelling at any one of the factors.

The value proposition of the digital value chain extends this traditional view of business, using technology as a prime but not exclusive vehicle for doing business, redesigning business explicitly for the digital marketplace, while leveraging the role of digital assets. The key to participating in a digital value chain is not that the traditional rules governing customer needs or the generation of profit have been minimized; on the contrary they have been magnified, because utilizing technology has raised the bar on what it means to be perceived as having a marked difference in how the firm adds value. Consequently, financial services firms must expand the definition of a digital value chain to include non-digital processes, and balance both a virtual delivery of product offerings with the physical delivery of services, resulting in a click-and-mortar strategy, as discussed in Chapters 25 and 26.

Financial services firms must re-examine the value they add to transactions and determine what the primary added value is, if it will remain valuable over time and if it is perceived by customers as a clear differentiation in the market. When formulating a strategy to derive a value proposition, organizations should consider the following factors:

- Technology will continue to alter consumer interaction;
- A clear value proposition to your customers is not an option;

- Do not confuse customers with choices for choices' sake;
- Brand identity must be distinct and identifiable;
- Brokered services must show your value added;
- Mature markets are often areas of great change;
- Major changes in the market create many new opportunities;
- Digital value relationships spread risks and costs.

CHAPTER I

Designing the Twenty-first-century Financial Institution for Value

Competing in the twenty-first-century business landscape requires that financial services organizations rethink not only product offerings but also the very nature of how value is provided to customers. New market entrants hungry to acquire customers are rapidly rising to meet the competition head on by commoditizing prices and providing convenient technology access to products. Previously, technology-differentiated companies with deep pockets provided a competitive buffer between competitors. Now technology is within easy reach of any potential market entrant, blurring the lines between added value and customer service. The combination of skilled talent and technology, coupled with the ability to shift resources to take advantage of opportunities, is the essential ingredient for being competitive. A highly skilled employee needs little direction other than a clear understanding of the desired end result, reducing the need for a hierarchical organizational structure.

In the last quarter of the twentieth century, giving away a small household appliance when a customer opened a new bank account was considered to be practising customer service. This form of marketing and customer retention worked simply because the time taken to switch to another financial services company with the same basic bureaucratic processes deterred most customers. In the 1990s, consumers started examining the total value in a relationship as new Internet technologies, implemented by new market entrants and traditional financial services organizations, made switching convenient and easy, forever changing the ratio of gimmicks to service. Customers are continually raising the bar on what is considered an acceptable level of services, sometimes by simply moving to another provider. Unfortunately, many organizations are unable to detect unhappy customers until too late in the process, having to repair a damaged reputation instead of proactively preventing it. Customer retention is the key measurement of the effectiveness of the customer service process and its success is directly linked to two factors within the firm: the talent of the individuals and the structure of the organization.

Organizational Structure

The new standards in customer service demand a realignment of organizational structure to provide a comprehensive blend of customer relationship management (CRM) and efficiently executed products. The Internet has created an overnight onslaught of new competition and is just as rapidly exposing poorly executed customer service processes in both new and incumbent market players. The Internet magnifies poorly designed customer service processes when organizations simply apply the new technology to an existing process, in many cases making small companies look big and big companies look unintelligent.

People are the financial services organizations' greatest asset. Yet they are continually organized in structures which prevent them from attaining the business agility needed for the twenty-first century. Unfortunately, many financial services companies are labouring under a compound bureaucracy, which is the result of inheriting the functions of fiduciary processes born in the Middle Ages, with compartmentalized, organizational hierarchies that were the product of the post-Industrial Revolution's assembly line.

If one studies the evolution of medieval bankers and the development of merchant guilds, one soon realizes that the fundamental structure of an organization is hierarchal, yet the amount of knowledge possessed by each individual is extremely high and centred, requiring process focus, not single-activity focus. As Marjorie Quennell, a specialist in late medieval history, claimed:

In the Medieval period the arts and crafts were much more representative of the whole community than they are now. The craftsman learnt not only the practical details of his trade, the way to use his tools, and to select materials, but was taught as well to design his work; and all his fellows did the same, working together on much the same lines – all interested in doing good work, and trying to find better methods and designs. All this accumulated knowledge was handed down from generation to generation, and formed what we call tradition and it resulted in the work being extraordinarily truthful. The man in the fourteenth century was not content to copy the work done in the thirteenth, but with all his fellows was trying to improve on it; so if we have sufficient knowledge, we can recognize the details, and say this place must have been built at such a date.[1]

Craftsmen and medieval merchants possessed knowledge of the total process which was a product of their apprenticeship. In the early 1900s, after Henry Ford's implementation of the assembly line, individuals moved towards specialization as a direct consequence of the effect of compartmentalized thinking.

As a result of the assembly line, organizations have compartmentalized discrete functions, distancing the individual from the entire process. For example, few people engaged in the mortgage business can explain the nuances of the mortgage process, a mortgage bank, mortgage bond, mortgage debenture, mortgage lender, mortgage Real Estate Investment Trust (REIT), endowment mortgage or mortgage-backed securities or, more importantly, the underlying value proposition to the customer, or how these products operate with each other.

In sharp contrast is the example of medieval masons, who, as a result of total process knowledge, were able to build insurmountable structures without the need of calculators, computers and in many cases even blueprints. A master builder could describe to the mason that he needed a wall to connect this structure to an adjacent structure, and the mason's accumulated empirical knowledge allowed him to understand the task without the need of technical specifications. The mason was able to sort out the height, width, length, type of material, mortar, jointing, framing and all other aspects of constructing a wall simply because he knew all aspects of performing and directing the process of constructing a wall, from quarrying, transporting, cutting, shaping, carving and assembling the stones and finally installing the stonework.

A simple test for any financial services firm is to find the number of people in the firm who can clearly explain the entire process of what is considered the key competency in the product offered to customers.

Building Agility

As we have seen previously, the opportunity for financial services firms to do more with less requires, in the first place, increasing the working knowledge of each process that offers a value proposition and jettisoning the single-area specialization. In today's job market it is difficult to make a substantial investment in the skills of individuals. However, firms that rethink the social contract between employer and employee may find that, like the investment made in acquiring customer loyalty, the investment in a company's employees yields both loyalty and productivity.

The structure of the organization its business procedures and the skill of the employees all play a vital role in the execution of business processes. Technology provides the tools to reshape how business processes are executed and improved over time, and subsequently it can alter the organization's structure by increasing the capability of the individual. Today's organizations fall into three broad categories of structure; a value chain in which the focus of the organization is the production or fulfilment of a product; a value shop whose focus is to bring together resources to complete a specified task or event; and/or a value network in which the capabilities of the organization are a node connecting a series of processes or acting as a nexus in which to aggregate processes (see Figure 1.1).

A firm that is a *value chain* typically has a traditional, hierarchical organizational structure focused on the production or fulfilment of a single product or product lines. The underlying business processes support the value proposition by simply adding value to achieve a new product. Almost all processes within the firm follow a familiar pattern, and perform a set of tasks that add value and distribute or sell the product. Examples of this are manufacturing companies, or financial services products such as mortgages.

Alternatively, a *value shop* comprises a radically different matrix structure in which both a line organization and cells of specialization are brought together as combined resources to complete a specified task or event. These organizations are often focused on a single opportunity or a group of opportunities that may be temporary in nature with a specific desired end state. For example, the production of a movie in which a range of talents is brought together for the creation of a single feature and the same talents may be brought together for a second movie. Equally, a subset of the talents used for the first opportunity may be used with the addition of other talents for the second opportunity. Consultancy companies are typically organized in this way and can rapidly mobilize resources to respond to a client's needs.

In contrast, a *value network* takes on the structure reminiscent of a medieval guild in which the capabilities of the firm are organized in cells of competencies. These cells act as nodes of capability, connecting a series of business processes or aggregating a collection of processes. The value proposition of the value network lies in the organization's ability to marshal resources to fulfil a process and/or opportunities that may or may not be delimited by time. The focus of this type of organization is the

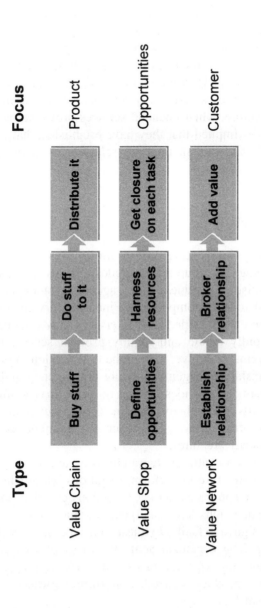

Figure 1.1 The focus of value

customer or, more specifically, the requirements of a customer's changing needs expressed as a relationship between two parties. A participant in a value network finds that the key asset is the relationship between the parties, and the value proposition resides in the continuous reduction of cost as well as the increase in trust between the two parties, which reduces the need for activities such as requests for proposals and other activities that are related to selling. Value network participants often act as relationship brokers, in which the referral of a relationship is backed by the trust of another relationship. Recommending a client to use another value network partner implies a level of quality and trust within an existing relationship. Therefore, when financial services providers recommend an insurance firm, it is implied that they have established that the insurance firm is reputable and has an ongoing relationship with the financial services firm.

Value Creation Agenda

Simply reshuffling the existing organization provides little value as a prelude to reshaping the culture and attitudes towards a customer-focused orientation. Establishing a value creation agenda is paramount to meeting the challenges of today's competition. Financial services organizations must examine their value added in the services they provide, develop a capability to rapidly create and deploy product service offerings as customers' requirements evolve, realign the organization in order to make customer relationship management a core competency and establish a network of partners that provides a broad range of service offerings. Easy to express in words, difficult to perform in practice: financial services organizations are often unsuccessful when transitioning between evolutionary organizational structures.

During the last two centuries, hierarchical organizations encapsulated the discipline and structure to perform operations but left little room for interpretation of exceptions as market conditions changed. In the last ten years, matrix organizations have emerged, aligning products with associated processes designed to facilitate transactions that were packaged into a product offering. The organizational structures of financial services companies fall into one of three broad categories, each with a distinct value proposition; product focused, opportunity focused, or customer focused (see Figure 1.2).

Applying these organizational structures against the framework from Treacy and Wiersema's *The Discipline of Market Leaders*,[2] it can be

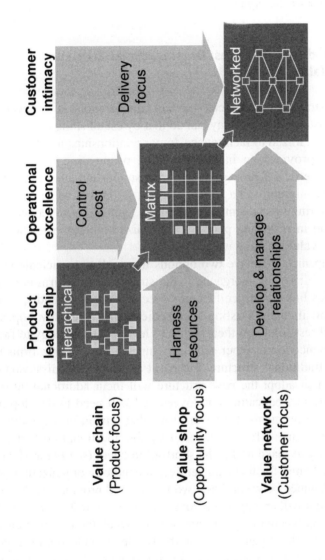

Figure 1.2 Operating models and organizational structure

argued that each organization has the opportunity to excel in the areas of product leadership, operational excellence and/or customer intimacy. However, organizations tend to fall into these categories due to the combination of focus and structure. Theoretically, it could be argued that a financial services firm that adopts the traditional hierarchical structure and tries to achieve customer intimacy could find achieving this goal extremely difficult, because of the organization's structure.

Operating Models and States: Organizational Structures to Support Value

The essential strategy for financial services organizations is to develop a value-added customer focus. They can do that by establishing a network of competencies organized to facilitate customer relationships in which every distinct group provides an individual value proposition to either the customer or the efficient processing of the customer-initiated transaction. In all cases, the migration to a network organization will be an enormous challenge, requiring investments in leveraging technology to reduce operating costs, and in reskilling people to optimize core competencies and work in a new, value-creating way.

Hence, companies will have two options in which to participate in the value network. Firstly, by reorganizing the structure of the firm into cells of competencies linked with collaborative technologies. Secondly, if they elect to remain in their existing hierarchical structure, any hopes of competing will rest solely on their ability to leverage technology to facilitate the interconnection of other cells of competencies. Clearly, firms that remain in the traditional structure will be at a competitive disadvantage. Organizations that adopt the new structure will incur additional up-front costs in training and educating employees and will need to develop new performance measurements. However, firms that remain in the traditional hierarchical structure will be hampered by the additional cost of technology necessary to make up for the shortfall in talent (see Figure 1.3).

The new challenge for financial services technology organizations will be to strike a balance between these two factors and provide a technology infrastructure that will anticipate the long-term trend to restructure the firm as competition and technology alter the way in which the firm participates in the value network. Organizations on the whole are indeed transitioning between states of structure as the combination of technology and customer needs continues to evolve. Technologies that facilitate communications, collaborations and co-opetition are essential to make the transition

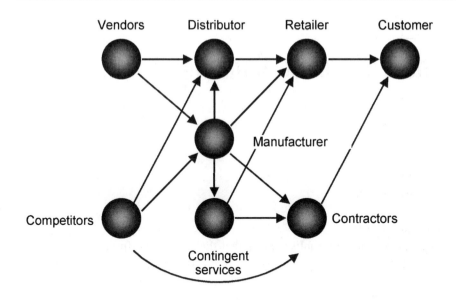

Figure 1.3 A value network

between operating states, and, as said above, the ability to leverage these technologies will be the fundamental building block to compete in a value network.

The financial services industry is in the early stages of restructuring, caused by the early effects of disintermediation promoted by Internet technologies, transforming them into a value network in which cells of competencies (represented by either an entire firm or a department within a firm) offer a product or service that fills a market niche or the needs of a market segment. These cells of competencies are manifesting themselves as new market entrants, previous functions within financial services firms in connection with a niche market, joint ventures with technology firms and retail merchants, and co-opetition agreements with competitors to service market segments. In order to compete in this newly evolving landscape, many firms will be challenged not only to redefine their value proposition to customers, but also to restructure their organizations.

CHAPTER 2

The Future of Banking: $E = mc^3$

Today's media continually claims that the key to the future of banking is new delivery technology coupled with customer relationship management (CRM) software, the next weapon in the technology arsenal to fend off new market entrants and preserve eroding market share. Technology pundits have predicted that the consumers' appetite for gadgets that deliver convenience-driven techno-banking will reduce their sensitivity to fee rates and other financial services charges. The precognition of customer behaviour may be true in a rapidly growing economy, but, under adverse economic conditions, customers typically retreat to the fundamentals of a firm's value proposition. The perception of value is relative to the customers and their immediate needs or long-term goals. This relativity of value can be demonstrated in the rise and fall of the stock markets during the dot-com surge and retreat.

However, the rise of technology and its influence on consumer groups and business is clear. Products and services must evolve to meet and in many cases lead the changes in lifestyles or business climate. The future of banking resides in a simple but strategic formula: $E = mc^3$ (financial products' evolution = innovation mobility + competency + capabilities + customization).

Evolution

Financial products' evolution is the rate at which products can be developed and introduced into the marketplace, predicated on sensing market demand and harnessing capable resources organized under business processes that are easily modified to incorporate changes in demand. Financial products' evolution is not a new phenomenon; its occurrence can be observed as far back as the Middle Ages. Just as medieval markets evolved from local ad hoc places to buy and sell products into well-organized fairs that were centres of commerce, the underlying financial services technology continued to evolve to meet the changes in the characteristics of exchange. As markets matured during the later Middle Ages, the introduction of the widespread use of coins led to a reliance on mints and the transformation of merchants into merchant banks and eventually into the financial super-companies of Florence in fourteenth-century Italy. The transformation of the markets resulted in the creation of new financial instruments to reduce risk, secure transfers and generally facilitate the expanding reach of business. Letters of credit, fair letters, bills of exchange, marine insurance, life insurance, overland insurance, share dealing, dividends, indentures, letters obligatory, assignments of revenue and a variety of loan products that addressed the Church's ban on usury are the foundation for most of the financial services offerings of today. It could be argued that very few new financial services products have been invented since the Florentines.

During the emergence of the financial super-companies of fourteenth-century Florence, technology played a key role in shaping not only the direction of the companies themselves, but also the markets they served, causing an impact in the economy of medieval Europe. How medieval financial services firms used technology such as double-entry accounting, construction costing, maritime partnerships, loan contracts, marine insurance, issuing cheques, bills of exchange, letters of credit and the tally was dictated by the activities of their customers, the merchants. This raises the question that Hunt and Murray posed:

> 'What did the international merchants do?' The answer is 'Just about anything that would turn a profit.' To illustrate this point one can use Pegolotti's *Practica* as an example: under the rubric 'spices imported from the East' no fewer than 288 items, including threads, waxes, rock candy, glue, elephant tusks, tin sheets, and asphalt, in addition to the seasonings, dyestuffs, perfumes and medicinal products that one would expect.[1]

Medieval bankers were driven by the need to generate profits and diversified into a wider variety of merchant trades, wholesale materials and retail goods. These activities were to finance the exchange of goods, but in many cases they were merely reverting back to their merchant roots.

Financial services companies must strive continually to bring new product offerings to the ever-changing relationship between consumers and business. The key to survival in the new eEconomy is mastering product innovation and streamlining the cost of operations. Product mobility consists of sensing market trends, developing a deep understanding of technology and orchestrating these forces into profitable opportunities in which excellent customer service and lower operating cost are by-products, not goals. Unlike our medieval counterparts, the pace of product introduction is measured in days, not years.

Innovation Mobility

The three essential ingredients of innovation mobility are: developing core competencies purposed on rapid deployment; establishing infrastructure capabilities that are quickly connected and integrated into complete product offerings; and creating technology that allows mass customization of these products into offerings that seamlessly enable the customer to select options that meet specific requirements or lifestyle needs. Financial services firms are facing a dichotomy between introducing an ever-widening range of products while lowering their cost of operations, resulting in a balancing act as to where to invest to achieve these goals.

Developing Core Competencies

Competency in core and non-core services is an essential ingredient at the heart of twenty-first-century financial services. Highly skilled people will separate brand-loyal customers from bargain hunters and reduce customer turnover. A recent review of two hundred financial services institutions found that over 60 per cent mentioned people as their greatest asset, yet announced large staff cuts at the first sign of an economic downturn. The dictionary defines competency as the 'quality of being adequately or well qualified physically and intellectually'.[2] A sharp contrast to most branch employees who enter a financial institution with high career goals and find that the investment in their training often falls far short of the changes in financial services products. In the future bank, individuals across the firm, especially those branch representatives who have direct contact with customers, will have to be highly trained in every aspect of the products offered and capable of answering complex customer enquiries. Yes, technology can be greatly leveraged to provide the information to answer a query, but training in the fundamentals of each product offered and, more importantly, in how to assemble or bundle products together as a solution set to a customer's problem is vital.

As technology becomes less expensive for non-traditional sources to provide banking services, and because technological offerings can be rapidly duplicated, the essential component to a core competency will be skilled people as the greatest asset to be leveraged.

Establishing Infrastructure Capabilities

Here again, the dictionary defines capability as:

> the quality of being capable; ability; a talent or ability that has potential for development or use; often used in the plural: a student of great capabilities: the capacity to be used, treated, or developed for a specific purpose.[3]

Capabilities do not just happen; they are developed as a strategic intent and produced to support a business process delivering value to a customer by interaction. Corporate capabilities start at the management team as a vision of a suite of services or a set of products that are then brought to the market by identifying a value proposition to a market segment and developing a business process that fulfils that requirement. The underlying business process is then refined and modified to reflect the normative or most economical set of steps in which to execute the desired outcomes. Then an exception process develops as conditions test the boundaries of the process design. The normative and exception processes come to life when people are inserted into the execution of the processes. The productivity of the processes and the return on investment are directly proportional to the efficiency of the process design and the talent levels of the individuals employed to execute the process. Many failed start-up organizations are demonstrations of management teams that had spectacular process designs, and yet fell short on fundamental skills such as cash management.

Developing Mass Customization

The mantra of the new age of the Internet economy and particularly of eMarketplaces is mass customization. The dictionary defines customization as 'to make or alter to individual or personal specifications'.[4] This definition provides a foundation in which to place this fourth variable of financial product innovation into context by identifying the root problem, knowing what the individual specifications are or guessing the needs of the customers. Mass customization is a western philosophy that places the individual and his or her needs at the centre of the product consumption universe and is the nirvana of individualism. Customization should not be interpreted as unlimited consumer choice, but as an opportunity to allow customers to provide direct input into financial services product design using technology as a feedback mechanism. For example, financial services products can be simply designed to present a menu of products to facilitate business in an emerging eMarketplace. A collection of these products can be organized to facilitate small start-up firms; within the collection, start-ups in a specific industry may have services grouped together as used by other start-ups or linked to other services most often used by firms less than one year old. Technology can be employed to present a wide palette of service offerings and lead a customer to find the combination of services that fit their individual or business needs by pairing options into what appears to be a customized solution.

Even with a highly complex manufacturing process, the automotive industry is adapting to the concept of mass customization with a build-to-order strategy that requires redesigning the manufacturing process and re-educating the consumer. As we will see below, the concept of build-to-order has direct applicability to how customers engage complex financial services offerings, as a customer can assemble a customized solution from an offering consisting of both a menu of prepackaged options and individually priced options.

$E = mc^3$

So how does a financial services company capitalize on product evolution? By seeking out sources that provide insight into how technology can be applied to their business, developing a process that senses and evaluates market trends and determines the potential return on investment to service specific market segments or niches, and creating core teams of cross-functional people who continually assess these factors in order to introduce new products. However, these factors alone will not guarantee success. In fact, new technology focused on retail delivery is only half the equation. Technology infrastructure and the ability to rapidly integrate new technology into the infrastructure are paramount in bringing products to the new consumer. The real endgame is to employ technology to leverage skilled people who can innovate and service customers as requirements change.

Financial services firms are often overwhelmed with the obligation to develop a product offering that caters to a mass customization market-place. Frequently, they overlook the obvious, that there are only a limited number of ways to do banking. Giving consumers customization choices does not translate into giving them infinite options. It simply means creating a comprehensive navigation through a preselected set of options, giving the consumer the feeling that he or she is in control of what services they are buying. Financial services firms can learn much from the model of customization developed by the Ford Motor Company. Ford's website presents the consumer with the capability of designing a vehicle to their own specifications (see Figure 2.1).

Using the Internet, customers select the type, model and style of vehicle and navigate through a series of Web pages that allow them to select either prebundled or individual options. This provides the customer with a wide range of options and creates the sensation of individually designed trans-portation. In reality there are only a limited number of options that can be coupled together, but the magic of the selection process provides a buying sensation that is individual and satisfying.

Financial services firms can offer the same type of ability to select and bundle products, while developing a profile of customer behaviours by allowing customers to enter into the same type of process with services tailored for individual or business needs. This type of product navigation requires a presentation of lifestyle scenarios through which a customer can begin the navigated journey. For example: a small business has a cash flow problem stemming from an inability to collect receivables. In this case, while in the act of selecting product options (or being presented with recommended options that others in the same predicament have chosen), the business may realize that outsourcing the collection of receivables is an option that was previously thought to be cost prohibitive.

Technology will continue to create conditions that provide low-cost entry for new market entrants in the financial services sector. Conse-quently, the marketplace for financial services is fragmented and customers do not have a single point of contact to compare financial services offerings from providers in a simple, easy to navigate environ-ment (or portal). This creates an opportunity for financial services com-panies to reinvent banking and target consumers who are shopping for services that meet the needs of their lifestyles. Surprisingly, brand, company and product identity is now an integral part of how technology is crafted into a new product offering.

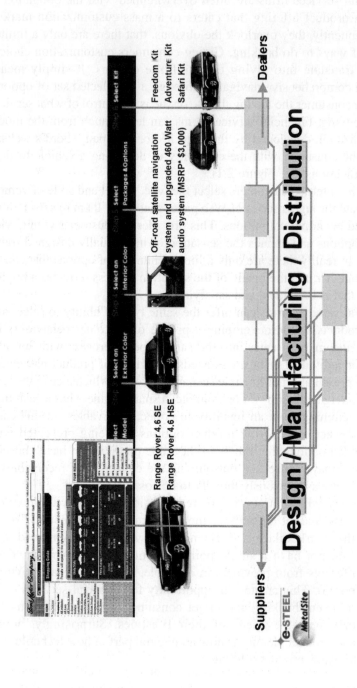

Figure 2.1 Ford's build-to-order process

Niccolò Machiavelli's *The Prince* provides insight into why new market entrants can seemingly pose a potential threat to long-standing customer relations. In Machiavelli's words:

> So let a prince set about the task of conquering, and maintaining his state; his methods will always be judged honourable and will be universally praised.[5]

In modern terms, traditional financial services organizations consider that technology is an end justifying the business means, holding people within the firm as low-value commodities that can easily be reduced in bad times and oversubscribed during upturns in the business cycle. New market entrants are founded on a different interpretation of Machiavelli, in which technology is a means to a business end or state of operations, one in which people are the essential component and technology is commoditized. This can be validated by the insistence of venture capital firms to know and understand the founders of a venture and the individuals of the management team, in some cases in lieu of understanding the technology that supports the venture. In traditional organizations, it is the cost justification of technology and labour that drives the decision to enter into a new product development cycle. Organizations such as Microsoft understand that talented individuals are the key to driving product mobility, and that products are transitory in nature. The transitory nature of technology – and adaptability of organizations and products – is not simply a refurbishment of old products; it is the opportunity to rethink the product and how it is used by the end customer. The key to unlocking the potential to rethink the product/organization relationship is to ask the question: Does the available new technology together with the organization's value proposition change how customers work and conduct business? Microsoft senses the market and adapts the products to recast the nature of work versus the simple acceleration of traditionally defined work. For example, Microsoft Word started as a repaving of the traditional typewriting functions and matured into a product that integrates many other functions such as spreadsheets, graphics and tables to reduce the labour associated with the integration of the components. The next evolution of this type of product incorporates the need to collaborate during the creation process and mass customize the distribution of the final output.

During the next twenty years of Microsoft Word evolution the original premise of typed pages to mimic a typewriter will be lost while the nature of how organizations communicate will be drastically altered. This process of product and organizational adaptation is neither as apparent nor evident in financial services markets, and developing the ability to harness these two forces is a core competency that needs to be developed. To underscore this, one can postulate if Microsoft will be selling Microsoft MS-WORD version-83 in the year 2030, or will financial institutions still offer current accounts that were founded as a mechanism of medieval merchant banking?

Deriving Value from Technology

The medieval value proposition for financial services technology was simple: it applied to either the back office (for example double-entry accounting, bills of exchange) or the customer (for example letters of credit, indentures) if it could be applied to reduce the operating expense or improve transaction speed. Like today, technology revolutions altered the nature of medieval financial services when technologies such as coinage and the introduction of the zero as a mathematical placeholder increased the processing power of calculation over the use of Roman numerals.

Unfortunately, today's financial services technology organizations have been deluged with continual requests for more technology services to be implemented in shorter time periods, along with a growing shortage of skilled personnel. Moreover, delivering these technology services is forcing technology organizations to be more creative in their approach and embrace concepts such as outsourcing, application service providers (ASPs) and co-opetition. Technology groups and their business counterparts are rapidly learning that it is the relationships of technological groups or centres of competencies that are the building blocks to facilitating the value proposition. In outsourcing, in which a function of the business or technology organization is transferred to another operating entity for execution, it is well-defined, measured processes that make the transition, leveraging the relationship of the two parties. Many ill-defined and loosely measured outsourcing relationships result in the eventual deterioration of the relationship due primarily to decaying expectation management. From many failed outsourcing agreements, organizations have learned the valuable lesson that the best processes to outsource are ones that are accurately measured and monitored so that expectations can be met consistently. The emergence of ASPs,[6] in which a component of technological capability is no longer hosted within the firm but at a remote technology management organization, is clouding the issue of the application of resources to the value propositions. The ASP service offering is often misconnected with the technology service bureau of the 1980s, and its potential to reduce operating costs and leverage technology is yet to be fully explored. The ASP relationship requires a great deal of specificity and understanding about which generic functions of a financial services product lend themselves to this delivery mechanism and how a firm's value-added activities relate to the end use of the product. For example: if one is a small banking institution that outsourced the core banking technologies, delivered standard products such as current accounts, loans and other retail applications via the Internet using an ASP, what will the employees do other than customer service? Even more complex is the issue of co-opetition in the area of technology and how it can be applied to the reduction of cost without reducing the ability to attract and retain customers. Co-operative ventures can be as technologically uncomplicated as merely linking similar products together to form comprehensive product offerings, to intermixed products in an open exchange or marketplace competing on value-added functionality, each as its own independent entity. Nevertheless, these relationships that cross traditional boundaries in many financial services firms permit technology organizations to supplement the workforce, allow for the development of a process to create capabilities that rapidly 'cobble together' technology-based product offerings in conjunction with new demands by consumers and business.

So, what is the future of banking? Put simply, it is rethinking the value proposition to your customers on a regular basis and developing an organization armed with technology that can rapidly capitalize on market trends. These tall sounding words could easily be found in any corporate mission statement, often translating into elusive goals that are unattainable when market conditions change faster than the organization's ability to adapt. Indeed, organizations often overlook opportunities to rethink their offerings and are surprised when new market entrants show up with innovations that change the fabric of the market. The combination of low-cost banking software and the Internet signalled an early warning sign of disintermediation in the financial services market that was dismissed until new market entrants began a rapid erosion of traditional banking customers. The new competitors simply copied existing banking products and brought them to market as a lower cost alternative, coupled with the speed and convenience of the Internet.

As traditional products continue to be commoditized, the next generation of financial services offerings will stretch beyond the boundaries of traditional banking products and readdress the value added by the intermediary firm. For example: Do customers still need savings and current accounts, money markets and other short-term instruments that originated in the nineteenth and twentieth centuries? These accounts represent the consumers' quest for higher interest-bearing accounts for short-term funds to the detriment of the financial services firm. Many traditional banking products are processed and administered by often disassociated applications, resulting in the customers' central information (for example name, address, phone number, date of birth) being replicated and stored, in extreme cases, in each and every product processing system. In a variety of financial institutions, the resulting computer systems may contain the same customer name and address for each account opened, resulting in additional cost in the maintenance of the account and processing transactions. Is it more cost effective to administer one universal cash account that combines these offerings into an account with graduated rates that incrementally match accumulated daily balances? The answer is obviously yes; however, the database consolidations and modifications to legacy systems often make this level of innovation beyond the reach of many traditional organizations trying to reduce short-term cost.

The future of banking is the adoption of a process that enables the organization to sense – think – innovate – brand – service, not simply to continue to apply technology to legacy products in the hope of reducing operating cost or luring new customers. This process combined with the $E = mc^3$ formula invites financial services firms to rethink not only their products, but the structure and capabilities of their organization and its ability to add value as an intermediary. This is not to say that financial services firms that do not rethink their value proposition will be forced to close their doors; nonetheless it will result in ever-decreasing profit margins as traditional products continue to be commoditized.

Balancing the Two-part Equation

The product value in financial services is a two-part equation – service and technology. Services are easily attributed to the revenue-generating aspect of the value equation and are often determined by the market's perception of their worth to a customer. Technology, on the other hand, is mostly associated with the reduction of cost, and can be viewed and broken down into a four-part spectrum consisting of bands of hardware and software combinations spanning back office systems, devices to interconnect business processes, mechanisms to interact with external entities, and devices used for corporate and consumer delivery (see Figure 2.2).

One can observe that technologies that perform core banking functions and Internet working are reaching a level of stability due to the overall

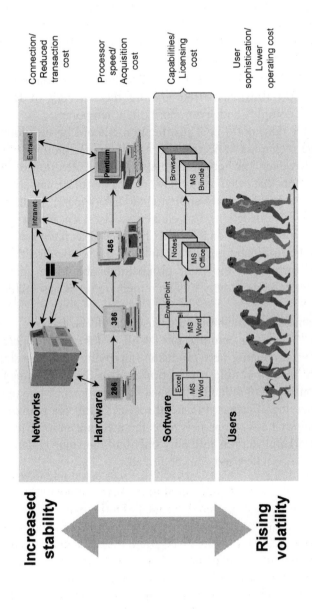

Figure 2.2 The stability and volatility of technology

maturity of infrastructure technologies. What is important to note is that core banking systems are undergoing a silent revolution from traditional batch processing to continuous real-time processing without a major re-development of associated systems. In fact, the relative stability of core banking systems allows organizations to refocus on new delivery mechanisms and concentrate on integrating new technologies. Alternatively, end user computing devices such as PCs, personal digital assistants (PDAs), mobile phones and other consumer-driven technologies continue to be volatile, with short lifespans often making the delivery of financial services products complex and, even more often, temporary.

A value proposition, not a cost justification, should be developed for each part of the technology spectrum to assess the technology's overall applicability. However, services decompose into a collection of tightly coupled components that often do not have clear lines of demarcation such as brand, business process, staff ability, customer demand, partnerships, rates and customer satisfaction. The elements of service are an intrinsic part of the value proposition and need to be viewed as having a defined contribution to the fulfilment process. Items that cannot be directly attributed to the performance of the value propositions should be questioned and clearly understood as to why this incremental cost is associated with the process.

Lines of business and technology groups should be looking at technology as a mechanism to optimize one or all of three areas: increasing market share by introducing new products; improving customer satisfaction by moving from a simple transaction intermediary to managing a financial relationship; and reducing the cost of operations by streamlining processes and service offerings. Financial services firms are realizing that although technology has been perceived as the mechanism to differentiate oneself in the marketplace, it is in reality only half the value equation, and can easily become complex and commoditized.

CHAPTER 3

Pervasive Computing: Really Getting to Know Your Toaster

The avalanche of technologies developed in the last twenty years has conditioned consumers to expect a new wave of devices in ever-shortening cycles, yet the pervasiveness of technology is the least understood aspect, and its implications for a global society are only just beginning to come to light. Studying the application of bio-integration to the socio-economic fabric of human relationships and the interface to contemporary business has barely begun. It is apparent that the consumer's love affair with electronic gadgetry is far from over; in fact, it could be argued that it is only just starting. The rate of technology adoption is increasing with each new generation of potential users. Although all members of society do not share this affection for technology, the pervasiveness of technology continues to impact each individual either by direct participation or as an indirect consequence. The pervasiveness of computing has many implications for financial services companies, and in some cases distracts from a clear value proposition.

Is new technology spawning a revolution in how we work and live or is our lifestyle driving the need for new technology? The architect/philosopher Richard Buckminster Fuller noted in 1980 that the time between the creation of a technology and its practical adoption by society varied by technical category and application. In his words:

> My half-century experience also discovered the natural, unacceleratable lags existing between inventions and industrial uses in various technical categories, which occur as follows: in electronics – two years; aerodynamics – five years; automobiles – ten years; railroading – fifteen years; big-city buildings – twenty-five years; single family dwellings – fifty years.[1]

This commercialization time lag in technology represents the time span necessary to educate the population about the benefits of new technologies, convince society of the improvements that such new technologies bring and allow the business infrastructure to reach a point of production that will make it economically viable. Architects incorporate the practical advantages of new technology into structures that shape our behaviour, while architecture involves employing a more complex process of changing social taste. The matter of adoption of any sort of technology by individuals is an exercise in shaping the behaviour of consumers as new technological marvels emerge.

The same technological time lag can be equated to financial services products and the technologies found in the four bands in the technology spectrum (for example ATMs, credit cards, retina scanners, and the Internet) and should be a critical part of strategic technology planning. Individual technologies can be plotted along a maturity curve and compared to a similar curve indicating the level of social acceptance. The delta between the curves represents the opportunity to experiment and refine the application of the technology as well as a barometer to set the expectations of the firm on the return on investment (see Figure 3.1).

Technologies mature at a predictable rate determined by the innovation of their components. However, social acceptance of technology occurs at a rate that varies from culture to culture or even within the socio-economic classes in one given culture. For example, the use of mobile phones for

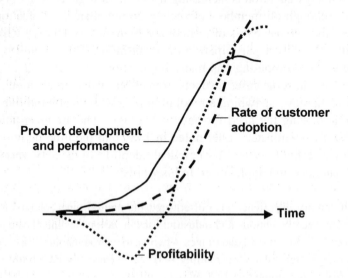

Figure 3.1 Technology maturity and social adoption curve

banking is more popular in Scandinavia than high-tech Boston, Massachusetts. Furthermore, there is a synergistic relationship between technology, people, and how people work in the lifecycle of technology creation, adoption, impact and design. Fuller's observation on technological latency brings into question the accelerating rate at which society is adopting technology. Technological visions such as Microsoft's Home of the Future and the Halifax's Future Retail Bank are early indications that the nature of work will radically change during the next twenty years. It can be argued that not only will the nature of work change, but where one works will undergo a transformation. For example, retail banking will need to rethink how branches are designed in order to accommodate the shift from a transaction to an advisory business, which will indeed be different in each culture serviced. Organizations such as BWA\Chiat\Day, which have radically altered the way in which people think and work by inventing work spaces that stretch beyond the conventional designs of today's business, inadvertently provided financial services firms with a glimpse into the future of financial services.

Technological gadgetry – and the pervasiveness of computing – carries with it a familiar technology banner, resembling the messages from the early twentieth-century electric companies about removing the complexity of life and enabling users greater work efficiencies, that it will provide members of our modern society with additional leisure time. Alluring words, which should be remembered as you carry your laptop, mobile phone and personal digital assistant (PDA) on your next family vacation. Stripping away the marketing hype, pervasive computing is capable of placing the user in the centre of the technological universe, allowing the individual to control the amount of intrusion permissible by other members in the connected society.

Technology is as pervasive as you will allow it to become. Business looks at pervasive computing as a new method of interacting with consumers, whereas consumers should view it as a way of employing technology to perform tasks on their behalf. The underlying dilemma that pervasive computing brings to the surface is the new balance that individuals must strike between work, leisure and social interactions. The product of this balance is a redefinition of when, where and how people work. A strong argument can be made that the impact of technology will be the redefinition of the socio-economic contract with business and a re-examination of the nature of work. It is not incomprehensible that the result of society embracing pervasive computing is anytime, anywhere work. Technology is redefining where and how organizations work by removing the need to be in a specific geography, at a specific time. Many financial services firms, organized under traditional hierarchical command and control structures that were established because of the need to regulate the activities of subordinates, will find moving into a matrix structure difficult unless ample investment is made in training and education. In today's world, manufacturing, consulting and research organizations are realizing that the ability to act (on an idea, customer problem or a host of business challenges) unfettered by work hours, geography or corporate bureaucratic structure is not creating more leisure time for employees; in practice it is enabling a freeing up of work time, resulting in additional capacity.

The proliferation of technology also creates opportunities to redefine the structure of organizations and establish new functional disciplines. A new skill that individuals will need to develop is striking a balance between these two diametrically opposed forces of work and leisure. As the lines between work and play become blurred, there may be opportunities for co-mingled activities to occur. For example, an employee working at home for some portion of the week can order supplies for the office and home at the same time on the same Internet site using two different payment technologies, as well as communicating with colleagues and customers on the telephone and Internet while performing many other traditional in-house tasks without commuting.

Described in a business context, pervasive technology operates within a framework which can be represented by a diagram comprising four levels of conductivity similar to concentric circles in which you are at the epicentre. Individuals can add 'layers' to their epicentre as they grow more accepting of technology and more adept at using its capabilities.

Level One Technologies

The first level is composed of smart devices equipped with microprocessors, called appliances, which are attached to you and facilitate your lifestyle, including home devices, wearable computing and biometric feedback mechanisms. These devices are basically automated methods of recognizing a person based on a physiological or behavioural characteristic. For financial services companies, these devices provide new avenues for secure transactions because of their ability to identify a single individual or entity (see Figure 3.2).

Level one technologies centre on the point of interaction or an interchange of value, either monetary, informational or data. Micropayments, billing data, usage information and other transactions can be used to develop a profile of customer behaviour in retail banking applications. The

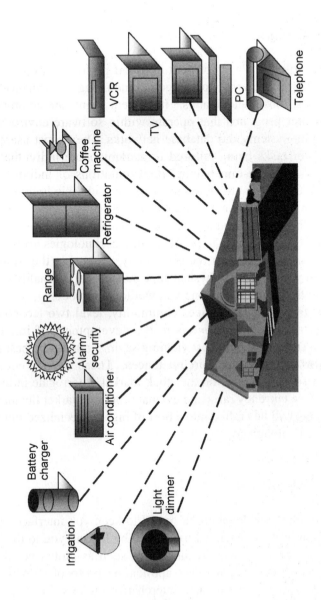

Figure 3.2 The interconnected microprocessor home of the future

same model can be applied to small businesses and other entities such as government departments, not to act as Big Brother, but to optimize operating expenses and plan future budgetary requirements.

Level Two Technologies

Level two technologies that represent you and perform duties on your behalf are commonly referred to as agents, including bio-enhancement, intelligent agents, robots and avatars.[2] Intelligent agents are autonomous, adaptive computer programs that operate within software environments such as operating systems and database networks. They assist users with routine computer tasks being tailored to accommodate individual user habits. Avatars are three-dimensional representations of individuals in cyberspace that users may utilize to represent themselves in both form and task. At the moment, avatars are inanimate objects.

However, in the near future they may be animated to further express the personality that end users wish to portray. These technologies give you the ability to represent yourself in the eEconomy, proposing the following question: When you select the physical appearance and personality of your avatar, will it reflect you or someone you would like to be?

Concerning the financial services community, level two technologies are a treasure-trove of opportunities in the development of intelligent agents that can seek out the highest yielding savings rate or the best mortgage terms to fit individual circumstances. These agents could be employed to assess conditions on the stock market, interrogate individual securities, analyse currency rates and evaluate foreign market fluctuations. Intelligent agents will be crafted into a host of highly specialized functions that have yet to be imagined.

Level Three Technologies

Mechanisms on the third level are designed to keep you interfaced to the relentless stream of data generated by society by linking you to the information that is relevant to you. Technologies such as global positioning satellites (GPSs), bluetooth, wireless application protocol (WAP) and a host of new devices will act as data interchange brokers. Interface technologies are an integral part of the following example. With your smart card's stored value-chip in your mobile phone, you approach a cold beverage machine, make a selection and then transmit digital currency to it by pressing a key on the phone. The machine accepts your token and dispenses the beverage, sends the token to the bank via its cellular modem and transmits the reduction in inventory to the beverage distributor. In this scenario, cash has moved from your account to your card, from your card to the dispenser, and finally to the accounts receivable of the beverage company, eliminating the need for physical cash pick-up, armoured car services, lock box operations and a suite of support services.

Level three technologies present financial services firms with an opportunity to facilitate transactions across markets, suppliers, consumers, nations and all parts of the Internet. Put simply, these technologies are the tools of the twenty-first-century intermediary. The fees associated with these types of transaction will obviously be commoditized over time and command very thin margins, indicating that operational efficiency will be the key factor in sustaining long-term viability.

Level Four Technologies

Finally, fourth level prescriptive technologies, called regulators, are designed to keep you within the designated limits of a process or a set of rules in society. They include radio-controlled ankle restraints, anti-theft devices for automobiles and the pet chip, an electronic dog tag that is inserted under the skin of your pet. These technologies can act both passively (a GPS-linked automobile that is reported stolen can actually engage a listening device to monitor the occupants of the car) and actively (a beverage machine can detect if it is being vandalized and signal the police).

The application of these technologies to financial services is in its infancy. One can imagine microsensors embedded throughout an automobile providing an insurance adjuster with the data to assess damage incurred during an accident.

Data, Information and Everyday Life

Another aspect of pervasive computing is the challenge that it creates for data replication and information usability, including establishing corporate data-sharing policies to regulate the level and detail of information being passed to value chain partners. One can speculate that if there is a direct relationship between data and value, the underlying value of information will be commoditized or worth less over time. Every piece of information has a half-life of usefulness to the individual or organization that assigns its original value. For example: for a stock trader, the value of up to the minute stock price information is extremely high; that same data on the following day is less valuable as a single piece of data, although it may still be valuable when plotted with similar pieces of data to form a chart or graph. Ultimately, to the stock trader, the individual stock quotation is almost valueless at some point in the future. However, as that same element of data becomes less valuable to the trader, it increases in value to a stock analyst or fund manager. One can conclude that there is a direct relationship between information and its perceived value which is relative to who set the value on the information. This relationship between information and value is critically important to financial services organizations because of the nature of the data, received from third-party sources, passing through the business process within the firm to value chain partners. Surprisingly, organizations are continually disappointed when they discover the often dysfunctional state of customer data that was in many cases a critical element in merger or acquisition negotiations. Often the value of the customer data is drastically reduced when the labour cost associated with bringing it up to date is applied.

Regardless of the data produced by these new technologies, it is difficult to predict how people during the next five years will use these technologies in everyday life. The more information that is collected about an individual, the greater the possibility that it can be mishandled and simply increase the cost of operations.

The Intent of Technology

Often the purpose of a technology's initial design is derailed by the necessities of business or the way it is embraced by society. For example, the developers of television thought that its primary application was to give everyone the opportunity to receive a college education at home; however, today's television programming schedules are a long way from that ideal. From the noble ideal of television's forefathers, its use was quickly transformed into an entertainment delivery device supported by product advertising, moving to its present state as a mechanism for selling products interrupted by entertainment programming. In order to draw a parallel between the pervasiveness of technology in everyday life, one can examine the pervasiveness of product advertising on television. Television programming was merely supported by product commercials that provided the viewer with a view of life with the product in 10–30 seconds. Now, the products are simply integrated into the programming, noticeable as the actors or actresses in the programme strategically hold a beverage can so that the audience is able to read the label.

Financial services organizations are presented with a wide range of opportunities to leverage these technologies into product offerings that supplement our everyday lives and streamline core banking services. Pervasive technologies provide a financial services firm with the opportunity to rethink what they offer, how it is delivered and, more importantly, why a product or service offering is valuable to a customer. The long-term implications of these technologies are to change our view of technology as an asset and begin to manage it as a liability. This is not to say that technology should be treated as a liability; on the contrary, the management of technology should be as if its value declines over time. So as to put this concept into perspective, the legacy of banking technology is rooted in the high capital equipment cost that was an investment with a useful lifespan, requiring maintenance and support personnel. Thus, the typical classification of technology as an asset depreciating over time while providing a mechanism for improved information flow. However, technology is advancing at an accelerated rate, making older technology not only less valuable, but commanding a higher cost to maintain. Despite the rapid decay of technological value, technology is still regarded as an essential asset of the organization, one without which it cannot function. The idea of treating technology as a liability is not an oversimplification of the balance between technology investment and technology deployment; it is merely to say that the technology should be viewed and managed differently from the way in which it was managed in the past. This can be seen in the following example: there is a fundamental difference between the strategy of an equity fund manager and a bond portfolio manager. Both specialists are managing assets with strategies that come from two very different philosophies on investing. Taking these conditions into account, the management of the technology liability will be different from core back office systems to end user or consumer devices. If one considers that consumer retail delivery devices, such as PDAs, PCs, WAP phones and many others, will continue to experience a high turnover due to the nature of the innovation of devices and the demand for new technologies by consumers, it can be concluded that the delivery of retail banking products using these technologies will have a half-life much shorter than a core processing system. Simply, the rate of the half-life of technology is proportional to the distance to the end user. Core systems are replaced at a rate of five to ten years and retail end user technologies range from six months to four years.

The key althought to consider when treating the management of technology as a liability is that each technology should be handled according to its application to the business process that it serves and linked to a realistic expectation of a phased retirement. Again, the closer a technology is to the consumer, the faster the rate of decay and the greater the tendency to overmanage the asset. For example, a consultant was engaged to review the operating cost of the technology group within a large bank, and found an ongoing cost of warehousing a stockpile of outdated PCs because they were a depreciated asset. The cost of warehousing these non-functioning computers, coupled with the cost of the labour associated with inventorying and tracking these assets, was greater than the new replacement value. Put simply, for the amount of money being spent on storing these outdated PCs, they could be purchasing new ones, as indeed they were.

Pervasive computing amplifies the fact that technology is ever changing. A general rule can be applied to thinking about managing pervasive technologies: the closer the technology is to the end user, the more it will be subject to change. Therefore, the key to providing pervasive technology services is a robust architecture that anticipates a continuous change of delivery platforms. The by-product of combining pervasive computing with evolving Internet technologies is to rethink core banking operations and redesign how banks work.

The Dark Side of New Technology

It is not hard to imagine a darker side to pervasive technologies as the intrusion into everyday life moves from something controlled by a consumer to an action regulated by a governing authority. Combinations of technologies have been coupled together to allowing a pet owner to pinpoint a lost pet using GPS technology. A pet owner can elect to have this technology implanted under the skin of a cat or dog (in the case of farmers, sheep, cattle, horses) to determine where an animal is located if it becomes separated from the owner. Several organizations have discussed making this technology available to parents, allowing a similar transponder to be implanted under a child's skin to eliminate the problem of missing or abducted children. It is not beyond the range of Orwellian thinking to imagine the next evolution of this technology – a governing authority requires the insertion a GPS chip under the skin of citizens to monitor their actions and whereabouts. Regardless of the intent of these technologies, they will continue to raise questions about ethics, morality and social consciousness, creating new social responsibilities for business while redefining the relationship between technology and a diverse global population.

For financial services firms, another dark side looms in the distance. In a connected environment in which a customer's home provides massive amounts of usage data, for example lights, computer use, phone use and other data-supporting activities, the need to secure and encrypt this data arises because a criminal monitoring the data will know exactly when people are not home.

From a positive viewpoint, a variety of these GPS technologies could be employed in the physical world and cyberspace to track a variety of illegal activities, in order to reduce money laundering and drug trafficking, for example. As governments continue to develop new responsibilities for financial services providers to know the sources of depositors' funds, these technologies have an enormous potential to be used as a regulatory mechanism.

Regardless of the final evolution of the pervasiveness of technology, its potential over time to alter the social contract between employees and employer, taxpayers and governments, customer and financial services institutions is as predictable as the effect of radio, television and the PC. The adoption of a technology will fundamentally interrupt the traditional relationships between parties and market forces, and, as has been proven, a planned design will not be able to reconfigure the way in which these relationships are maintained and executed. In conclusion, the implication to financial services is to develop a clear understanding of these trends, interpret how value can be added and create services that facilitate the transition.

CHAPTER 4

Convergence and the Changing Landscape of Financial Services

Competing in the world of twenty-first-century financial services requires that traditional financial services organizations rethink not only their product offerings but also the very nature of how they provide value to customers. New market entrants, hungry to acquire customers, are rapidly rising to meet the competition head on by commoditizing prices, often by offering unprofitable terms to lure customers, and providing convenient technology access to products. During the last forty years of computing, technology-differentiated companies with deep pockets established a competitive buffer between opponents because the cost of the technology put it out of reach of smaller firms. Now eBusiness and Internet banking technologies are within easy reach of any potential market entrant, blurring the lines between added value and customer service. The differentiator is now service vis-à-vis a tightly coupled integration of technology to create added value by excelling at the customer service process.

A Framework for Thinking

Technology should be considered disposable, a temporary state of capability that requires a continual process of adaptation to add value when conditions in the business environment change. The closer the technology is to the end user, the greater the volatility, due to personal preferences. The ramifications of technology on society have generated new business issues that cross moral and ethical resolve, personal and corporate security, individual and national privacy, local and international legislation, resulting in a continual re-evaluation of the relationship between work activities and social commitment.

Consequently, the greatest area of change is the rising expectations in customer service made possible by technology. Organizations that travel naively down the technology path, rapidly installing customer relationship management (CRM) systems, often discover that unless there is a comprehensive redesign of the customer support process and associated functions, technology simply facilitates the discovery of a poorly designed customer process. If CRM is a keystone in the new arsenal of competitive weaponry, careful attention to detail must be observed in designing the new customer experience. Strategically, customer service operations must represent an efficient, streamlined organization that can respond rapidly to changes in a customer's expectation. Technology provides this flexibility and enables business agility, only if the business process is optimized and the corresponding organization is highly skilled.

In the near future, value propositions will have to be focused on making customers happy, a concept that is still unfamiliar to many financial services institutions, as telephone banking customers enquiring about their balance will discover. Humor Space, providing a comical, yet realistic look from the customers' point of view in the 1998 publication of 'The Near Future of Public Utilities', provides a perfect example to the ideal of a value proposition: [1]

RING...RING

'Hello. This is Bell Atlantic-Nynex-MCI-TCI-America Online customer service.'

'May I help you?'

'Yes, I'd like to report a problem with my telephone.'

'Our records show you don't have local phone service through us.'

'How do you know who I am? I didn't give you my name.'

'We have... ways.'

'Well, I'm pretty sure you have my phone service.'

'Our records show you have long-distance, cellular, satellite TV, Internet access and your MasterCard through us. Your phone service must be through one of the other three big communications companies. Have you looked at your bill?'

'My bill is 134 pages long.'

'Oh, you're one of our light users. But we'd be happy to become your local phone provider. If you sign up, you get one-third off long-distance calls made on your cellular phone to friends and family members who have an Internet home page.'

'It's tempting, but I just want my phone fixed.'

'Fine, sir. Just a reminder: Next time you need to contact us, try our Internet site. And when you get there, you can sign up for a free showing, through your satellite TV system, of Hamlet starring Bell Atlantic-Nynex-MCI-TCI-America Online CEO Ray Smith.'

'Thanks. Goodbye.'

This portrayal of the customer services representative demonstrates how an organization focused on cross-selling products continues to offer opportunities for the customer to make a purchase without actually addressing the underlying problem. Although humorous, the passage above is an example of customer alienation, in which the customer services representative is not listening to the request but simply following a pre-scripted method of handling requests which often compounds customers' frustrations. This is an essential lesson for any financial services firm endeavouring to expand to a full spectrum of service offerings that cover many products.

Sometime in the Near Future... Customer Choice Doesn't Mean Customer Confusion

Across the globe, many financial services firms are working to develop a comprehensive suite of services designed to offer customers a financial services superstore or one-stop-shop acting as a consolidator of banking, insurance and other services, targeted at facilitating a lifestyle or community of consumer behaviour. However, in this quest for market supremacy in wallet share, organizations sometimes confuse customers with so many options that navigating them is a daunting task. Once again, Humor Space provides insight into the complexity of service offering navigation:

Click. Dial. Ring.

'Good morning! This is SBC-Pacific Telesis-Sprint-GTE-Little Caesars.'

'Little Caesars? You do pizza?'

'You buy it over phone lines. It's content. Would you like one? You get a medium with two toppings when you order HBO on cable.'

'Uh, no. I called because my phone line isn't working right.'

'I see. Do you have your phone over your cable line or do you have your phone over a phone line.'

'A phone line, I think.'

'OK, then that's not SBC-Pacific Telesis-Sprint-GTE-Little Caesars. My file shows that you get cable TV and video games on demand from us, but in your area, we only offer phone service over cable lines. If you use a phone line, it must be one of the other companies.'

'Thanks. I'll call them.'

'And sir? We're testing some new products in your area. We're offering electric service and natural gas service for 10 per cent less than the public utilities. One-stop shopping. We want to provide you with every-thing that comes into your house and connects to a device or appliance.'

'No, thanks. Bye.'

Click.[2]

Competitive pressures and changing market forces demand that financial services firms develop this broad collection of service offerings, acting as a single source for consumers and business to find services that supplement corporate activities and individual transactions. Unfortunately, the missed opportunity is not in the presentation of this dizzying array of offerings; it is in the development of a clear, concise mechanism to get rapidly to a preselected collection of similar service offerings. Content portals or brand entry points allow customers to navigate through product and service offerings from the perspective of the customer, therefore reducing confusion and providing a clear path of offerings formulated to specific business activities or personal lifestyles.

Sometime in the Near Future... Brand Recognition Must Be Clear

Unlike banking brand development during the latter half of the twentieth century, the competitive landscape of financial services demands a re-examination of the composition of a brand and its relationship to products and services. Financial services firms that apply a single brand strategy to both cyberspace and the physical world miss the opportunity to leverage an array of branding strategies that strengthen existing products and introduce new services. Clifton and Maughan put the challenge of branding into a broad perspective:

> Whichever way you look at it, brands today are the most demonstrably powerful and sustainable wealth creators in the world. The term 'brand' and the practice of branding are not only being applied across the full spectrum of businesses; they are now being applied across any type of organisation that seeks to create a relationship with its audiences over and above day to day process and cost.'[3]

Developing a click-and-mortar strategy will require the development of a strategy that presents a dynamic product offering and a stable operating firm to the customer. Stability can be achieved by creating a strong anchor brand that represents the elements of trust, security and financial know-how, reinforced by a physical presence and market awareness at the global and regional levels. A dynamic product brand incorporates the changes in the marketplace and quickly adapts products to reflect a change in the customers' requirements. Financial services firms, while expanding their product offerings, participating in joint ventures, mergers, and eventually eMarketplaces, will need a cohesive strategy for branding that will determine the limits of how global the reach of the organization is and how valuable the products are to the local markets that they serve. However, in any rebranding effort it is easy to alienate customers during the transition period; consequently, careful execution of customer migration is essential to retaining customers during the process. Once again Humor Space provides an oversimplified but effective view of the problem:

Dial. Ring.

'Hello. Endorphin Enterprises.'

'I'm sorry. I must have dialled the wrong number.'

'You're probably in the right place: we just changed our name. We used to be US West-UUNet-Universal Pictures-Ameritech, but that got pretty cumbersome. I guess they wanted to call it UUUUSA, but then decided to start fresh. So we're Endorphin Enterprises.'

'Clever.'

'Personally, I thought we should call ourselves Youse Guys. Get it?'

'Yeah, that's good. Um, I was calling because my phone line doesn't seem to work right.'

'Ohhhhh. What services do you have with us?'

'I'm not sure.'

'We offer everything: local, long-distance, cellular, cable TV, satellite TV, Internet access, music on demand and so on. But so does everybody else these days.'

'Yes, well, it's gotten a little confusing. I've already called those two other companies with long names.'

'Oh, right. OK, see, it looks like you don't have anything at all with us. Now, we could make your life easier by giving you all the services so you'd know who to call. Except in your area, we only offer movies on demand over the Internet, so that could be a problem.'

'No, really, I just want to get my phone fixed.'

'My guess is you must have your local phone service through AT&T. That's the only other company left in the business.'

'OK, I'll try AT&T.'[4]

Compounding the problem of developing brands, product offerings and managing the customers' perception of value in the financial services offering is the continued evolution of technology and the recrafting of products to meet or exceed the competition. Al and Laura Ries outline eleven key components in developing an Internet brand that are easily applied to a 'click-and-mortar' strategy for organizations struggling with how to synchronize a brand to a value proposition, and put the effect of the Internet on the financial services industry into perspective:

> What's important to keep in mind is that the Internet will change your business even although you don't have a website, you don't do business on the Internet, and your product and service will never be sold or advertised in cyberspace.[5]

Sometime in the Near Future... How Far Can We Go With Brokering?

Synchronizing a brand, preparing for a brand or product transition and embracing a continuous wave of mergers and acquisitions in many cases can lead to customer flight and severely damage the perception of a brand, even though the underlying value proposition remains the same. For example: a traditional bank with headquarters in one Central European country acquired a smaller competitor located in a neighbouring Western European country as part of a growth strategy. Immediately they replaced the logos, signage and other visual images of the acquired bank and began converting customers to the new operating entity. The value proposition presented customers with new product offerings combined with the power of an established brand and superior service. However, during the succeeding weeks, customers left the bank in droves simply because the 'foreign bank' had little appeal to local customers who preferred a local-close-to-home feeling institution.

During the process of any growth plan involving the reshaping of financial services organizations, the key elements in the strategic manoeuvre are joint ventures, the reconstituting of services and/or the development of new product offerings and the migration of the customer to the new operating state. In fact, the design of any transition that requires a migration of customers needs to be constructed from the customers' viewpoint. A final instalment from Humor Space again demonstrates the extreme of the branding/product dilemma:

Click. Dial. Ring.

'Hello. AT&T. Bob Allen speaking.'

'Bob Allen? The chairman? I'm sorry. I wanted customer service.'

'No problem. Hold on a moment.'

Pause. Rustling sounds.

'Hello. Customer service. Bob Allen speaking.'

'Mr. Allen, I really just wanted customer service.'

'This is it. We spun off everything but my office. It goes totally against the megamerger trend. Our shareholders love it. I'm getting paid $55 billion this year.'

'Well, sir, my phone line doesn't work right, and I think I need someone to come fix it.'

'Be right there, as soon as I can find my tool belt.'[6]

It is vital to remember that outsourcing a primary or secondary business function does not mean abdicating one's relationship with the customer.

Many organizations have confused transferring the processing of an account to a third party with that of managing the account relationship. Customer retention is an essential element in long-term relationship growth strategy and in many cases is more economical than customer acquisition. Unfortunately, technology is a double-edged sword that can be used to retain customers but also to help them to change financial services providers:

> The Bankers Automated Clearing System (BACS) has introduced a new system which will transfer details of the new account electronically to companies which receive payments by direct debit and standing order. Before the direct debit transfer scheme was introduced, information was sent through the post, and it is hoped the new system will make it quicker and easier for people to change current account providers.[7]

Simply, it costs more to acquire a new customer than it does to keep an existing customer, and now technology enables customers to be less loyal to a set of product offerings that are not perceived as delivering value for money. The challenge for financial services firms will be to develop customer segments and devise plans that retain customers for greater periods of time. By connecting products and services into a comprehensive set of offerings, the key feature that customers will demand is a consolidated view of their relationship with the institution. Ideally, what financial services organizations will achieve is the consolidation of financial data into a clear understandable format that provides the customer with a collected view of accounts and reduces the amount of time needed to spend on banking matters, giving to the consumer the most valuable of commodities, time.

Aligning Structure

However, the new standards in customer service introduced by new market entrants such as Virgin Money demand a realignment of organizational structure to provide a comprehensive blend of CRM and efficiently executed, technology-enabled products. As said above, the advent of the Internet has changed the frame of business, introducing new competition and exposing bad service faster than before. It is the competitive level at which a firm elects to compete that determines the organizational structure necessary to achieve the desired output, not the applied technology. Technology is the means through which a process can be enhanced by automating one of its specific components; however, let it be noted that it is the organization that sets the rate at which business is conducted.

Simply reshuffling the existing organization provides little value as a prelude to reshaping the culture and attitudes towards a customer-focused orientation. In establishing a value creation agenda to meet the challenges of today's competition, financial services organizations need to examine their value added in the services they provide, develop a capability to rapidly create and deploy product or service offerings as customer requirements evolve, realign the organization to make CRM a core competency and establish a network of partners to provide a broad range of service offerings. As said before, this is easier said than done. The transition from a product or process focus to a customer focus requires an intense reorganization of the company's structure, and a huge investment in re-educating employees in all categories.

As seen before, the vital strategy for financial services organizations is to develop a value-added customer focus by creating a network of competencies structured to facilitate customer relationships. Reskilling personnel to become relationship managers with a deep understanding of process and reducing the operational cost will be key ingredients in this proposed transformation.

The challenge for financial services companies is the migration from a traditional, historical, hierarchical, product-focused organizational structure to a more customer-centric structure in order to stay competitive with the ever-evolving level of customer expectations. This transition to a networked structure anticipates participation in an interconnected collection of financial services, represented by the rapidly emerging list of financial services portals on the Internet such as BanxQuote.[8] A network structure allows the financial services organization to move rapidly in and out of partnerships and alliances while segmenting internal operations in order to optimize the harnessing of resources when conditions change.

Moreover, the blending of a refined customer service process, highly skilled individuals and a cacophony of technology does not always guarantee success. Financial services are just beginning to feel the impact of a rising set of customer expectations that reflect an individual's appetite for cultural and regional preferences. The products and services of a truly global financial services company will need to be configurable to a variety of product combinations that respond to regional preferences. For example, a larger percentage of US households' long-term wealth is tied directly to the performance of the NYSE and the NASDAQ, rather than to their European counterparts.

In order to develop an agenda to compete in the twenty-first century, financial services organizations should embrace a simple formula that has appeared in various forms from an array of sources: *think global* (that is, consolidate operations, core services, economies of scale, streamline processes, franchise products); *act regional* (that is, tailor product combinations, partnerships and alliances, call centres, Internet portals); *look local* (that is, branding, branch operations, customer touch points, interchange with consumers and merchants).

Each one of the above levels requires a clear definition of business process, brand, product offering and other aspects of the business in the formulation of market strategies. Moreover, each one of these levels presents financial services firms with not just a degree of competitive pressures, but a host of new opportunities.[9]

Financial services organizations are well placed to be the catalyst for initiating social and economic change by providing a comprehensive suite of services that transcend geopolitical boundaries and facilitating preferences that are indigenous to local cultures and individual requirements for banking services. The face of banking and other related financial services stands at the crossroads in our relationship with money and wealth. Financial services organizations that are quick to adapt will enjoy a competitive advantage and will reap short-term profits; organizations that rethink the nature of our relationship with money and design products for lifestyles and services for sustaining lifestyle events will be well positioned to compete in the future.

Even a small financial services institution can participate as a global player if a market niche can be developed and a superior service level can be achieved. However, competing at any level requires that offerings have a clear value proposition and are targeted at specific market segments. For example: a recent study by Verdi & Co found that in selected US markets 35 per cent of the younger customers recorded above-average use of tellers, compared with only 30 per cent of customers aged 30 and older. In the race to automate and downsize retail operations, many financial services firms are confusing a customer's computer literacy with financial competency. Customers do value the self-service of fundamental banking and trading transactions, but are often undereducated in the financial instruments available to them and, more importantly, in how to tailor their use of financial products to facilitate their lifestyles.

Having customers who can use self-service transactions does not mean that there is no longer a need for a strong physical presence; in fact, the demand for branch locations is counterintuitive. Customers will use self-service technology for basic transactions but often feel more at ease with face-to-face meetings when developing financial plans. The financial services industry has identified that its long-term value is in the customer relationship, and one should not assume that the interactions will be exclusively technical but perhaps more personal.

CHAPTER 5

eInsurance: Staking a Claim in the New World of Insurance

At the dawn of the new millennium two colossal industries are poised at the crossroads of enormous change. Armed with technology, they are presented with an opportunity to rethink the fundamental business which comprises their core services. Banks are rapidly expanding into the insurance marketplace in search of new sources of fee income (or just commissions) and insurance companies are racing into the financial services arena on a quest for new sources of revenue. The clash of two titans in the financial services sector reads like the conflict between the gods that inspired Homer to write the *Iliad*. In this classic work of Greek literature, we learn that the gods were quite happy celebrating the wedding of Peleus and Thetis, until suddenly Eris, the goddess of discord, who was angry because she had not been invited, threw a golden apple into their midst. She said: 'The fairest of all gods shall have it!' Hera, Aphrodite and Athena each thought herself the prettiest, so they all ran to pick it up. When they realized that they all wanted the same apple, they became angry and started a huge argument that ended in the seige of Troy.

Consumers looking for financial services product offerings and insurance policies are watching the gods of business bring a plethora a co-mingled, co-branded, rebranded, cross-industry, co-operative and ultimately confusing collection of products to the insurance and banking sector. Storm clouds may be forming over Mount Olympus, with so many organizations selling the same services and literally banking on technology to be the key differentiator in their competitive strategies. Although technology is also the enabler of this new wave of products and services, more importantly, it is the catalyst for change: real market differentiation starts with the customer.

Organizations that are engaged in this quagmire of customer services should subscribe to a simple but effective insurance business strategy. Technology can be employed to optimize the three fundamental components of insurance:

1. the act, business, or system of insuring

2. the state of being insured

3. the means of being insured.

These insurance industry components require a level of technology investment to sustain long-term viability and are only achievable by a close examination of the key business drivers in the business of insurance.

The first component, purely from a business perspective, focuses on the organizations engaged in bringing insurance products to market which are deeply involved in the first set of activities, the system of insuring. Technologies can now replicate the existing insurance process and remove process steps, duplicate data, speed up claims processing and incrementally reduce operating cost. The key to these technologies is to develop a predictable infrastructure that offers an easy integration of successive new technologies. Thereby, a technology infrastructure works at its optimum when it is invisible to the participants in the process. For example, electricity is an infrastructure technology that is only really noticed when one experiences a disruption in the service. Like the silent servant of electricity, insurance is not a product that is uppermost in the mind of a consumer until he or she has need of it.

The big opportunity to organizations providing insurance products is to rethink the process or act of insurance: origination, underwriting, claims processing, settlement and a host of other activities. Today's technology provides a framework for global standards in insurance data structures, tokens or encryption formats, methods for processing and a variety of delivery mechanisms connected via a predictable infrastructure. Core banking, networks and other interoperative technologies are achieving a level of stability which allows organizations to couple specialized technologies with core business competencies, offered as complete solutions to customers. The net result of a solid infrastructure is the company's ability to participate in the emerging eInsurance marketplaces.

These electronic marketplaces, such as Chicago-based e-insure.com, offer a portal into the insurance market to receive quotes on auto, life, home, health, business, small business and specialty insurance. Portals provide a window for consumers to view products and make selections;

eMarketplaces provide avenues of exchange between parties. Incorporating both into your product offering is essential to developing your brand. It is not only what product is offered, it is where it can be found and with what other products it can be associated that are important to develop the brand.

The by-product of the marketplace is the emergence of standards to interchange data between providers and customers. For example, a customer could provide his or her personal information to a central register and provide encrypted tokens in order for each selected provider to acquire the data necessary to process an application. Conversely, an insurance provider could provide the customer with a token that will open a specialized banking product based on his or her lifestyle.

A customer-centric viewpoint is the focus of the second component, the state of being insured, reflected in the operating philosophy of the IMRGlobal organization which does business in the UK, France, Asia and the US: insurance is a unique industry, its products are promises; its resources are people and information.[1] Put simply, the state of being insured is peace of mind. Technology can be employed on behalf of the insured to monitor the policies held and compare them with those of other people at a similar socio-economic stage of life, reviewing the coverage quarterly using life events. For example: when finalizing your latest mortgage, a refinancing intelligent agent or insurebot assesses your homeowner, life, property and other policies and provides you with recommendations grounded in statistics from other individuals with similar circumstances. Fidelity's eMarketplace insurance portal, Insurance.com,[2] offers unbiased advice on how life events such as moving, marriage and sending children to college impact your insurance needs.

The opportunity for organizations is to engage technologies that make insurance invisible, like electricity, a silent servant that requires little or no direct effort. People depend on insurance; but, like the complex technologies associated with delivering electrical power to each appliance at home, you only notice when it stops working. Organizations offering insurance are only just beginning to explore the technologies that change insurance to a customer-centric product. Unlike infrastructure, which is maturing to a state of predictability, the emergence of customer-centric products will undergo many changes in the next few years. The essential use of technology will be to make customer service easy, convenient and painless, remembering that customer service is typically used when a customer feels that he or she has left the 'state of being insured' and has a problem to resolve (for example an accident, a birth, a change of job). Reducing the amount of time it takes to go back to the comfortable feeling of being covered by insurance is the cornerstone of customer centricity.

The final component to insurance is the means of being insured. Means, in the case of insurance, is best thought of as a combination of wealth, market intelligence and life event planning. Wealth is the ability to meet the financial requirements to be insured. Market intelligence is acquiring information and knowledge that lead to decisions on being insured. Life event planning is incorporating insurance with an anticipatory approach to your financial conditions within your socio-economic group.

Organizations such as Hong Kong-based Internad Limited[3] provide an example of how to acquire information in the Asian property marketplace by acting as an intermediary to provide research to security brokers, property consultants, developers and institutional investors across the globe. As insurance organizations rise to the awareness that their market differentiation is information made available by technology, information portals that cater to customers, providers and all members of the insurance value chain will be a prime factor in developing a corporate partnering strategy.

The difficulty for financial services firms wanting to move into the insurance market, and for traditional insurance providers, is that technology is altering the nature of insurance products. Insurance and the act of being insured must change from being reactive (the result of something happening) to being proactive (the eventual fulfilment of a forecasted condition or event).

> Insurers hear from their policyholders when major life events happen – births, illnesses, new houses, new cars, retirements. Banks and brokerages, by contrast, interact with customers far more frequently. As a result, bankers and brokers – many of whom now sell insurance – are getting their marketing messages in front of customers more often than are insurers. How can executives in a low-transaction industry such as insurance raise Web site visibility and win back customers when high-transaction competitors have greater access to them?[4]

The *Dictionary of Banking and Finance* defines whole-life insurance as 'a policy where the insured person pays a fixed premium each year and the insurance company pays a sum when he dies'.[5] It is not difficult to rethink the term 'whole-life' to be a series of connected policies that continue for the duration of your whole life or a set of insurance relationships that provide an integrated suite of coverage that adapts to changes in one's lifestyle. Given that financial services customers can be categorized into both markets and market segments, the attributes of the demographic profiles that comprise these delineations are measurable and somewhat predictable. Nevertheless, lifestyles are a way of living, with traits that reflect the behaviour of an individual shared by a social group. Within that lifestyle, life events that can be attributed to the social group are relatively predictable, not always the timing of the event, but the nature of conditions that trigger an event. For example, a married couple may or may not have children; if they do have children, they may or may not go to college.

Unfortunately, proactive life event planning remains the area in which most consumers fall short of realizing the maximum value of insurance. This brings to light a new opportunity for both financial services companies and insurance organizations, titled 'educating the customer'. Easy sounding, it often takes an enormous toll on the long-term viability of many organizations. For example, if one examines the aftermath of the dot-com boom and bust, one can see that the majority of these companies' expenses was advertising and marketing. Educating consumers as to how to engage in business on the Internet resulted in many organizations simply running out of cash before consumers could become comfortable with using the Web to supplement everyday life. Like other technological innovations, the early Internet pioneers were the ones out in front of the brick-and-mortar firms, receiving all the media arrows in the back. The opportunity here is for financial services firms to partner with an organization within the industry to educate the consumer base on the new state of being insured. Software companies that are focused on wealth management will develop tools for addressing the coverage needed to support the lifestyle of individuals.

Like Homer's gods and goddesses, financial services firms and insurance companies will be creating a lot of thunder in the race for cross-selling services to consumers in all demographic sectors. The challenge that twenty-first-century financial services firms will face is how to develop a brand that is based on the three primary components of insurance while developing an insurance/technology agenda that incorporates the revolutionary changes necessary to achieve customer centricity. The first item on the agenda must be a clear product offering that is simple to understand, convenient to use, accessible all the time, anticipatory in design, cost effective and, above all, perceived to be invisible to the consumer. Like electricity, the fidelity of insurance lies in its ability to achieve invisibility to the consumer. One can imagine an advertising campaign in the future with slogans such as: 'ReallyBigFinancial.com anticipating your every move since 1999' or, 'Insurance so complete you can have an accident with confidence'.

One thing is clear, technology, branding and customer service are the foundations of any insurance offering. These aspects, coupled with marketplace partners that combine value-added financial services, are only the beginning of the journey into the new millennium of financial services. Financial services firms should not be asking if insurance should be offered, but rather how, when and by whom, and how will it be branded and how will it add to the customer's perception of trust. For this reason, the first criterion in offering insurance products is to find out whether it adds value to the current suite of product offerings, and if the inclusion of the new offering changes the customers' perception of the institution as a trusted advisor and lifestyle facilitator. A customer's perception of a trusted advisor is not someone who is continually selling them a product, but someone who advises them on the right products and, more importantly, the right time to purchase the product. The key message is to move from a product-centric to a customer-centric focus, in which insurance is a product which adapts to the changes which occur during a customer's entire life.

CHAPTER 6

Capital Markets: Global Aspirations, Regional Values and Local Fears

The classical definition of a capital market is 'a place where companies can look for long-term investment capital'.[1] However, the behaviour of capital markets across the globe responds to the investment populations that they serve and the companies for whom they are building markets. To say that all capital markets are merely mechanisms for businesses to acquire various forms of financing, or to say that an investor in one market is like all other investors – simply looking to achieve the greatest possible returns – is to underestimate the diversity of the markets themselves. European markets behave differently from Asian, African, Australian, North and South American markets. The allure of globalization tends to homogenize these into a global pool of capital that marches in lock step with the rises and falls in the United States markets, although events such as the 11 September 2001 tragedy cause a ripple effect throughout capital markets worldwide, a longer term examination of the markets reveals that each market has its own market vitality, unique style of investor and types of company interaction that defines the market personality or tenor. This tenor is not to be overlooked in developing local, regional and global value propositions, because it is a critical element in developing the niche market opportunities and subsequent localized value propositions.

Developing a multi-regional value proposition depends on having market intelligence on the tenor of the local market and the attitudes of investors willing to invest in business endeavours. For example, a company in the United States wanting to establish a joint venture in Brazil may elect to raise some or all of the equity financing in the local Brazilian market, leveraging the relationship with the venture partner in the local market. Why? In some cases, because it is less expensive, fosters local interest and public relations, legitimizes the relationship in the local market and, in many cases, future local investors could become part of the customer base. Of course there are many risks associated with executing this type of strategy, one of which is of course the fluctuation of the local currency. However, this could be an early indicator for what is to be the future, as more customers and businesses adopt a global perspective on access to capital and investments. Regardless of any risks, global travellers are beginning to ask questions along these lines: If my home is valued at £150,000 and this value can be certified by a local financial institution for a mortgage, can the mortgage be serviced by a lender in the United States or some other location where interest rates and fees may be more palatable?

From an investor's perspective, capital markets offer opportunities for direct participation in a wide range of firms engaged in providing services to every conceivable type of business. To corporations, capital markets give access to the capital needed to fuel growth and expansion. These two perspectives share one common theme: expansion of access is directly proportional to an underlying, unseen current of technology adoption and infrastructure implementation.

Global Aspirations

The dot-com boom-to-bust cycle has reduced investors' appetite for risk, so that they direct their funds to less risky financial instruments or investments, ultimately slowing growth. Under adverse conditions, investor sentiment plays a significant role in providing access to capital; global companies seeking major sources of capital as an alternative to bank loans. Now that the market has demonstrated the fundamentals of how to use Internet technologies to participate in a global marketplace, companies will be returning to capital markets to secure funding for expansion, armed with new, value-driven propositions.

Not surprisingly, small to medium sized companies with global aspirations are beginning to embrace less traditional criteria such as intangible assets and non-financial performance measures, as part of their valuation. How companies operating in a globally connected economy are valued by investors will evolve, as the internal metrics of performance are refined in the second wave of the eEconomy. One key by-product of globalization will be redefining how a company's value is measured and to which market it is ranked as a value exchange member.

If the trend to globalize capital markets into 24-hours-a-day, seven-days-a-week utilities continues, the competition for capital will follow a predictable market maturity model. Like a phoenix rising from the ashes of failed dot-com companies, capital markets are anticipating predictable growth merely because money continues to seek higher returns over time.

Regional Values

What are the idiosyncratic attributes of marketplaces around the world and can they shed light on how eMarketplaces will work in the future? Unfortunately, the nationalistic behaviour of investors retarded the growth of pan-European market concepts such as the EASDAQ[2], resulting in not attracting as many issuing companies and investors as originally hoped. Investment behaviours in pan-European exchanges have demonstrated that investors' appetite for a diverse portfolio is not as aggressive as originally thought. The lesson learned is that the French invest in what they know, that is, French companies; German investors typically buy German-based firms; and very few investors put capital into companies and products that they do not fully understand. The cornerstone of understanding is information on the conditions of the market, the stability of the country, and the performance of the company. Providing information is understandably a product of a suite of technologies that range from infrastructure to consumer devices.

The continued proliferation of technology will facilitate a revolution in regional capital markets (initially expanding services by removing the traditional trading times, then offering additional investment opportunities by modifying the requirements for listing). Critically, these revolutions are linked to the pervasive delivery of information on all levels and to all market participants. The evolution will occur in two stages: firstly, by linking exchanges in a network of interconnected marketplaces, and ultimately, establishing an interlaced global capital market that provides investors with opportunities for their investment literally to follow the sun.

Already local organizations are preparing for a connected future by establishing guidelines and other policies to encourage market growth and avoid any illusion of an ill-managed regional market offering. For example, the mission of Kenya's Capital Markets Authority[3] is to promote the development of orderly, fair, efficient, secure, transparent and dynamic capital markets in Kenya within a framework that facilitates innovation, through an effective but flexible system of regulation for the maintenance of investor confidence, and safeguards the interest of all market participants. The same can be said of the Egyptian Capital Markets Authority:

which monitors market activity and facilitates capital growth by requiring disclosure, encouraging more secure institutions for trading securities, and promoting the introduction of markets for new investment instruments.[4]

Local Fear

The primary difficulty is how to understand the underlying value proposition of the company. How corporations report their value, market conditions and, more importantly, their performance is paramount to gaining investor confidence. Fear of the unknown is about lacking data. The thirst for data on how capital markets of the future and their listed companies will behave has set the stage for the emergence of an organization such as The Center for Ethics, Capital Markets and Political Economy,[5] a non-profit organization established in 1994 to provide a discussion forum and information resource for those who believe that moral concerns should be taken into account in economic and political thinking.

Consequently, on a global level, an organization such as the International Monetary Fund has a Dissemination Standards Bulletin Board[6] which provides access to the Special Data Dissemination Standard to guide countries, that have, or might seek, access to international capital markets, in the dissemination of economic and financial data to the public.

The Path Forward

Regardless of which vision of the future you subscribe to, capital markets are changing and will continue to change over the next few years due to the continual advance of technology and the appetite of investors to find new opportunities for their money. For financial services institutions, the opportunity is to provide a suite of products that are steeped in infrastructure and can be used as capital market conduits to a new class of sophisticated investors, who have a new appreciation of how companies generate value.

Banks will continue to play a vital role as an intermediary, and perform the central function of assisting firms that need debt contracts in lieu of equity contracts to support reorganization or restructuring. Traditional banks and financial services firms with legacy banking functions will continue to provide services that evaluate risk at the local level. Risk management is a growth area; as eMarketplaces mature the requirements for capital will change, as firms of varying degrees of maturity engage in transacting business across international and regional boarders. Interestingly, a reduction in regulations, to spur competition in capital markets, may result in a redefinition of international and national regulations in order to establish the minimum requirements of what constitutes a bank, financial services firm, insurance firm, or banking functions within non-banking firms. For example: Will non-banking firms be required to carry deposit insurance? Will the Federal Deposit Insurance Corporation of the USA offer services to banks globally and become the Global Deposit Insurance Corporation? Only time will tell. As the market for capital redefines itself, there will be a realignment of services to facilitate the capital needs of small and medium sized companies.

The new economy has the potential to act as a liberating force in capital markets for a whole generation of individuals who typically would not have access to opportunities beyond their traditional marketplaces. Technology provided by financial services organizations gives individuals everywhere an opportunity to participate in new sources of global economic growth. Through technology and a network of interconnected financial services providers, we have entered an economic global village.

CHAPTER 7

Introducing eMarketplaces[1]

Markets, marketplaces and eMarketplaces all share a common function, set of behaviours and ultimately the same future. Hunt and Murray said:

> A market at its most basic is simply a meeting place of buyer and seller where the needs of one are satisfied by the surplus of another.[2]

The emerging eMarketplaces are mechanisms that facilitate the exchange of value between two or more parties electronically. This new phenomenon offers financial services organizations a broader range of new product and service opportunities to support the exchange of value between parties. Unfortunately, as previously discussed, financial services companies are finding it increasingly difficult to define a clear value-added service that they can provide to this cyber-exchange and, even more worrisome, to differentiate their services from those of emerging competitors.

From a historical perspective, Hunt and Murray assert that diversification and specialization were the ancient Roman responses to the vagaries of crops and climate. The Roman market experts were attempting to supply a consistent flow of foodstuffs to a growing empire. This was a deliberate action to reduce the cyclical nature of local crops by distributing foods that did not grow in a particular geography at various times of the year.[3]

Like the ancient Romans, financial services institutions need to use the elements of diversification and specialization to deliver multiple services in each type of eMarketplace, therefore participating as an aggregator of services. If they fail to do so, they risk becoming a commodity offering within the realm of content providers. For example, an eMarketplace that acts as a broker for consulting contractors could provide cash management services to both parties and eliminate internal accounts receivable and accounts payable functions. The value proposition to the consulting company is clear: the payable/receivable functions offer lower operating cost and reduce time for collections, thus improving cash flow. If the same financial company provides services to both parties in the eMarketplace, managing the cash flow in transit is a clear opportunity to grant added value.

An eMarketplace reflects the needs of the community that it serves, and it must adapt to the changes in the demands of individual parties engaged in the exchange of value. The basis for value creation in financial services organizations will be their ability to adapt services in order to meet the changing needs of the market participants.

The value propositions of financial services firms became more apparent during the medieval period as markets matured and diversified into fairs. Here again, Hunt and Murray provide a historical lens in which to view the dynamics of the marketplace:

> In successive centuries, market networks grew to embrace regional and inter-national areas, but more distant market relations brought greater problems of transport and payment, making the direct exchange of one commodity for another increasingly difficult. The incentive for traders to adopt coins as the medium of exchange thus became more and more compelling, until the truth can be said, 'no mint, no market'.[4]

Comparing the medieval marketplace to the Internet eMarketplaces reveals the same basic elements in the cycle of market maturity. The formation of the Open Financial Exchange Consortium,[5] an organization formed in 1998 by Microsoft, Intuit and CheckFree establishing a protocol for exchanging information between financial institutions and consumers designed to facilitate data for personal financial management applications and electronic bill payment and presentment, is the modern equivalent to establishing a medieval mint.

Hunt and Murray's view is that as the marketplaces in the Middle Ages matured, they transformed from their early ad hoc nature as a casual event lacking laws of conduct into an organized, regulated place of exchange with fixed times, which resulted in a basic need for law and order on the roads and waterways to sustain the necessary support infrastructure. This parallels with the Internet eMarketplaces maturing from individual websites to connected eMarketplaces. Internet-based eMarketplaces are easy to establish with low-cost technology, but they often lack the rules of commerce and the necessary business infrastructure to engage in inter-national trade. World governments are just beginning to understand the impact of market regulation, taxation and the fundamental aspects of facilitating eMarketplace activities across borders.

An eMarketplace Action Agenda

The emerging eMarketplaces represent the next evolution in market adaptation, presenting an enormous range of opportunities for financial services institutions to develop new areas of fee income and transaction-based revenues. However, to establish market credibility and quality of service in a rapidly changing competitive market, these opportunities again require a clear value proposition. Any firm that wishes to compete in the eMarketplace needs an action agenda that spans a host of business, technology and organizational issues. It is important to keep in mind that the value proposition to the marketplace and the resulting financial services product offerings will have to evolve as eMarketplaces mature. Organizations are often surprised when a new product falls from popularity and, in many cases, profitability, leaving behind a management decision that often pits new product introduction against customer alienation. Financial services firms, like their medieval counterparts, need to develop financial products that adapt to changes in the marketplace, lifestyles and basic requirements of the markets. For example: a banking product created as a loss leader should be designed from the viewpoint of the customer using the product. Opening a savings and current account as a student should result in a seamless transition to credit, mortgage and investment services as the conditions of the individual's life change. Financial services organizations should be the trusted advisor, not simply the cheque casher. If the customers' perception of value is high, the transition cost between these life events should be minimal. If the value perception is extremely high, the need to look beyond the institution to 'price shop' is greatly reduced.

The fundamental ingredients for developing a sustained value proposition are very often based on common sense:

■ Know your added value and how it complements the market it serves;

■ Create mechanisms for market sensing;

■ Rebrand products to reflect your identity;

■ Build capabilities for rapid market reaction;

■ Develop competencies in customer relationship management (CRM);

■ Leverage technology to facilitate transactions;

■ Improve your aptitude to manage relationships;

- Change offerings and approaches as the markets mature and evolve;

- Develop relationships with providers of technology and services.

Strategy Must Mirror Maturity of the eMarketplace

Capitalizing on opportunities emerging in eMarketplaces involves a flexible approach that reflects the stages of market maturity, calculates the rate of technology innovation and the speed of customer adoption in the marketplace. These three factors, market maturity, rate of technology innovation and speed of customer adoption should be the essential ingredients for strategy development. In order to succeed, companies will need to have a clear understanding of how these factors influence the product offering, and, more importantly, in many cases drive the design and direction of the product and its overall value proposition.

As the eMarketplace matures, firms must be able to adapt to the changing conditions. The associated financial products and services must evolve rapidly to meet demand. Financial services companies have a unique opportunity to lead the market because many services sought by consumers (for instance wealth management for the newly affluent) are predictable and can be anticipated.

Each phase of eMarketplace maturation offers initial opportunities for financial services firms. The inception phase, for example, offers opportunities for partnering, experimentation, definition of an operating model, exploration of new channels of customer acquisition, branding, portal establishment, product definition and bill presentment, to mention only a few. The second phase of maturation, called growth, offers an array of prospects, such as refinement of the operating model, introduction of core banking services, rebranding of products and services with maturing partnerships, revenue/profit sharing model with channel partners, consolidation of retail services, wealth management and anticipatory payments, among others. Finally, the last phase, maturity, offers opportunities in driving down cost, optimization of processes, CRM, customer order fulfilment, and several comprehensive wealth-generating strategies.

Technology innovation will continue at an ever-increasing rate, providing a multitude of mechanisms to deliver financial services products and improve the quality, cost and productivity of the organization. Financial services firms need to understand how technology enhances the value proposition of the product offering, and how it affects the customer in receipt of that product offering. In many cases, the point is not whether the technology is applicable, but to which market segment it does apply, and how it will add value to the existing offering.

The phenomenon of technology advancement conflicting with either market factors or consumer adoption can be seen in the automotive industry, which continually incorporates technology, sometimes missing the mark with vehicles such as the Dymaxion car in 1939, the Edsel in 1957, the German Amphicar in the 1960s and the Sinclair C5 in the 1980s. Financial services firms need to be cognisant that technology allows the creation of almost any type of product offering, but does not necessarily guarantee that customers will value it. The speed of customer adoption is the relative rate that a specific market segment will adopt a technology (or product) as an integrated part of value proposition. If the utilization of a technology is perceived as more valuable, the rate of adoption will increase. For example, using the Internet for share trading was adopted rapidly by investors because its value proposition was clear: easy access to information to initiate a trade; lower cost; the ability to initiate trade transactions 24 hours a day (for execution later); and the convenience of self-service.

An Agenda of Strategic Actions

Most eMarketplaces are still in the inception phase, although a few early leaders have entered the growth phase. In the strategic action agenda, the three most critical components are creating a value proposition, developing core competencies based on technology and selecting the right partners.

Creating (and more importantly, adapting) a value proposition has been the Achilles heel of many of the dot-com failures. It cannot be overemphasised that developing a value proposition is paramount in establishing any eMarketplace and critical for the long-term viability of any participant in an eMarketplace. Like their brick-and-mortar counterparts, eMarketplaces are built on three primary models of operations – the eProcurement model, the dynamic commodity exchange, and vertical exchange (these are analysed in Chapter 29). Financial services organizations contemplating services for these markets should seek to integrate or eliminate steps required in processing transactions for members of the exchange.

Developing appropriate competencies traditionally has been understood as creating compartmentalized and discrete activities that add value. In eMarketplaces, financial services institutions can provide a suite of services that centre on activities such as originating, brokering and passing transactions; aggregating, consolidating and managing transactions; and providing extra-market interchange. Still, providing products and services to eMarketplaces is only half the challenge. The more significant challenge is innovation mobility, that is, being able to harness resources quickly to capitalize on technological change. Essentials are rapid deployment; building infrastructure capabilities that can be quickly connected and integrated for complete product offerings; and technology which enables mass customization so that consumers can readily select product options designed to suit their lifestyles.

The final component of an eMarketplace strategy is the selection of partners to perform or support the value-added service. The contemporary business climate allows few companies the luxury of performing all aspects of the services brought to the marketplace. A key feature of the eMarketplace model is its capacity to readily be disaggregated into its components, making specialization a viable strategy. Insurance companies are effectively product specialists, relying on a network of brokers and agents to distribute their product. Credit card companies are good examples of infrastructure specialists, providing a consumer pathway between buyer and seller. The lesson is to develop a network of capabilities that fulfil a value-added service to the eMarketplace and manage it as a performing asset.

Should Traditional Banks Participate in eMarketplaces?

With an eye towards the past, Hunt and Murray remind us that during the Middle Ages it could be said that 'by the thirteenth century all fairs were markets, but not all markets were fairs'.[6] Describing the next set of business decisions faced by financial services firms on eMarketplaces, where to participate and at what level of market maturity, is a twenty-first-century challenge. Obviously, the earlier a firm engages in an embryonic marketplace, the greater its opportunity to influence the direction of the market as it matures. However, financial services firms have been taken aback by the flight of customers to new market entrants.

Not only should financial services institutions participate in eMarketplaces, but they should also take a leadership role in providing a suite of services designed to drive down corporate operating cost by leveraging technology. The new eMarketplaces represent a collection of converging technologies that are just beginning to grow. Technology has played a key role in reshaping the delivery of banking services as well as the underlying processes that support financial services product offerings. The new eMarketplaces demand services that transcend typical lines of business within a financial services company and require the establishment of new relationships, sometimes with organizations previously viewed as competitors.

Providing market-enabling services can include, but is not limited to, products such as cash and multi-currency management, seamless customer relationship management, fulfilment integrated services, synthesized data recast to partners, aggregation services and market interoperative services. Financial services firms that are engaged in designing value propositions for these products should then develop a baseline of thinking by keeping in mind the following common characteristics inherent in today's competitive market:

- Participants interact more frequently, non-linear;

- Process steps are repeated often;

- Streamlining reduces steps;

- Value may be added through the interaction of a community of customers;

- There is value in linkages with similar products and services;

- Product cycles are shorter, measured in periods as short as weeks, days and hours;

- It permits mass customization and the perception of singularity.

The opportunities for a financial services organization to provide value in eMarketplaces will be limited only by the degree of innovation that the financial services institution applies to the marketplace and its ability continually to adapt those services as the market matures. Initially the fertile ground for financial services companies to add value is in the introduction of products that facilitate the exchange of value and move away from traditional fee generation. For example: providing cash and multi-currency management services requires moving from being simply a transaction broker to providing a suite of services that maximize the use of funds for the depositor. Therefore, demonstrating a seamless customer relationship that enables a single representative to guide a customer across all products requires a radical alteration of the organization, the competence of its employees and the convergence of key technologies.

CHAPTER 8

Web Projects, Infrastructure and Value Propositions

At the beginning of the twenty-first century, financial services firms continue to struggle with methods to determine the value of infrastructure and, more importantly, Web-based projects. Simple infrastructure is the backbone of an organization providing financial services, and the cost of infrastructure is often difficult to attribute to a single business unit, function or product. Traditional cost justification of infrastructure as a single investment event with a predetermined return on investment can be regarded, under certain business conditions, as a waste of time. The business agility and rapid market entrance displayed by many dot-com companies demonstrated that larger organizations engaged in a process of business case justification, and many times annulled any potential savings once the cost of the justification process was factored into the return on investment equation. The problem existed because the process itself continually hindered the ability to get to the market quickly. The strategic approach to infrastructure is to embrace the concept that corporations cannot exist without infrastructure. It is a question of asking how much infrastructure is necessary. Specifically, it is a problem of what level of infrastructure is required to deliver a basic financial product, a superior product or a competitive product.

Determining Value of Infrastructure and the Web

Providing a basic set of products or services is far easier today than ten years ago. This circumstance, applied to the Internet world, led to the rise of the dot-com companies. This new business trend trumpeted an often unspecified amount of profit improvements, the potential to expand market share, the ability to improve the connection to the customer, and the opportunity to maintain parity with competitive offerings. A rising interest in the new, misunderstood, often mystical Internet provided a convenient justification for investments in technology as a mechanism to facilitate corporate growth agendas. The technology organizations of financial services companies, weary from the Y2K experience, found business units eager to embrace the rapid deployment of technology. Fortunately for technology vendors, many of these projects required infrastructure to support multiple technologies and facilitated additional infrastructure purchases. The fall of the dot-com companies has changed the sentiment of the marketplace seemingly overnight, and firms have retreated to more traditional attitudes on justifying technology purchases.

The change in attitude in technology purchases reflects investors' sentiments in the equity markets, but it also presents an interesting paradox. Despite the fact that it is counterintuitive, downturns are the best times to make investments in infrastructure. Unlike an investment in the stock market, the underlying value of technology as a mechanism for leveraging a business process does not lose value as market factors rise and fall. The current change in business climate finds many vendors eager to extend solutions at prices (or with partnered capabilities) unheard of during the previous 24 months.

Delivering a superior level of service introduces a simple lesson learned from the dot-com experience: customers expect a higher level of performance at a price point that is defined by the market and that reflects a value proposition palatable to market conditions. The past few months have also revealed that when market conditions are right, the combination of economically priced technology and an idea that either fills a market niche or defines market behaviour will be fertile ground for new entrants. The disillusionment of eCommerce is making the case more difficult for justifying technological infrastructure and other Internet projects using traditional methods. Investing during a market downturn in Web-based projects that entail additional infrastructure requires a rethinking of the perception of value and its relationship to return on investment.

The New Formula for Value

Traditionally, return on investment (ROI) looked at the result of a project's associated resources and labour as a one-time event rather than the product of a continuous process. Today's business clients dictate that the Internet is not a luxury channel to market or an alternative path to the customer but a prerequisite for conducting business in the new century.

As a result of the dot-com phenomenon, funding for individual projects now elicits closer scrutiny, restricting an organization's ability to react to changing market conditions. Projects that engage the Internet as a mechanism for exchange should look towards two simple methods of reconciliation for the use of corporate funds: return on investment for justification and return on process (ROP) for value creation.

A competitive level of value creation, which is becoming synonymous with long-term viability, and justification are two very different concepts that are simply tools to provide data with which to support a business decision, often evolving more than technology. How we describe what is valuable is often a result of our perspective on the relationship of one item to another.

Previously, technology used in the delivery of financial services offerings needed to be viewed as investments that paid for themselves by reducing the cost or labour. The business reality in financial services companies is that in many cases technology is such an integral part of the business that it must be justified on value creation.

Cost Justification versus Value Creation

Organizations such as IBM have re-engaged the classic DuPont return on investment model by altering its application to the process of business. In 1914, DuPont bought 25 per cent of the stock of General Motors Corporation. Finding complex accounting systems that required a mechanism to untangle the accounting of the operations, Donaldson Brown, an engineer tasked with cleaning up the car maker's tangled finances, developed a model that can be applied to establishing value in infrastructure and Web-based projects (see Figure 8.1).

The DuPont ROI model still helps companies to visualize the critical building blocks in return on assets and return on investments. This model is a way of schematizing the information so that everyone can see it. Designed to give you a picture of where you have put your resources, it also allows people to understand how they can have an impact on results. Flexibility, a hallmark of the expandable DuPont model, enables the technology strategist to run what-if scenarios.

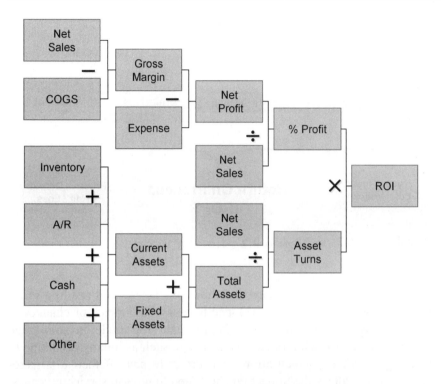

Figure 8.1   DuPont ROI model

Return on Process (ROP)

A by-product of the reengineering wave that many corporations embraced in the 1990s is a greater awareness of the process of business. Integrated supply chains, customer fulfilment process and distribution process are examples of processes that extend beyond the business enterprise. Business processes that are integrated with other businesses in a global economy take on the characteristics of organic processes. They require a structural framework to facilitate the organizational and technological adaptation that must occur periodically as market conditions change.

In addition, when organizations connect with each other by providing linked banking services, using the DuPont model to measure process results is even more revealing as a mechanism to measure value. It works by modifying the model to redefine fixed assets as processes, and then

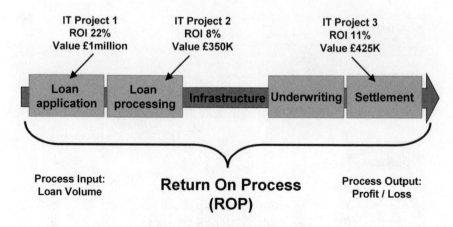

Figure 8.2 The ROP model

applying the associated resources to those processes. As a result, a series of what-if scenarios can be developed to assess the impact of changes in the business environment. For example, regarding modelling mortgage acquisition and servicing processes, a change such as linking eBanking to mortgage servicing, which allows consumers to pay off their mortgages early, would address the impact on short- and long-term service revenues. This information could be used to streamline operations in sub-processes that would be made redundant (see Figure 8.2).

Organizations that are experimenting with the DuPont model to measure process results and service processes are reviewing these issues as customer acquisition versus customer retention, revenue growth versus cost reduction, business process fragmentation, airline yield management and even manufacturing vehicles.

Linking to a Value Proposition

Internet technologies that are employed to facilitate a business process can use ROP as a method of measuring the fragmentation of the underlying business. A value proposition to the customer must be clear, with a return on the overall product or service being greater than the sum of its parts. Value creation is not simply a cheaper price, or a higher degree of service; it is delivering these things profitably. In the past few years, the race to eCommerce meant a suspension of fundamental business sense. Technology can be applied to virtually any business process with the express intent of providing value. During the dot-com rush, there were many stories of companies that were taking customers' orders via the Internet, printing the orders on paper, and retyping them into the old back office computer. Such an application of eCommerce simply added cost to an already over-burdened process. The Internet technology was window-dressing for the firm that wished to be perceived as a player in the eEconomy.

A variant of the DuPont ROI model used by a financial services company can be used to illustrate not only a return on process, but also to perform what-if scenarios for establishing and operating an Internet banking offering. The flexibility of the model lies in the fact that assets and resources can be attributed to both direct process and associated overhead processes for a comprehensive profile of cost and returns. This type of modelling provides snapshots of future operating states that can then be incorporated into a business scenario. For example, the Internet bank can be modelled at start-up, at 1,000 customers, 10,000 customers, or comparatively with one partner, two partners or with outsourced resources and multiple delivery technologies. Any of these snapshots can then be organized into business scenarios culminating in grouping scenarios into a business plan (see Figure 8.3).

People and technology play an interchangeable role in this type of scenario planning, because it can be applied at many points within the process. For example, internal personnel associated with a process are to a partnership relationship as technology infrastructure is to outsourcing. The variations of technology and personnel resources are almost unlimited. The art of applying technology to this scenario plan is striking a profitable balance between these variables while still providing value added to the customer. Organizations in the quest for return on technology investment often lose sight of the balance and value equations.

The application of technology should follow a simple rule: apply technology to obtain a leveraged return, not just a recovery of cost. One method of measuring the value created by infrastructure and Web technologies is to employ performance metrics that monitor the underlying process throughput. For example, the cost of processing an invoice at a large multinational company was £17 per invoice generated from the purchasing system. Implementing new technology to facilitate the purchase of frequently ordered items could reduce the cost to £1.50, with a clear return of investment. However, a change in the business process, eliminating the need for purchase orders under £700 and allowing employees simply to use their credit cards to make these small purchases as expenses, reduced the cost to £0.17 with a clear greater return while using less technology. If the purchasing function and the accounts payable functions were outsourced, an even greater return could be realized.

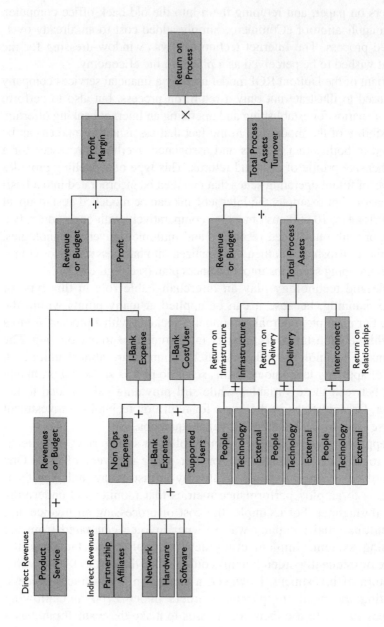

Figure 8.3 Internet bank ROP model

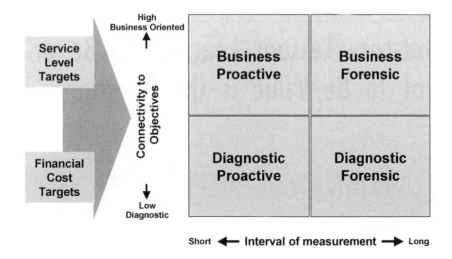

Figure 8.4   Process performance metrics

Understanding the overall process and developing points at which to measure the performance of the process is essential to gaining insight on where to apply technology for maximum return. The essential thing to consider when measuring a process is that the more frequent the measurement, the more proactive actions can be taken in the performance of the process (see Figure 8.4).

Developing process awareness and a deep understanding of the processes which support the business in addition to the business's value proposition is a key skill that needs to be developed not just by the business analyst, but by everyone connected to the process. Familiarity with the process will be the foundation for the discovery of operational improvements by individuals within the process, made possible by information that measures the process and records its results.

Financial services organizations looking for market distinction can employ models and performance metrics that measure process as a mechanism to discover their value propositions for customers. At the same time as the price or performance aspect of technology continues on its evolutionary path, technology will no longer be the defining factor in a firm's value proposition. A technological infrastructure that facilitates a dynamic business process, coupled with performance metrics that enable firms to react to changes in the business climate, is the new basis of value propositions.

CHAPTER 9

Dot-com Lessons Learned: To Be or Not To Be, Value is the Question

When is a bank a bank? Is a store still a store or is it a retail portal? If doing business on the Internet is called cyberspace, should traditional brick-and-mortar channels be called terraspace? If there is only one lesson to be learned from the dot-com phenomenon, it is a reacquaintance with the language of business. The common belief is that technology is both a catalyst for business and the driving force behind society, the results of which have ushered in a new language for the eEconomy, often blurring traditional definitions.

In order to assess the implication of the dot-com phenomenon on financial institutions, one must review the events that shaped how businesses behaved during the last few years. The majority of companies that failed during the dot-com boom-and-bust cycle did so due to significant shortfalls in management skills, coupled with the inability to adapt as market conditions changed. The enormous hype generated by the press aggravated the situation by propelling the market in the early stages only to diminish it later. This is market Darwinism in full bloom, with many lessons to be learned for financial services organizations embarking on the path to providing global services.

Sensing the Market

Many organizations doing business in the eEconomy witnessed changes and downturns in many firms with which they competed, and paid little regard to analysing the impact of these changes on the marketplace. Companies assumed that the competition simply had an inferior product or service. Too often, they failed to consider the value that their own products or services brought to the market and the degree to which they provided value, assuming that they were market-proof or impervious to changes in business demand.

History has proved that at the advent of most new markets or industries there is a rush of organizations bringing a wide variety of products to a limited number of buyers. For example, the popularization of the automobile in the 1920s brought over 200 small and large companies into the automobile production business, only a few of which still exist. Yet, a century later, there are only a few market winners operating in a commoditized market with thin margins.

Unlike previous business cycles, which waned over longer periods of time, one reason why companies failed in the dot-com bubble was insufficient capitalization. Raising cash was easy during the market hype surrounding the dot-com boom, but sustaining the perception of double-digit future returns that were only achievable long term proved to be greater than the market could bear, and investor enthusiasm waned along with investors' cash. This is the new economy language for 'going broke' or 'becoming cash challenged'. Business is about making money, that is, the positive result of the simple equation of how much your company is spending each month subtracted from the revenue received from external sources. If the result is negative, then your company is 'burning' money. Savvy organizations that received funding often assessed the total investment received divided by the monthly burn rate in order to establish when they would be out of cash, unless a rise in revenues could propel them into a cash positive position.

Like the introduction of any new business cycle, the dot-com phenomenon has introduced a host of new words and meanings that now must become part of our thinking in financial services delivery:

- *Reorganizing:* 'We need to conserve cash and although we claim people to be our greatest asset, they are easily jettisoned to improve the bottom line.'

- *Realigning:* 'We need even more cash.'

- *Restructuring:* 'We are telling our investors we need cash.'

- *Right sizing:* 'We really need cash.'

Putting aside the humorous aspect of the new language, the business implications are clear: that a sustainable value proposition is what drives long-term viability and, in most cases, the ability to leverage technology within an organization and to its external customers is a core competency that must be developed. Many of these terms are indicators that the need for cash in the short term is so great that management has to assess the worth of risking the long-term health of the organization.

The Basics

The unanswered question presented to many companies was whether the money would last longer than the attention span of the investors. Along with that were issues too often ignored or dismissed as being unimportant by the investment community: is the underlying business value proposition presented to customers viable long term, and is the product or service valuable?

Vilified by the press, most organizations blamed their business models because business models cannot defend themselves. Regardless of the intended business model, consumers need to believe in the value of a product or service in order for a business to survive. When there is clear value, the consumer realizes it and is willing to pay the price, even at a premium. Many organizations started with a simple value proposition and were encouraged by the competitive nature of business to engage in expansion, cross-industry products, acquisitions and the maintenance of an ever-increasing growth agenda. These organizations were engaged in a process of diworseification,[1] that is, the practice of taking a good business and expanding it beyond the market's appetite for its products and services, coupled with growth occurring faster than the management team's ability to adapt to business conditions. The essential learning from the dot-com saga was twofold: firstly, do not create business models that get in the way of the consumer experience and, ultimately, consumer acceptance; and secondly, keep the business models like the initial idea or product – simple and straightforward.

One dot-com success story is Asiatravel.com, an Internet portal that has focused on a single niche market and has mastered its market position. A viable enterprise since 1995, it is only now entertaining a public offering. Its competitor Asiatravelmart.com is also a successful organization demonstrating its viability in the marketplace. Both these organizations share a common theme: focus on a niche, present products that are valued, and provide sterling customer service. They have jettisoned the typical travel agent-based model and adopted a market-place model.

Reengineering Revisited

Has the dot-com phenomenon cleared the way for a reengineering revival? Yes, the chief stumbling block in the reengineering of the 1990s was the lack of applied technology to fulfil new ways of envisioning business. The acceptance of the Internet as a viable medium for business calls into question the very structure of how businesses work. When is a bank a bank and what are the products needed to be a financial services institution?

A bank is a bank when it acts as a financial intermediary with its focus strictly on banking, and its products reflect the basic concept of holding money for depositors, lending money at interest and facilitating the transference of money. The overall focus of a bank is money and the fees that can be generated as a consequence of transferring money between parties. Key to defining a value proposition for the twenty-first-century financial services firm is to change the focus from money to customer.

Retail products and services have to be transformed to facilitate customers' changing lifestyles and made proactive to lifestyle changes instead of reactive to life events. For example: the retirement and eventual demise of the baby-boom generation will see the second biggest transference of wealth between two generations since the Black Death in the 1340s. The spending habits of recipients of the medieval wealth transference reveal an upsurge in the purchase of luxury goods during the second half of the fourteenth century, as a result of the increase in purchasing power of the surviving population.[2] Today's rising product is wealth management, which is appealing to the segment of population that has been involved in creating the wealth, but is not the foremost concern of the generation due to inherit this wealth.

Moreover, predicting the behaviour, spending and savings habits of two generations of consumers must be viewed in the context of empirical data from the field. Exactly how the markets will be affected by the generational wealth transfer is an area of debate among scholars, economists and futurists, as demonstrated by Mankiw and Weil. In an article published in 1989, they projected that housing prices would decline by 47 per cent in twenty years, based on the assumption that the baby-boom generation would reduce its consumption as it got older.[3] Although the study and its arguments were criticized by economists, most accepted the observation that the housing demand of baby boomers would decline. Therefore, predicting when generational behaviours happen is more complex than an understanding of how behaviour impacts the market. The difficultly for financial services firms is designing product offerings that match the changing lifestyles of multiple generations who often present very different attitudes on financial matters.

Commercial financial products have to enable businesses, by reducing the cost and time spent on transactions, to provide services that mirror the business agility that firms are trying to achieve. As stated above, the Internet is rapidly changing the landscape of who can provide financial services and how consumers and businesses gain access to financial services. Contemporary access pathways have been labelled portals, ISP, electronic markets, and constitute new ways of doing business. Oddly, these new intermediaries bear a striking similarity to the role of the inns in post-Black Death Europe, which operated along the trade routes in Belgium during the second half of the fourteenth century. The development of support services to facilitate commerce reflects the maturity of the trading routes and may provide some insight into how value propositions are developed as the Internet matures. According to Hunt and Murray:

> Inns played a key role in the movement of goods along the overland trade routes of medieval Europe, and innkeepers provided not only lodging, but also warehousing, expert help with local governments, and even emergency financing. The last medieval inns of Bruges were unique in providing all these services plus brokerage, banking, and finance on an ongoing basis – in short all the services necessary for doing business.[4]

Did fourteenth-century Belgian innkeepers decided to get into the banking business on the spur of the moment? No. They simply identified a market niche and supplied the services that were valuable to their customers. It can be argued that these innkeepers were the medieval equivalent to today's supermarkets and retailers who are moving into traditional banking services.

The Lever of Technology

Each new technology presents a degree of opportunity to rethink the underlying business process that it services. The potential of the technology is proportional to the degree in which it changes the business process; breakthrough technologies eliminating the business process altogether. Technology falls into four broad categories when applied to a business process: disruptive, streamlining, compressive and channelling.

Harvard University Professor Clayton Christensen describes *disruptive* technologies as technologies that challenge sustaining technologies; they are used to improve upon something that you are already doing.[5] Disruptive technology introduces a radically new way of doing things, or a way of doing new things – precisely because it focuses on the customers and those customers almost never value a disruptive technology in its initial stages. Christensen explains that customers are conditioned over time to buy products that are offered from traditional sources, and that they are never immediately receptive to changing their structure to buy a new product. Customers that value a product offering will be institutionally inclined to stay with their current structure, and therefore the incumbent product. Disruptive technologies change the course of an industry and are often counterintuitive to how a technology is employed by traditional service providers. For example:

> Thomas Edison turned down the radio because it had no commercial value; Western Union turned down the telephone because management thought 'it will never be more than a toy'; Thomas J. Watson Sr., founder and head of IBM, turned down the computer; and Kodak turned down the Xerox copier.[6]

Streamlining technologies are typically combinations of hardware and software that eliminate isolated steps in a business process by reducing either the total time of process or the resources to execute the process. Technologies that eliminate process steps are often misplaced during the original implementation, until the nature of their utility is realized. For example: when ATM machines were first implemented, they were inside the branch, and their sole purpose was to reduce the traffic of transactions to the tellers; they were only available during banking hours, that is, they offered no alternative to customers needing cash after banking hours were over.

Technologies that are *compressive* in nature collapse entire processes or redefine the structure of a process by radically reorganizing the steps necessary to fulfil the process. For instance, home grocery shopping eliminates the need for the consumer to go to the store, thereby reducing the need for checkout people if and when the volume of shoppers switches to online ordering. The next logical step would be to automate the grocery store to anticipate people rarely visiting and high-tech automation could fulfil the orders, further compressing the process. However, firms such as Streamline and Webvan learned that unless the volume of transactions is able to generate revenues or cost savings that can sustain the operating cost of an automated grocery experience, the viability of the operating model is questionable. These technologies and their logical, final implementation may simply be ahead of demand, primarily due to the customer's unfamiliarity with them.

Channelling technologies focus a process or consolidate processes into a single focus, often resulting in the redefinition of the process over a longer period of time. Technologies such as customer relationship management concentrate the information, transactions and actions required by several products and processes, aggregating them into a new process with a symbiotic relationship to the original processes. Over time, the use of the new data on customers and their transaction behaviour will lead to a recrafting of the original processes.

Today's business climate situates financial services organizations in a unique position to rethink their business operations, product offerings and brands. While the definition of a financial services company becomes blurred with the redefinition of the marketplace, organizations can define what they are offering to their customers and through which medium the service will be delivered. Technology is the key to viability, not in the traditional process-automation sense, but as a broad business utility. The technology of providing financial services should be viewed as a spectrum of capability, from core banking systems that provide support to the back office through connective technologies that facilitate transactions and communications, to delivery technologies that provide service to the end customer. This spectrum of technologies makes it clear that most financial services firms will not be able to go it alone. Partnerships, affiliations and co-branding are only a few of the multi-tiered relationships that need to exist to provide services in the new economy.

As the new eMarketplaces are being redefined, the underlying suite of financial services presents a seedbed for interconnective services that employ technology-enabling business to transcend geopolitical boundaries. These technology-laden infrastructure services will have a dramatic effect on international taxation, regulation and transactions, which comprise the exchange of value between nations. With each generation of new technology, financial services firms have the opportunity to rethink how they work and what services to bring to the marketplace. A fundamental rethinking can be achieved by employing technology to leverage the way in which value is created and the role that the organization plays in the exchange of value. It is not hard to envision a new role for financial services organizations that develop along three distinct areas: transaction utility, business facilitator and value negotiator.

Transaction utility acts as a conduit for business transactions and merely exchanges value from one party to another. This service is similar to today's back office transactions when transferring funds between a savings and a current account, but, in this context, on a greater scale, providing a pathway and clearing service for transactions that originate and terminate between two parties.

A *business facilitator* provides a higher value-added service by incorporating the knowledge and wisdom of the institution to the very process of business. Services that streamline processes within a business, such as accounts receivable, payables, payroll, purchasing and other transactions that can be aggregated, give the financial institution the ability to provide an essential service, that of cash management.

The least understood area of services is a *value negotiator*, in which a financial services organization acts as the facility for several international marketplaces and also as a transaction consolidator and broker to other marketplaces. In that sense, firms such as Worldwideplastics.com are providing these services with a value proposition that is based on the potential compression in business time and the economies of scale on cost. For example, a financial services firm provides the utility and facility for a marketplace in Europe, Asia and the US; or a new client in Europe, that has outsourced its payable and receivable accounts, wants to do business in the US. The marketplace that is serviced in the US is a marketplace that can be introduced by the financial services institution with ready links to clear multinational transactions. This reduces time to market for the underlying companies simply because the financial services organization can provide the necessary international infrastructure to do business.

Reaping the Harvest of the Dot-com Phenomenon

A true test of a corporate vision and value proposition is measuring the rate at which investors flee during the early stages of a change in the industry. The dot-com phenomenon reacquainted most firms with the fundamentals of business: it is not hype, but profit that drives companies and their investors. A more significant lesson is that technology infrastructure plays a critical role in participating in today's business marketplace, when technologies' reach can be extended through partnerships with resources outside the traditional boundaries of financial services firms. Although first mover advantage is often the goal during the formation of a new marketplace, it is frequently the prudent management of cash that creates the environment for long-term viability.

Like the automotive and the pre-Internet economy eras, the lesson for financial services firms bringing new services to the marketplace is clear:

adaptability to changing business climates is the core competency that requires development in order to survive. The ability to sense the market and quickly bring to market product offerings that reflect consumer needs is the desired operating state that can only exist by leveraging technology to deliver services. Even if counterintuitive in today's business climate, investment in technology and a fundamental rethinking of products and services are essential steps for long-term survival.

PART III

Global Viewpoints

Individuals in the financial services sector are now grappling with globalization, which is commonly translated into 'sameness' of product offerings, sometimes carrying a very negative connotation. One could claim that the globalization of economies and financial services does not act as a detrimental force on cultural, social and political aspects of society, rather being a force to galvanize financial markets to raise the standard of living worldwide. Unfortunately, many financial services firms are labouring under the misconception that all financial services are created equally and technology will be the only mechanism for market differentiation. A tendency to marginalize cultures and local values diminishes opportunities for new market entrants to develop niche sub-segmented markets. Monitoring global trends, or, more importantly, observing how organizations meet the challenges of global, regional and local competition, provides a mosaic of solutions, product ideas and service offerings that financial services companies must develop in order to compete. This section examines whether globalization is a question or an answer for large and small financial services organizations.

Industry forecasters predict a broad palette of seamless, integrated, global financial services designed to facilitate an individual's needs across geopolitical boundaries. Individuals participating in the new economy as twenty-first-century global citizens are experiencing a disconnected and bureaucracy-divided collection of financial services that are bound together by marketing hype. For example, a US citizen moving to the UK finds that opening a savings and current account is a labour-intensive process, as establishing credit is even more challenging because your credit history is not transferable even within the same institution. It is even more frustrating for a depositor or investor in a global bank to find out that he or she is unable to receive a consolidated statement of holdings while owning accounts in the same bank on multiple continents.

Financial services are hamstrung by a legacy of geopolitical regulations designed to protect depositors, which, coupled with bureaucratic processes dependant on fee income, often act to inhibit private individuals engaged in a global lifestyle and limit the abilities of small businesses trying to expand into regional markets.

Spurred by new market entrants, traditional banking firms have started to realize the potential of a channel to market represented by the small business market and its ability to embrace Internet technologies. Small businesses – especially one- or two-person shops or home-based freelancers – are not always well suited to a bank's product and service offerings, which are laden with fees designed for larger retail and corporate clients. Financial product offerings need to reflect the requirements of small business, with more specialized products and services that address the problems faced by entrepreneurs, such as managing cash flows, financing, retirement plans and settlement for transaction beyond their immediate marketplace. Unfortunately, small businesses and entrepreneurs have been classified by many banks as requiring high-touch services and generating little fee income. However, this niche market is rapidly learning how to use the Internet to expand their product offerings around the world, often without the assistance of a financial institution. Small businesses eager to expand are turning to other sources for business services, such as using credit card networks as the intermediaries in facilitating the collection of international payments.

One aspect of globalization is its similarity with the financial product requirements of small businesses. The requirements of small to medium enterprises (SMEs) are representative of the new types of service that need to be developed for financial services firms to create clear value propositions. Ironically, the characteristics of the SME market segment, with lower transaction volumes per customer, are often a deterrent to traditional banks looking for fee income. However, the ability to work with a small group of customers who have a greater tolerance for experimental services creates the ideal environment for prototyping new products in the financial services industry. The hidden value to this market is that small business people want to establish long-term relationships with a financial institution, and they are used to experimentation. This combination of factors is a key ingredient for the development of prototype products. Additionally, small businesses naturally tend to have a tolerant mindset when experiencing problems during implementation, and they are more amenable to assisting in design. If products are to be developed to service the needs of this market sector, it is simply a matter of rescaling, not reinventing, the product. Therefore, the small business market niche can be used as a development partner in the creation of new product offerings, and may well provide an avenue for a process of product refinement which requires less total investment than the process of product development for larger, multinational organizations. The basic needs of small businesses are similar throughout the world and are more easily cloned and applied to generic financial services offerings than their larger corporate counterparts.

Globalization of Financial Services

Globalization is not simply selling products in a variety of regions; it is participating in a global economy, membership in a community without borders. This necessity for businesses to forge relationships with customers regardless of the geographical location of either party will continue as businesses continue to seek new avenues to market. Financial services firms are in a good position to provide services to facilitate this growth, but are in danger of disintermediation by new market entrants and other industries if they do not act wisely and quickly. This is not to say that financial services firms will cease to exist; however, it does indicate that the need for traditional banking services will be overshadowed by more contemporary services designed specifically to enable businesses to engage in global trading activities. In basic terms, financial services firms risk being excluded from a rising set of niche marketplaces that have the potential to evolve into the mainstay of global business activity over time.

Businesses large and small are looking at improved services and a better value for money from financial services firms. Technology is enabling even the smallest of companies to compete in a global marketplace and also increasing the awareness that each type of business has banking requirements that are indigenous to its industry or market segment.

Financial services firms are faced with the dilemma of providing an integrated suite of business services and new product offerings for consumers while trying to reduce operating cost. Compounding this demand on resources to create both types of service, the most visible avenue has been that of the retail banking customer and small investor. In a global marketplace, investors are seeking to maximise their returns; for that reason, financial services firms need to build an environment that enables the fluidity of money, seeking returns in all capital markets equally driven by returns and risk. A new class of globally aware citizens is emerging, one that has a greater tolerance for risk and is now looking to invest in long-term opportunities across the globe without having to commit to large initial sums.

With the need for new retail product offerings and high-touch commercial banking services raising the level of competition, financial services firms have to develop not only a clear value proposition, brand identity and the ability to adapt services, they will also need to examine the root causes of globalization, understand those market trends and leverage technology to create competitive products. The perceived reasons for globalization have been that big business is chasing lower labour rates in developing countries as a method for cost reduction, or that large corporations are simply trying to expand their market share.

The Economies of Scale Myth

The myth of economies of scale is one issue that is often listed as a benefit of globalizing to a firm. In many cases, the opportunity to consolidate purchases to acquire greater discounts from suppliers is a stated justification to invest in computer technology and additional capacity. However, in many cases, it has been observed that organizations tend to develop an additional bureaucracy to co-ordinate the purchasing activity. In extreme cases, the extra steps introduced into the business process, coupled with the additional overhead cost, actually eliminated the perceived benefits that were used to justify the consolidation. For example, in several large financial services organizations the purchase of personal and laptop computers was centralized to reap the economies of scale and secure a volume purchase of several models of computers. The intent was twofold: to negotiate the best purchase price for computer hardware and attempt to standardize the model of computer in order to reduce the cost of maintenance by the internal technology group. However, close examination of the process revealed that over the course of a year the continued fall in computer hardware prices in the retail stores meant that the volume purchase deal was more expensive than purchasing the same equipment from retail outlets. In fact, it was realized that, given a set of minimum specifications that were required for computers to operate under the corporate infrastructure, end users were more adept at making purchases than the centralized technology group. This resulted in a corporate policy change that empowered end users to acquire their own computer hardware, as long as it matched or exceeded the basic configuration specified by the technology group. Seemingly, there were a number of procedural actions and education steps required to make the transition but in the end the savings were greater than the previous bureaucratic process. Additionally, the technology group discovered that since a large majority of global end users had already purchased PCs for home and family members, they were more aware of which retail outlets had the best prices and best service policies.

In an economy of scale, there is a simple fundamental rule which summarizes its principle and goals: the more a company produces, the lower is the average unit cost. If one examines an economy of scale as applied to financial services, one realizes that, for example, there are no economics of scale to an ATM that only serves three customers per day, because the investment cost is greater than the cost of providing the service via the teller window. However, if the ATM services four hundred customers per day, the economy of scale is realized by the avoidance of incremental teller cost. The key to addressing the issue of economies of scale is to find the optimum rate at which the product or service can be updated and return a profit.

It could be further argued that the value of economies of scale is inversely proportional to the size of the bureaucracy created to obtain the desired savings. Therefore, the expressed goal of reaching an economy of scale is not always a desired state when applied to an organization operating globally. Financial services firms need to achieve the optimum rate of throughput without the incremental cost of additional labour and overhead.

Technological Literacy

The higher rate of technological literacy across the world can be attributed to a by-product of globalization, which is cultural awareness and an extension of communications. Put simply, individuals across the globe have not only learned to use computers, acquire new technologies, install software and interact with each other, but also to integrate the use of technology into their lives and business actions. To financial services firms, the rising global computer literacy rate is a double-edged sword. There is an enormous opportunity to reduce operating cost by outsourcing some transactions, previously conducted in branch and back office operations, such as name, address change, transfers, equities trading and other retail activities, directly to the end user. Technology which enables self-service has a distinct appeal to customers in several market segments, and can be used to strengthen the overall global brand of the product offering. However, this can lead to an additional technology cost and, in some cases, an increase in the cost of maintaining Internet websites, language translations and content development.

The Globalization Phenomenon

In short, globalization is not simply a big business phenomenon; it is the product of the world's communities reaching a higher level of communication and interaction. Globalization in and of itself is not the homogenization of culture, but rather the ability of cultures to reach out beyond their borders to touch other global citizens. However, globalization is also an economic phenomenon that is the by-product of the growing interaction between geopolitically bounded economic systems in which trade, capital and investment flow to facilitate local economies.

The opportunities for traditional banks, financial services firms and new market entrants lie in the need for business and people to trade, invest and interact in a global network of financial services in order to establish clear value propositions that service defined market niches and segments. The implications for financial services firms are threefold:

- Provide tailored customer services that are designed to match the needs of different business types;

- Become a provider of information that can be used by small businesses to make key decisions;

- Provide an easy pathway for businesses to conduct activities with a wide variety of global partners.

A key learning is that the fundamental process of businesses – selling products, receiving revenue, paying bills, executing payroll, providing pensions and other basic activities – will remain the same, while a core set of services that establish a baseline of operating functions for a business will reflect a normalized business process. New services designed to meet the idiosyncrasies of different business types must be addressed, due to the rapidly changing nature of how business is conducted as the global marketplace embraces co-opetition and other forms of competitive collaboration.

Without venturing into a philosophical discussion, it can be argued that in the context of identifying patterns for business opportunities, globalization is not a modern phenomenon. Machiavelli's *Discourses on Livy*, written in 1531, furnishes a very modern approach to an old problem:

> Anyone who studies current and ancient affairs will easily recognize that the same desires and humours exist and have always existed in all cities and among all peoples. Thus, it is an easy matter for anyone who examines past events carefully to foresee future events in every republic and to apply the remedies that the ancients employed, or if old remedies cannot be found, to think of new ones based upon the similarity of circumstances.[1]

Hence, societies in general exhibit a basic need to expand as a function of their rise in their cycle of maturity. The extension of trade beyond one's borders can be observed in many societies throughout history, from the empire of Alexander the Great, the Romans, the Mongols, the Incas, the European states of the fifteenth century and the European nation states of the nineteenth century, all demonstrating the need to interact with other cultures and placing economic activity at the heart of the exchange. Like the Amalfi merchants, the Medicis and countless other organizations that facilitated commerce of the past, today's financial services firms share a common set of opportunities to extend the reach of business and clear the way for the by-product of globalization – a raised awareness of the cultures and values of the world's peoples.

Financial services firms can build standardized products, facilitating business-to-business and retail banking customer transactions, that incorporate an awareness and respect of cultures into the branding of financial product offerings, and in the options available within the services offered. As a consequence of combining the forces of globalization with technological evolution, any financial services firm or new market entrant has the opportunity to become a global provider of financial services. It has been observed that the ability to service the full spectrum of market segments is directly proportional to investment in both technology and people. One can therefore infer that the tendency for small companies to appear to be global players typically falls within the confines of a niche global segment. For example: a small regional bank operating in the United Arab Emirates could easily become a significant financial services provider to the niche sector of the Islamic banking market segment of affluent Muslims in, for example, Dubai and Abu Dhabi as well as providing services across the globe.

Finally, it is important to note that, for financial services firms, the opportunity to go global depends on developing a robust, standard product that contains sufficient options to allow the product offering to be located or tailored to meet the needs of a specific culture or micro-segment within the market.[2] Globalization is not the act of making cultures homogeneous, as so often stated by those who distrust and fail to understand this phenomenon. Globalization is merely the act of linking geographically separated groups of people, presenting a heterogeneous array of cultural awareness. Financial services firms have a distinct value proposition in providing the conduits of commerce and other banking services that can act as a cohesive force for stimulating business and increasing the wealth of individuals worldwide.

CHAPTER 10

Developing Trust, Brands and Services in African Banking

The cornerstone of the banking industry is an implied trust, a recognized brand and a distinctive value for money. In Africa, financial services firms, looking to expand in the local markets in order to offer new services to small businesses and attract foreign investment, are discovering that the key to success is creating a multi-threaded strategy that is based on developing a strong brand image and a stable, predictable infrastructure. Multi-threaded strategies combine the business and technology agendas into a series of targeted service offerings delivered to correspond with the rebuilding of infrastructure, while addressing market needs. This concept could be applied to any financial institution; yet, African banks are in a unique position to take advantage of this, because the reduced volume of their existing infrastructure allows them to migrate quickly to newer delivery technologies and, more importantly, establish an infrastructure based on Internet-enhanced, third-party products. Basically, with fewer components of old infrastructure to undo, they are capable of making the migration from legacy systems more easily than the same size organization operating in the US. This is not to say that there is less to do, or that the banking processes in Africa are not as sophisticated. On the contrary, the advantage of African banks can be largely attributed to a more risk-adverse approach to technological adoption than their western counterparts. Nevertheless, this more guarded approach to technological implementation has placed African banks in an enviable position; now they are poised to take advantage of new technological innovations at a substantially lower cost of investment than just five years ago. However, simply being in a better position than a competitor does not necessarily translate into an improvement on bottom line performance, it merely presents an opportunity. Thus, African banks making the transition to full range financial services firms need first to address the brand and image part of the value proposition to customers.

The Development of the African Brand

African banks can find valuable market insight by consulting Nigel Saul's view on England's King Richard II,[1] who faced the problem of how to change the perceived loss of royal power after the actions of the Appellants in 1387. Richard's reign during the 1390s was a determined effort to reinstate royal authority, not by military action, but by a set of actions that resemble the elements used in a modern product or brand strategy. Oversimplifying, it could be argued that King Richard's methods could easily be employed today in any firm in the advertising/marketing/public relations arena, simply because they address the fundamental and intrinsic nature of brand identity and perception management.

In the case of Richard II, the use of language, ritual and iconography created the market of what it meant to be regal, the individual brand being the sovereign himself. This link to imagery and language is still the fundamental building block of branding strategies today, in which the use of logos, images and words define contemporary products and link them to the corporate brands they represent. However, the introduction of the Internet as a new viable market means that financial services firms can profit from adopting the same basic methods employed by Richard II.

African financial institutions need to develop strong brands based on implied and expressed trust, and adherence to regulation and safety, while presenting customers with a clear value proposition based on two key principles targeted to two very different market segments: the local market and the global market. To the local markets, the services and product offerings need to be at the same level of sophistication as their European and North American counterparts. In fact, it could be said that the above, coupled with the social-demographic differences that are indigenous to each region of Africa, means that the level of customer service needs to be even higher. This suite of product offerings and higher level of customer services will be required to stem the rate of customer flight to larger global institutions, increasing their share of the local markets. At the same time, African banks need to portray to global markets the image of an easy, secure and efficient access path to emerging marketplaces in order to attract investors to local capital markets. Once again we can turn to the methods of Richard II for insight into how to achieve this multi-faceted set of goals. As Saul said:

> If he was to re-establish his authority and power, Richard needed not only to build up support and win friends, but also to do something more: to convince his subjects that he was mightier than he was.[2]

Richard's method was clearly to create an image. As said above, the use of iconography, ritual and, most importantly, language distanced the king from his subjects. In effect, the combination of royal iconography and the introduction of phrases such as 'your highness' and 'your majesty' further developed the idea that the king was indeed above the rest of society. Richard's commissioning of portraits, heraldry and iconography provided the physical links that individuals could relate to and offered a relationship to the king. In developing a branding strategy for African banks, a combination of technology and service based on an implied and expressed trust is paramount to growing the business and retaining customers. Therefore the brand has two key elements to meet the competitive challenges of the international and local markets: image, which is the customer's perception of value, and a technological infrastructure, which is the mechanism for realizing shareholder value.

The Image of Value

For most financial institutions, the brand of services must reflect the overall value proposition to customers, and needs to exemplify the values of the organization delivering the service. The new value proposition in financial services is a relationship not only with a place in which to bank, but also with an advisor who guides customers through the rising tide of financial product offerings. African financial services firms will develop an image of value on three fronts: the Internet or virtual world, with integrated services offerings that are easy and convenient to use; the physical or local world, with a reinvention of the brand network targeted on all demographic sectors; and, finally, the interconnected partner network, providing and receiving value from brokering services with affiliated institutions.

As previously said, in each distinct avenue, the brand must carry a clear value proposition to customers in the cases of Internet banking and the branch network, and, in the case of interconnected partners, a differentiated product that is indigenous to a geography or emerging market opportunity that must be formed elsewhere. Advice for developing a strong image of value is best expressed by San Jin Park of Samsung Electronics:

> I think a brand is an embodiment of the comprehensive promise made by the company to the outside world. It's a proposition of the value provided to customers by the company, and it's all the underlying corporate activities that support that proposition. All these constitute a brand.[3]

Therefore, African financial institutions with aspirations of growth are challenged to reinvent themselves locally while engaging global channels and new market entrants. However, image and brand are only the first step in a solid value proposition; delivery technology driven by a robust infrastructure is, as we have seen, the execution part of the value equation.

Leveraging Technological Infrastructure

The use of western banking technologies, more specifically US and European products, to demonstrate the stability of the technological architecture for the Internet and bank office can be leveraged to portray an image of technological parity with new market entrants. For example, a number of traditional African banks have turned to European solution providers such as Ireland's Kindle Banking Systems to avoid reinventing the wheel and reduce their overall technology development cost. Acquiring a core banking technology capability such as Kindle's BankMaster allows them to concentrate internal resources on enhancing the retail delivery mechanism and customer-facing aspects of their offerings. This hedging strategy is a prudent step in leveraging technology because it allows the smaller institutions to jettison resource-intensive activities previously assigned to core banking applications, and permits the redistribution of these resources to higher value-added activities with customers.

The key to supporting a value proposition that is predicated on reliable technology is to develop a predictable or seemingly invisible infrastructure. Infrastructure predictability is simply the adoption of a combination of mature technologies that provide a connection in which the transitory, end customer delivery mechanisms merely plug into. Technology is essential to build the key components of the brand value image of trust, security, privacy, efficiency and low access cost to markets; therefore, technology must be highly leveraged to be cost effective. Financial services firms need to partner with hardware and software vendors to develop joint competencies in establishing robust infrastructure and, more importantly, the ability to assemble product offerings rapidly (within three days) to accommodate the variability of change in the emerging markets. What must be remembered is that technology enables the value propositions; it is not the value proposition itself. That said, a value proposition for banking cannot exist without a predictable, robust technological infrastructure, which is often difficult to justify in its investment, but is essential to deliver value.

CHAPTER 11

The Asian Advantage: A Modular Approach to Business Agility

Asian financial services companies are presented with an opportunity to leapfrog their western counterparts by leveraging technology to establish a greater reach of services. This opportunity stems from the reduced amount of infrastructure that exists within and between financial services organizations operating in the Asian theatre and is clearly a competitive advantage. Strategically, less infrastructure means that there are fewer components of legacy technology to undo in order to integrate newer technologies into improving client services. This short-lived phenomenon gives Asian financial services organizations two opportunities to gain a competitive advantage: increase the ability to compete by leveraging technology infrastructures, and develop a strategic perspective on the returns from technology investments.

Expecting to capitalize on the first opportunity, Asian financial services firms must have flexible, stable, robust infrastructures that can easily adapt to changes in both technology and business services. Core banking operations must consider two variables in their strategic planning process: the ever-increasing level of business complexity and the rate of the organization's ability to absorb the pace of technological change.

Providing a wider array of products across traditional financial services boundaries, in addition to branching into non-traditional banking applications such as eCommerce, simply makes the process of delivering financial services more complex. As the new competitive marketplaces are being redefined, the underlying suite of financial services presents a seedbed for interconnective technologies that depend on an infrastructure that allows business units to do the following: rapidly introduce product offerings to the marketplace; uncouple existing offerings; and redefine services across organizational boundaries. The introduction of new capabilities such as mobile commerce, Internet banking, and a host of other retail/commercial services presents a cacophony of linking systems, often resulting in multiple back offices or loosely coupled applications. The essential competency that a technology organization needs to develop is a modular approach to systems, allowing them to turn applications on and off at the same rate of business change (see Figure 11.1).

Not to be confused with application software, solution sets are combinations of applications and infrastructure that are bundled into modules acting as building blocks of corporate competencies. For example: a bank operating in a specific geography can link a collection of customers, who use Internet banking services to pay their utility bills, and form a buying group to negotiate a more comprehensive rate structure, resulting in a new revenue stream, by acting as an agent of the buyer and the seller. The resulting suite of technologies to provide that service is a solution set, often involving a variety of vendors linked to a common core banking infrastructure. More importantly, solution sets supply essential components for business optimization and provide a framework in which to establish an operating level of business agility.

Unfortunately, the rate at which an organization can absorb changes in technology and business processes is often overlooked in strategic planning.

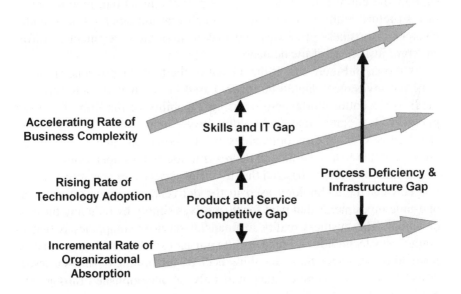

Figure 11.1 Ability to compete

The rate of technology adoption is increasing with each new generation of potential technology users. Taking advantage of the opportunities emerging in eMarketplaces requires a flexible approach that will reflect the stages of market maturity and the rate of technology adoption in the marketplace. Financial services organizations need to develop a holistic approach to enable operating business units to react rapidly to changes in the business climate and incorporate the rate at which their organization can adapt.

As discussed in Chapter 8, the second opportunity is to jettison traditional views on return on investment (ROI) and move towards a return on process (ROP). Traditionally, ROI looked at the result of a project's associated resources and labour as a one-time event rather than the product of a continuous process. Today's business clients dictate that the combination of the Internet, infrastructure and interoperating core banking systems is not a luxury channel to market or an alternative path to the customer, but a prerequisite for conducting business in the new century. As a result of the global economic downturn, funding for individual projects now elicits closer scrutiny, restricting organizations' ability to react to changing market conditions. Projects that engage the Internet as a mechanism for exchange should consider ROI and ROP for the use of corporate funds.

The following example of technology projects, each with a return on investment, rarely considers the incremental investments needed to support the entire process of mortgage processing. Often, investment in infrastructure requires a holistic approach that anticipates fundamental changes in business processes and makes strategic investment in infrastructure just ahead of the demand.

As shown in Figure 8.2, at the advent of the three IT projects, an infrastructure investment should be made, based on the incremental improvement to the entire mortgage-processing capability of the firm. The ROP perspective dictates that technology investments should result in an improvement in one or both sides of the equation, that is, either an increase in the loan volume or a decrease in the cost of operations.

It cannot be overemphasized that financial services organizations can no longer view the technology used in the delivery of service offerings as one-time investments that paid for themselves simply by reducing the cost of labour. The business reality in financial services companies is that in many cases technology is such an integral part of the business it must be justified on value creation. One thing is clear, facilitating business transactions in the twenty-first century will only be accomplished through the fundamental use of technology.

Ultimately, financial services firms need to develop the ability to leverage technologies that are directly and indirectly applied to a specific business process. A key learning is that the aptitude to leverage delivery technologies is directly proportional to the infrastructure that supports core business processes. A modular approach provides flexibility in making strategic manoeuvres, but it also requires holistic thinking to incorporate investments in infrastructure. Additionally, strategic investment in infrastructure should occur at regular, predictable intervals (annually, biannually), since the rate of business change is always rising. Investment in technology infrastructure should be a standard course of doing business, not a surprise that needs to be justified.

Infrastructure between Co-operative Partners

Investing in infrastructure becomes more difficult to quantify when partnering with other firms and/or competitors. However, in many cases it is easier to justify because of sharing the risk and cost. The continued emergence of collaborative eMarkets and other forms of digital co-opetition makes participation in these market channels a necessity, not a luxury. One such market collaboration of infrastructure is the China Financial Certification Authority, founded in July 2000, as a joint venture of thirteen commercial banks under the direction of the People's Bank of China. The value proposition for this co-opetition-enabling resource is a central clearing house for digital certification and a single source for eCommerce infrastructure mechanisms such as Internet banking, business-to-business transactions, eBill payment, brokerage services and other white label offerings.

Internet-based shared infrastructure is the first step towards an operational regional exchange or eFinance Interchange.[1] The regional exchange presents a value proposition to member banks as a channel to market, a supplier of best of breed capabilities, by aggregating technology suppliers and providing prepackaged services. This value proposition is predicated on the risk, return and cost of the underlying technology being shared by the member banks. In this environment, market differentiation comes from branding a collection of capabilities (in-house and partners) into a corporate competency.

CHAPTER 12

Taiwanese Collaborative Product Commerce

Financial services firms can learn valuable lessons from corporations operating in Taiwan, as they embark on a unique opportunity to leapfrog their western counterparts into an environment of collaborative commerce. Primarily due to the reduced amount of existing infrastructure and legacy systems, the technology gap that was considered a disadvantage in the 1980s is now a competitive head start in plugging into the emerging global commerce network.

Consumers, businesses, manufacturers, distributors and governments operating in the Asian economies are realizing that the new economy currency is not just information; it is collaboration or the exchange of content. More importantly, how information is exchanged between two or more parties has changed forever due to the advancement of technology. One example from the manufacturing sector, that provides insight into how new financial services offerings can be crafted quickly in a collaborative environment, is found with the alliance between the Hewlett Packard Company[1] and Parametric Technology Corporation[2] in the development of collaborative, commercial, product solutions. This type of technology-based solution is designed to build collaborative networks in which suppliers, designers, partners and customers come together on the Internet to create new products and services. The focus of the HP/PTC product offering is to decrease time to market for manufacturing companies and online exchanges. The online exchange concept, in which cells of competencies interact and exchange information to develop products and support a manufacturing process, is similar to the evolving relationship between financial services firms and the emerging eMarketplaces. In financial services, this type of product can be used to bring together individuals from various disciplines (for example mortgages, retail banking, insurance, the branch network and other groups) to assess rapidly the needs of customers and develop new product offerings. The interchange of product design ideas can then be targeted to market segments and prototyped in a specific geography to determine the viability of the offering's value proposition with a minimum of investment by the firm. Even more important is that this type of technology can be applied to external service partners in which co-branded solutions can be developed and brought to market with increased speed.

With declining margins, a ceaseless appetite for customer-initiated services and the continual appearance of new market entrants, present-day Taiwanese organizations, like their western counterparts, are speculating, on how to add value in a disordered and disorganized business climate. The culprit behind this fundamental shift in how organizations demonstrate value is a redefinition of what is valuable to customers and shareholders. Information, coupled with ever-expanding technologies designed to put data at the heart of the value exchange, will be key to surviving the next wave of business to be conducted on the Internet.

The foundation for the global eCommerce-driven economy is collaboration between firms and partnering in a network of value. Collaboration extends the boundaries of a firm's fundamental value chain to support a co-mingled set of operations in search of expanding markets, increased revenues or reduced operating cost.

Often mentioned as the overall leader in understanding customers' needs, Taiwan is typically referred to as lagging behind other nations in innovation, a necessary catalyst for rethinking value propositions. The opportunity presented to Asian nations such as Taiwan requires bold leadership to seize the moment during a widening economic downturn and invest in the infrastructure required to position firms for the next evolution of technology-based commerce. Exercising that opportunity can only be achieved by developing a corporate competence in collaboration, leveraged with a host of technologies.

The opportunity for financial services firms is to provide a new suite of commerce-enabling services as part of the growing emergence of business-to-business portals that are developing a value proposition based on simply brokering connective transactions between parties. Many of these portals are reminiscent of a matching or introduction service, acting as a conduit for finding a business partner or identifying needed products or services. Financial services firms should view these portals with the same eyes as the Medicis saw trade routes in the Middle Ages, that is to say, not as an invasion of domestic commerce and increased competition, but as opportunities to underwrite new possibilities of commerce. The new value propositions for financial services firms will reside in the formulation of services that reduce the risk of financing trade, lower the cost of transactions, reduce the processing time, act as a clearing house for such items as government paperwork and mitigate credit risks.

Taiwan, Hong Kong and other areas with long connections to the West have the opportunity to be the twenty-first-century Medicis, linking the East and West with a collection of services designed to facilitate business and, more importantly, the financing of business activity. In this newly defined market niche, there are numerous gateways forming with varying degrees of services, approaches and rates of success. The rising number of these gateways prohibits discussing an exhaustive list. However, AsianNet and the Asia-Pacific Economic Cooperation are two examples with contrasting approaches that merit closer investigation.

The first gateway is AsianNet, which acts as a mechanism to introduce goods and services within the Asian marketplace and provides global trade services. This marketplace acts as a gathering place for similar markets throughout the Asian region and supplies valuable links in order to reduce the barriers to trade through its close ties to the United Nations Trade Point Development Centre (UNTPDC), the China Foreign Economic Relations and Trade Committee, the China Chamber of International Commerce, the International Trade Association of Taiwan, Republic of China and the Korea International Trade Association (KITA). The AsianNet Trade InfoCenter's value proposition is to enhance the efficiency of international trade. In their words:

> Our goal is to enable users to access competitive trade-related information worldwide, a source of information which provides actual and potential traders with data about business and market opportunities, potential clients and suppliers.[3]

The second aspiring gateway is the Asia-Pacific Economic Cooperation,[4] which advocates meeting new challenges in the new century by achieving common prosperity through participation and co-operation. The goals expressed are not a value proposition per se, but are the base in which one can be developed, that is, sharing the benefits of globalization and the new economy, advancing trade and investment, and promoting sustained economic growth.

The three elements to the long-term viability of these gateways will be: knowledgeable people with at least one common goal and incentive;

technology to leverage communication to a public channel (one to all, recorded for later review) and a private channel (one to few); and a shared information space with access to past communications, access to past and current development products and mechanisms for the co-ordination of financial and non-financial data.

It can only be speculated if these Internet-based gateways will mature into viable mechanisms for financial services firms to reach new markets in Asia. The opportunity for financial services is to provide value-added mechanisms for businesses to finance trade, engage in commerce and offer commercial, investment and retail banking services. Historically, value propositions of trading hubs were defined by the physical location within a prearranged geography. It can be argued that a large part of the success enjoyed by financial institutions in fourteenth-century Venice was attributed to its privileged location. Geography in cyberspace is equally important, not as a representation of the physical earth with geopolitical boundaries, but as an environment in which to conduct business and engage in free trade.

However, like our medieval counterparts, a clear value proposition will drive business into these eMarketplaces. Hunt and Murray describe the primary conditions that are attributed to the successful adaptation of markets and fairs in the late Middle Ages:

> One cause certainly was the drive of businessmen to cut cost. A fair could reduce the overhead of bringing products to customers, because fixed costs were low (perhaps the rental of a bench and tent), and the flexibility of structure closely matched buyers and sellers. The more permanent and costly institutions in medieval cities could match neither the flexibility nor the lower cost of the fair.[5]

The characteristics of the medieval fair and its relationship to cost and flexibility are a striking parallel to the business conditions presented between the brick-and-mortar marketplaces and eMarketplaces of today.

The value proposition for firms providing financial services in Asia is twofold: to offer services within Asian geographical marketplaces and to facilitate connective pathways that integrate regional, commercial activities with other global markets. In order to capitalize on this potential new channel of services, organizations must develop core competencies in collaborative skills and technologies to respond rapidly to changing market conditions and tailor standardized product offerings to address the idiosyncrasies of local business climates. Collaboration, technology and niche products are the key to a successful firm in the Asian market.

CHAPTER 13

Lifestyle Banking from Down Under

In Chapter 3 we discussed how often ideas that are predicated on the use of technology are conceived long before society or customers are ready to accept them as valuable. The Australian financial services marketplace saw the rise and demise of co-opetition within financial marketplaces in AusMarkets Limited.

The Birth of an Idea

In November 2000, four of Australia's largest banks announced the formation of an Internet eMarketplace for the online distribution of wholesale financial products and services. Similar to the eFinance Interchange Model discussed later in Chapter 16, the formation of AusMarkets Limited by the ANZ Banking Group, the Commonwealth Bank of Australia, the National Australia Bank and the Westpac Banking Corp. endeavoured to establish an independent company to operate and manage a multi-contributor, multi-product platform. The value proposition for the customers of this marketplace was to offer large institutional and corporate clients a single access point for transacting wholesale financial products offered by each participant coupled with research, news, rates and portfolio analytics.

The Erosion of a Concept

Oddly, after a year of preparation and a six-month period of reviewing technology, the eMarketplace venture in Australia was put on hold. This was because the management team of the venture determined that the underlying business case to proceed was not directly convincing. The venture concluded that the viability of the value proposition had deteriorated during the course of the year:

> We conducted extensive customer research and understand clearly the proposition our customers require. The directors were unanimous in their decision to put this venture on hold and cited the deteriorating global economic climate and the difficulties being experienced by eCommerce ventures generally. Recent experiences of similar investment banking portals also suggested that the take-up rates being proposed 12 months ago were no longer realistic.[1]

It could be argued that the market is never ready for technological innovation and that the nature of entrepreneurship is what separates market innovation from corporate intention.

This is the fate of the post-dot-com boom: eMarketplaces now suffer a complete retreat from investment and start-up capital as the market moves towards ventures that only show rapid returns or more traditional justifications. This corporate behaviour needs to be placed in the context of the greater market/technology maturity, understanding that the motivations of the participants changed as the Internet matured from entrepreneurship into corporate channels to market. The primary motivation of early market creators was simply to capitalize on the potential behind the concept of disintermediation. In the exploratory process, the intent was to generate long-term profits, firstly by gaining market share and establishing a client base, and secondly by leveraging technology to reduce cost as the market reached a saturation point of competitors. However, investor's patience and market hype culminated in a market backlash that created a condition of Internet lethargy in the financial market sector.

Lessons Yet To Be Learned

Long before economic game theory had been developed to shed light on these types of corporate and market behaviours, the motivations of organizations under post-boom conditions are best understood by turning once again to a historical perspective. The Spanish conqueror Hernando Cortez, having landed in Mexico with a small complement of men, was certain that their ability to repel the vast forces of the Aztecs was limited. To motivate his men to excel beyond the limits of normal performance, Cortez carefully and visibly burned his ships to remove any notion of a retreat. The result of this action was that Spanish soldiers had no alternative but to stand and fight the Aztecs. As history records, the result was a bloodless victory as the Aztecs fled into the surrounding countryside. This same phenomenon was seen to some degree during the reengineering craze of the 1990s, when firms, facing clearly demonstrable declines or unprofitable conditions leading to closure, were quick to embrace the concept of starting from a white sheet of paper and rethinking their entire operating philosophy. On the other hand, large firms that endeavoured to reengineer and were laden with design committees and big project teams rarely witnessed their designs becoming reality. Therefore, this type of corporate behaviour could be summarized by saying that organizations with the most to lose take the greater risks and often enjoy the ability rapidly to adopt and innovate with technology.

Business in the twenty-first century is taking shape along two distinct fronts: the development of partnerships in an environment of co-opetition and a greater focus on customer fulfilment by ever-increasing levels of specialization. For financial services who find themselves in intense situations of cut-throat competition, studying the logic that governs the interrelationship between incentives, outcomes and strategic interactions should be used as a base for the development of market, product and brand strategies. For example: in the emerging eMarketplaces, early new market entrants were able to entice customers away from traditional banking companies by offering services that were tied to technology, with either higher interest rates or lower service fees. Because these new market entrants faced very low entry cost to the market, they were able to establish a presence on the Internet and compete head to head with larger, more established financial institutions. However, once the market reached a saturated level of competition and profit margins rapidly eroded to zero, the market began a consolidation to those organizations that could demonstrate a sustainable value proposition. The net effect of this consolidation is that the new financial eMarketplaces must offer a clear value proposition that can be understood as an integrated part of the long-term viability of a firm. Moreover, value propositions are now seeking specialization to address the specific needs of customer market sub-segments also observed in Australia.

What is interesting in the Australian market is that the refinement of financial services addresses the distinctive needs of the niche market of agriculture. Organizations such as BankWest[2] offer services that are tailored to support not only the individual farmer, but the entire supply and distribution chains of agriculture. For example, BankWest's Agribusiness is organized to incorporate all aspects of broad-acre farming from the production of raw food and fibre to final delivery of foodstuffs to the consumer. The value proposition for the customer is not only access to financial products and market information, but interaction with specialists, within the bank and its affiliates, who understand the nature of the problems faced in financing agricultural operations. This offering does not rest solely on leveraging technology. However, it does rely on the capabilities and competencies of a large network of relationship managers and specialized agribusiness consultants, who offer services in budgeting and farm management and have an understanding of the idiosyncrasies of the horticulture, viticulture, floriculture, aquaculture, silviculture and livestock production business. The highly specialized nature of these services allows BankWest to extend its financial offerings beyond the foodstuffs supply chain to include a greater diversity of agriculture production, including wineries, meat and seafood processing firms. However, to achieve this high level of niche market excellence, BankWest's success is predicated on having a customer base that finds these services valuable, added to which their investment in delivering market information, such as commodity price analysis, industry-specific analysis and monitoring land values, coupled with an extensive series of seminars, creates market demand by educating customers not only on their solution but the underlying problems faced by the industry. Here the value proposition to the customer is clear, targeted to a niche market sub-segment that understands the basic value added of the financial institution, and linked to a process of continuous education, which reduces the cost of sales on future product offerings. This is a good example of the second level of customer interaction which is discussed in greater detail in Chapter 25.

The next evolution of this type of market specialization can be a unified, intra-industry approach, thus avoiding the need to develop multiple, niche-specific networks which was the value proposition for AusMarkets Limited. The value proposition presented by AusMarkets Limited, in which a number of value-added financial services providers are aggregated into a single marketplace for convenient one-stop shopping for consumers and small businesses, is indeed not only viable but may simply be a technological innovation just slightly ahead of its time.

CHAPTER 14

The European Synconomy

Financial markets across the globe are becoming more accessible as a result of technological capability and the desire of investors to seek out new investment opportunities. In Europe, financial integration and deregulation are happening at a faster rate than many other markets due to the adoption of the Euro and the European Union's economic agenda. However, unlike the self-regulatory American attitude towards regulating commerce, the European mindset predisposes more towards legislation to protect economic activity. That said, the establishment of standardized investor-focused reporting mechanisms, coupled with a robust technological infrastructure, will give rise to market transparency, in this case the ability for investors to assess risk and return to make prudent financial decisions. The creation of a single market for capital across Europe has enormous implications and opportunities for financial services firms to demonstrate value propositions that interoperate in a heterogeneous collection of cultures and provide new levels of financial diversity.

The new connected European economy is evolving as a marketplace in which companies, customers and competitors collaborate on various aspects of design, development and refinement of product offerings in leveraging an operating synergy. A synergistic economy means a state of operation in which the behaviour of the entire marketplace is not predictable from the behaviour of the collaborating organizations taken separately. As financial services firms globally move into the twenty-first century, they must embrace a new state of co-opetition that enables them to compete and collaborate in all stages in the services' life cycle. Synconomy, a seemingly new phenomenon brought about by technology, describes a collaborative state of co-existing cells of organizational competency. Conceptually, it is reminiscent of the craftsmen guilds of the Middle Ages, whose continued quest for design improvement resulted in an extraordinary amount of accumulated design and process knowledge that has been almost completely lost in modern society. Put simply, medieval craftsmen were process oriented, not product oriented, which allowed them to learn not only the practical details of a trade, how to use tools and select materials, but also to understand how to design and collaborate with others within the guild to discover better methods and designs. This environment, underleveraged by communication technology, resulted in design innovations that spanned decades, making it easy for today's architectural historians to pinpoint construction dates of medieval building simply by observing the stonework. Today, in a synconomy, financial services organizations must develop complete process knowledge in order to balance the associated processes of a European-wide deposit market, inter-regional risk sharing, interoperable capital markets, diversification of multinational portfolios and new global capital sourcing for business activities. One of the first value propositions is the establishment of networked repositories of data on corporate performance to relieve the scarcity of investor information. A decentralized network of company information will need to cross national boundaries in order to keep emerging capital and non-capital markets from becoming detached from the mainstream global investor. Traditionally, the lack of information has hindered the growth of individual firms and protected small to medium sized local firms from stock volatility. Removing the barriers to information flow will make firms seeking global capital sources more susceptible to swings in investor sentiment concerning a region or market sector that could be unrelated to the fundamentals of an individual firm. Therefore, the second value proposition for financial services firms endeavouring to facilitate European and indeed global capital market fluidity will be to place individual corporate performance into the greater context of global economic activity.

In the evolving synconomy, the challenges of culture, labour, technology, consumer adoption, and branding must be considered in two aspects, integrated and differentiated corporate behaviours. In order to have market differentiation, firms operating in a synconomy must maintain a balance in the synergistic relationship between what is shared or integrated between partners and what is unique to a participant in an open marketplace. Collaboration between co-operating financial services firms is not a matter of if one should collaborate, it is an understanding of when, how and what to exchange. Fortunately, technology is removing the geographic confines of market collaboration, making exchange partners aware of the need to develop core competencies to address the issues of how to collaborate, what to collaborate on, and when to collaborate.

Regardless of the level of collaboration, any participation in the new co-opetition-based marketplace requires a clear, measurable, value proposition to customers, partners and shareholders.

The financial services industry in Europe is undergoing a redefinition which was brought about by technology, motivated by disintermediation and driven by market differentiation. In the race for market share, wallet share and industry dominance, many financial services institutions are developing brand and market strategies that often overlook the transitional state which the customer must endure as the industry reinvents itself. If one considers the classical definition of strategy as 'planning or directing an operation in a war campaign'[1] as the underlying premise for competition in the marketplace, it is curious to note that the word customer never appears in the description. One must remember that, in a war between different firms, customers are often viewed in the same light as civilians during political conflicts, frequently alienated during the process and, in many cases, commoditized to an acceptable level of casualties or losses. Machiavelli reminds us that

> whoever wishes to reform a long-established state in a free city should retain at least the appearance of its ancient ways.[2]

His view should be made a part of the contemporary transitional planning process.

At the heart of this transition in the industry are technology and the customers. Customers fall into two broad categories: individual depositors or investors seeking financial product agility (that is, the best products to serve their needs) and large/medium/small companies looking for business financial agility (that is, the right products to serve a changing set of needs). In this sense, financial product agility is derived from a value proposition that is supported by a combination of flexible banking software and a stable technology infrastructure architecture (financial product agility = flexibility of software + stability of technology architecture). Put simply, a dependable core banking system that readily accepts new and changing end user (teller or customer) delivery capabilities.

A distinct value proposition to small companies looking for business financial agility is to combine a rapid, flexible suite of product offerings with the relative stability offered in the currency and markets (business financing agility = rapid flexibility of financial services products = relative stability in access currency and markets). That is to say that banking product offerings need to be flexible enough to adapt to changing business conditions, while financial services firms offer a base of cash management and other commerce-enabling services that make currency and access to capital markets appear to be stable. Stability in this case is the underlying base service offering; even though the markets themselves and the currencies will continue to fluctuate, the access to those markets must be reliable and consistent.

During the formation of the emerging stages of growth within the European synconomy, financial services firms face two key challenges. The first is the core processing dilemma, and the second is that of process segmentation:

> Overall, however, the ability of large banks to innovate in the core processing area remains severely constrained by dependence on mainframe technology and the need for any new systems to be capable of processing massive volumes.[3]

Surprised by the speed of how new market entrants can suddenly appear on the market and enlist customers, financial firms have underestimated that legacy systems can be a liability when they encumber a firm's ability to bring new product innovations to market. Offering new co-branded, co-mingled and sometimes co-delivered product offerings will necessitate the acquisition of new core processing systems, core banking applications and other financial applications. Over the last few years, firms have raced to interchange between legacy systems and new Internet and other delivery technologies, simply because of competitive pressure. However, it would be naive to believe that present in-house developed and other batch core banking systems will continue to be a viable infrastructure over the next ten years. As technology continues on its evolutionary path, the cost of labour to maintain these systems and continually integrate new components into the older systems architecture will become cost prohibitive. Therefore, it is not a question of if today's core banking systems will need to be replaced; it is a question of when. Prudent firms are looking at the new array of core banking systems infrastructure and realizing that the economic downturn of the latter half of 2001 is indeed a counterintuitive time to lay the foundation for the next round of competition.

The second challenge is that of process segmentation, which necessitates the development of clear value added at each step in the overall process of delivering financial services to consumers and business. If the value proposition of a process or process segment cannot be readily identified, the process and products it services should be questioned. Processes with an uncertain value proposition or those whose value propositions depend on the organization's ability to perform the operation at a competitive cost should be valued in the context of the entire process. If a cost effective alternative is available on the market from partnering companies, the process should be outsourced:

> As developments in Internet banking and eCommerce change the economies of banking, so the structural characteristics of the industry will alter.[4]

The result of new levels of competition, the evolution of technology and the slow but steady adoption of technology by various consumer market segments will lead financial institutions to a radical rethinking of services and product offerings. This redefinition of the banking services has already begun with delivery technologies such as ATMs, EFTPOS, telephone banking, call centres, Internet banking, eCommerce and eCards, and CRM applications will eventually lead to back office core banking technologies. During this transition, institutions will have to address a reengineering or at least a complete rethinking of their core business processes from a value generation point of view. The revolutionary changes that will eventually lead to the revitalization of the products and services offered to European customers have already presented themselves. As the synconomy of European economic markets begins to emerge, companies will discover that the key to capitalizing on the new business environment will rest squarely on achieving a robust technological infrastructure and developing a high level of corporate agility.

CHAPTER 15

The Scandinavian Approach to mBanking

The many visions of mobile banking (hereafter mBanking) have led some financial services institutions to believe that instead of 'm' standing for mobile banking, it should stand for mystical banking, as in many cases the return on investments is as elusive as the Holy Grail. Successful in Scandinavia and so far failing to meet expectations everywhere else, mBanking offers two lessons: firstly, the successful implementation of the technological aspect of product offerings is directly proportional to the social adoption or saturation of the cellular phone technology; and secondly, the financial services product offerings' value proposition is directly connected to the demographic tastes indigenous not only to a specified geography, but also to highly fragmented market segments of technology adept customers.

Social Adoption

Industry sources have argued that the greater saturation of the mobile phone technology in Scandinavia is attributed to various social factors. Firstly, younger generations, who need to look fashionably 'in', have been using mobile phones instead of old-fashioned pagers. Secondly, in a more cost-oriented analysis, in Scandinavia the overall cost of owning and operating a mobile phone is lower than landline phones. Looking at the mobile phone phenomenon from a young person's point of view, the lower cost of ownership coupled with the convenience of moving house without changing numbers makes the technology flexible to a lifestyle. The ability to be reachable or merely to be able to communicate at any time, which is a basic desire in many customer market sub-segments, is moving mobile phone technology from a niche product to a mainstream commodity.

Europeans are leading the adoption of mobile technologies, and European financial services firms are merely replicating, not rethinking, retail banking product offerings. The overall success of mBanking has been less than the expectations set by the industry, primarily because of an overestimation of the adoption rate, but, more importantly, because of a lack of a clear and compelling value proposition to migrate to mBanking as a primary means of banking by consumers. Not to oversimplify the matter, but financial institutions have often overlooked the basic premise of mobile technology as it relates to a value proposition within a select demographic group. The value proposition for mBanking, that is, the aspect of convenience that it provides, is only applicable to customers in a very small segment of each demographic sector. The rate of adoption in different cultures also varies, making mBanking a less-obvious alternative to other types of banking.

The Mobility of People and Money

One observation to consider is that in the past one could dial a number and call a place, a physical location which was immobile, and the person one wished to speak to was either there or not there. Now, however, one is no longer calling a place; one is calling a person directly. The misconception of mobile banking is that the mobile device itself is driving customer demand because the customer is mobile; put simply, the person is mobile, and the money in the account is stationary and occasionally moves. A non-traditional way of thinking is that my money is mobile and I might be stationary even if I move during the day, my citizenship, my home and where I spend money are at fixed points. More specifically, currency in the new century is the mobile commodity, and technology, which will take many forms over the next ten years, will be merely a delivery mechanism for channelling money to stationary and virtual spending points.

However, the role of technology is only half the equation. As previously said, the social adoption of these technologies and the redefinition of what money represents are the limiting factors that will govern the success of offering financial services products to consumer and small business markets. So as to elaborate this point, a brief examination of the one value proposition associated with share trading for high net-worth individuals using WAP phone technology provides insight into one aspect of the mBanking problem. The expressed value proposition is that a high net-worth customer can be advised of share price movements continually throughout the day, and can act on these changes as the market fluctuates. This makes share trading easy, convenient, spontaneous and available literally anywhere, keeping the high net-worth individual abreast of his/her portfolio and the positions within the portfolio, so that corrective actions can be taken on a minute-by-minute basis.

Market Sub-segment Value Proposition

With such a clear value proposition to the customer, why has mBanking fallen short of the expectations generated by the marketplace? A closer examination of the value proposition reveals, firstly, that mobile share trading for high net-worth individuals only applies to a very small market segment; secondly, that a typical investor who wants to purchase or sell a stock at a predetermined price point can place the order via the Internet and simply wait for the transaction to take place; thirdly, that investors typically need additional information to confirm their overall attitude towards the transaction in the form of charts, graphs and financial analysis; and finally, if the investors have the propensity to continuously monitor shares and trade on them on a minute-by-minute basis, they would simply be at a computer performing these transactions, and only using the mobile when they could not get to their primary device. Therefore, although the value proposition to the customer is technologically capable, it is not robust enough to sustain it long term. This fact, coupled with an appeal to a very small target market, does not invalidate mBanking; it does, however, indicate that a greater degree of targeted strategy must be employed to ensure it as a viable channel to market. There will always be some sub-segments of the market that require this form of mobile share trading (see Figure 15.1).

To maximize technology's ability to enhance a value proposition, individual types of technology need to be applied to the social adoption of each device by market sub-segment. However, micro-market sub-segmentation can be taken too far and lead to choice overload, which may result in customer alienation. As Wiersema put it:

> Mere variety and multiple choices make choosing the right solution the customer's job. And that's a job they may not be prepared to handle.[1]

Therefore, financial services firms must strike a balance between providing customers with a wide range of products and organizing these offerings into logical associations. The tendency in the market today is to assemble products into offerings that facilitate customers' lifestyles. In any case, whatever the final product grouping, the value proposition offered to the target customer segment must be clear. Regardless of the delivery technology, the value proposition must exist and be compelling, and the technology should be viewed as the mechanism for product delivery and value realization. Figure 15.1 illustrates that for each customer market sub-segment, a value proposition must be developed for each technology. At the intersection of each technology and segment a value proposition must then be identified, assigned a specific worth (relative value to the organization, for example total projected earnings, ROI, or market penetration), and ranked to determine which collection of technologies can be employed to deliver financial products offerings. Typically, profit margins and transaction volumes have driven the technology deployment without considering where the market segments are on the technology-adoption maturity curve. The rate of social adoption often lags behind the market hype, and invariably some implementations are premature while other technology decisions are delayed until they no longer command a competitive advantage.

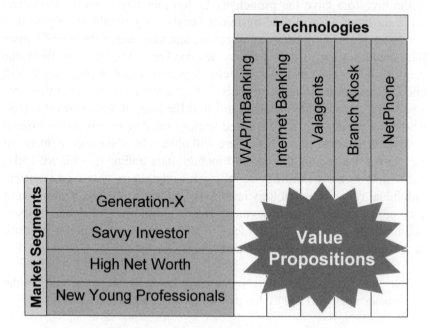

Figure 15.1 Application of technology by market segment

One technology that is in its infancy of social adoption is Bluetooth, which holds tremendous potential for facilitating micro-transactions and other traditional low-value exchanges. When combined with digital currencies, the value proposition it presents to consumers is the convenient purchase of goods or the exchange of a denominated value such as loyalty points without being connected to the Internet. For example: a mobile phone with a Bluetooth[2] chip could simply be pointed towards a vending machine and transmit the value of the beverage to the machine, which would then dispense the beverage. Since digital money is tokened and precertified as real, there is no need for verification via a communication line, unlike a credit or debit card that requires a physical link. Therefore, the value proposition to the merchant is the freedom of being connected to an infrastructure for micro-payments, especially attractive to small businesses because it eliminates the need for cash-handling services.

Another technology that provides insight to the evolution of ATM machines in the wireless environment is the introduction of Euronet Mobile Recharge,[3] which facilitates a customer's purchase of additional prepaid airtime. This technology authorizes a financial transaction, processing the recharge of the phone automatically, triggering a credit to the subscriber's prepaid account and generating a confirming receipt using the mobile phone SMS message capability. The longer term implication of this technology, when applied to certificated digital currencies, is that mobile phones, like ATM machines, could become electronic wallets with the capability to recharge or reload digital cash by initiating the same type of transaction to a bank account. The next generation of mobile technologies will see the integration or intertwining of mBanking and mCommerce capabilities, at which time the value proposition to customers will be more compelling purely due to the convenience in facilitating purchases traditionally associated with cash. However, the adoption or popularization will move in lock step with the implementation and mass distribution of digital currencies. Customers will discover the rising value of convenience when the number of places (such as merchants, banks, telecoms, airports, hotels) in which to interact reaches a saturation level in which digital commerce becomes convenient.

Often overlooked in assessing the long-term value of technology is the development of performance measurement criteria that can be monitored for the express purpose of timing the replacement to the next generation of technologies. With the continued acceleration of technological advancement, it can be argued that, in the case of retail banking delivery mechanisms, technology is a temporary state which provides the organization with a defined capability for a limited period of time. A key corporate competency is to know when to migrate to technologies that are linked to value propositions and synchronized with the rate of social adoption.

To contextualize technologies associated with retail banking functions for value creation, one should consider the relative maturity of these technologies in the following structure: an ATM is no more than a substitute for a bank teller; a debit card is a card that acts like a cheque, a credit card is just a prenegotiated loan in your pocket; and smart cards, stored-value cards or micro-payment technology is simply an electronic substitute for cash. Within that construct, mBanking is the collection of all these technologies, enabled by the new communications innovations that are increasing the availability of these services to the consumer. It could be argued that the value proposition for mobile banking to customers is convenience, and to the financial institution it is another step towards lower long-term operating cost.

CHAPTER 16

Eastern Europe Inc. Even Shakespeare said 'What's in a Name?'

The fragmented Eastern European marketplace presents an interesting environment for value creation that allows previously competing financial services providers to establish a co-branded, co-operative market presence for their products and services in a level playing field. Financial services firms have an opportunity to provide branded financial products under an umbrella of a pseudo-franchise of services theoretically labelled the eFinance Interchange Model. It is strikingly similar to the complex partnerships found in the Italian super-companies of the late medieval times, in which competitive organizations shared a common resource (for example a ship) to engage in long-range trade activities. The mechanism of a franchised service galvanizes the regional marketplace by providing a suite of mixed products (primarily retail banking services and commercial banking services in small and medium enterprises) that span competing firms in Eastern Europe. The essential ingredients of the model are: eMarketplace aggregation, brand management and a set of consolidated settlement services.

The volatility and tenor of the emerging Eastern European eMarketplaces, led by technology, are tempered with a note of caution in the development of co-mingled services. However, as these evolving markets undergo a series of transformations, a continuing focus on higher levels of customer service and increased aggregation of transaction data present Eastern Europe with a unique opportunity, that of the establishment of a co-operative retail banking marketplace (see Figure 16.1).

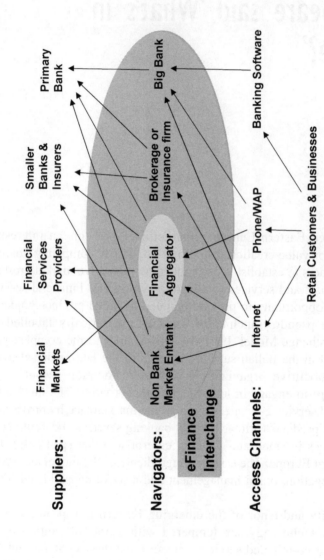

Suppliers:

Financial Markets

Financial Services Providers

Smaller Banks & Insurers

Primary Bank

Navigators:

eFinance Interchange

Non Bank Market Entrant

Financial Aggregator

Brokerage or Insurance firm

Big Bank

Access Channels:

Internet

Phone/WAP

Banking Software

Retail Customers & Businesses

Figure 16.1 The emerging market structure

As said above, at present the Internet-based banking services for financial services are fragmented and customers do not have a distinct point of contact to compare financial services offerings from providers in a simple, easy to navigate environment or portal. Europe, and more specifically Eastern Europe, is no exception to this condition, but is, however, in a unique position to exploit new technology to effectively surpass other areas of the world by providing a higher class of services via recently deployed infrastructure.

The value proposition for consumers, depositors and/or investors is the ability to select the best financial services product offerings to meet their needs. Specifically, the environment provides information on the offerings of financial products for many sources and ranks them for the best option for a customer and then facilitates the establishment of accounts with the financial services institution.

Market Aggregation

The growth of the marketplace will continue to introduce new entrants to the financial services market with a suite of product and services offerings that will continue to inflate the competitive situation. That said, the development of an eFinance Interchange Model in the arena of financial services offerings will pioneer a self-contained marketplace that will be an anchor point for providers, enabling them to both broadcast their product offerings and develop strong lines of customer service capabilities. Acting as a financial intermediary for depositors and investors, one or several financial services firm could develop an offering that provides an underlying structure to the fragmented marketplace. Early versions or nodes of an eFinance Interchange Model are already in use by firms such as ABN Amro in the eMarketplace.[1] As seen in Figure 16.2, the model acts as a gateway between ABN Amro and its affiliated partners such as Atlantic Mortgage, LaSalle Bank, LaSalle Home Mortgage, and Standard Federal Bank. Another example is Intuit's integrated Quicken product which links to their Internet Home Loan centre,[2] and aggregates conventional, alternative, home equity, jumbo and government mortgages from all 50 states in the United States.

The basic construction of the environment should be a simple framework that provides a customer with the flexibility of registering his or her information (name, address, and so on) that can be sent to a financial services provider at the same time as products and services are selected. Each financial services provider will depend on a prebuilt data exchange

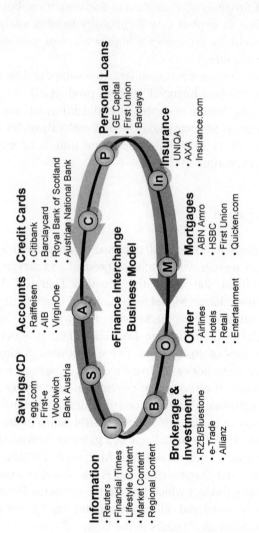

Information
• Reuters
• Financial Times
• Lifestyle Content
• Market Content
• Regional Content

Savings/CD
• egg.com
• First-e
• Woolwich
• Bank Austria

Accounts
• Raiffeisen
• AIB
• VirginOne

Credit Cards
• Citibank
• Barclaycard
• Royal Bank of Scotland
• Austrian National Bank

Personal Loans
• GE Capital
• First Union
• Barclays

Insurance
• UNIQA
• AXA
• Insurance.com

Mortgages
• ABN Amro
• HSBC
• First Union
• Quicken.com

Other
• Airlines
• Hotels
• Retail
• Entertainment

Brokerage & Investment
• RZB/Bluestone
• e-Trade
• Allianz

eFinance Interchange
Business Model

Figure 16.2 eFinance Interchange Model

format that will facilitate transactions. A data management scheme will have to be developed to support the interchange of data.

The ownership of the customer relationship will remain with the eFinance Interchange Model marketplace and information required by the associated financial services organizations will be brokered between the parties. However, the struggle of financial institutions for the ownership of the customer profile and relationship adds a level of complexity to the technological aspect of the model.

In order to facilitate the model, there is a technological underpinning that will act as a catalyst for the marketplace and facilitate transactions initiated by both the customers and financial institutions. As each financial services partner is added or removed, the data and information exchange formats will need to be created.

For example: ABC Bank requires ten items of information for mortgage origination and XYZ Bank requires fourteen items of information, of which only eight are common between the two firms. The marketplace will need to establish a baseline of the data that is available for interchange with all member financial services organizations. Creating a standard method of interchange is an often overlooked but vital part to be considered with any joint venture or co-mingled product. So as to participate in an interconnected marketplace, financial services firms will need to adopt a technology philosophy that views a spectrum of technology and assess the rate of change associated within each band of the spectrum.

The Technology Spectrum

The last twenty years of applying technology to financial services indicates that various technologies mature and change at different rates. These maturity rates can be understood by simple observation of the technologies associated with back office and core banking operations, which change less often and remain relatively stable for long time periods, whereas end user delivery technologies experience a higher degree of volatility and change due to the influence of purchases by consumers. Retail banking delivery technologies will continue to innovate at a faster rate due primarily to the number of financial services firms experimenting with them, and will require a higher amount of integration with existing infrastructures. Implementation of consumer-driven delivery technologies will also require a value proposition that is focused on the needs and desires of the end consumer. At the other end of the spectrum, the value proposition for core banking operations is shareholder value, the financial institution's ability to reduce cost strategically and establish an infrastructure which provides a stable connection to the back office and anticipates continual changes in the retail delivery end of the spectrum (see Figure 16.3).

It can be argued that within each band of the technology spectrum there are transactions that originate in one band and flow through to any and all bands. At each level of the transaction path, a variety of partnerships or relationships will be required, unless a firm is prepared to invest in all the technologies necessary to perform all banking functions. One alternative is to outsource each technology function to third parties that can deliver discrete components within a linked architecture. However, at this early stage of market maturity, there is no indication that any single application service provider (ASP) could perform all the required technologies for any large-scale endeavour. Seemingly, the ever-changing nature of this market may indeed produce a new ASP that has a wider selection and deeper capability to service the eFinance Interchange Model.

Technologically, the eFinance Interchange Model provides a framework in which to organize the interconnected technologies that will support a variety of transactions and formats required by financial services organizations participating in this type of exchange. Eastern Europe could be divided into three to five operating marketplaces and united into one aggregated market with today's existing technology. This unity of service may be as simple as one firm providing clearing services for all members. The growth of this variety of eMarketplace may only be hindered primarily by the unavailability of the technology partners and participating members. Ultimately, the ability to launch in multiple markets will depend

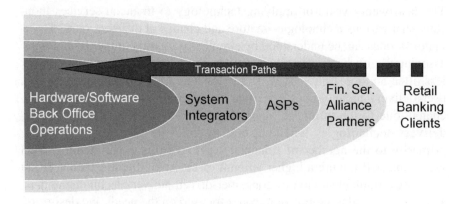

Figure 16.3 The spectrum of technology

on the legal and regulatory circumstances, as well as financial and operational implications, and timed by the perceived readiness of each marketplace. The value proposition that this eMarketplace offers to members is the capacity to provide services in multiple geographic markets to a wide variety of market segments with minimal investment in technology.

Developing a Brand by Sharing Technological Risk

In act 2, scene 2 of Shakespeare's *Romeo and Juliet*, Juliet speaks the immortal words: 'What's in a name? That which we call a rose, by any other name would smell as sweet.'[3] In an eFinance Interchange, one of the most visible concerns is that of financial services providers and product identity. Branding and the development of a clear market differentiation will be the essential elements in developing a strategy for participating in this market. In this case, a brand must be representative of a value proposition to the customer and reflect a distinct avenue to the value of the firm offering the product. In fact, the more companies co-operate with technological infrastructure, the greater the need to brand products clearly.

Financial services firms will participate in this co-opetition market simply to share the cost of providing infrastructure technology, allowing them to concentrate on more distinctive retail delivery mechanisms and to mitigate the risk of failure in implementing retail technology that is subject to changes in end user preferences (in this case, the customers). If collections of small to medium sized financial institutions elect to participate in this type of eMarketplace or Internet banking, the requirement to partner on infrastructure becomes clearer. The establishment of Internet-based banking with multi-channel access can be developed along two distinct fronts: either a capability provided generically by the ASP or a capability provided by the financial services organizations that is integrated by the ASP. Although access through PC/Internet and mobile telephones is desirable, the cost effectiveness may be difficult to spread across the financial services partners. It may be cost effective to allow each service partner to provide their own technology that is linked to the eFinance Interchange Model.

Providing integrated telephone contact centre support adds another level of complexity to the model. Support for this model will fall into two broad categories: financial services customers and financial services providers. Bringing in a high-quality, high-touch support function will require either the acquisition of a CRM technology tool-set coupled with a service organization that has a capability in each geographic market, or outsourcing the CRM to a third party. However, the multi-language requirement may demand the use of several CRM organizations linked via the ASP to provide service in all areas. Alternatively, the CRM function could be performed by financial services organizations locally and transactions simply routed through the eFinance Interchange Model.

Consolidated Settlement Services

To facilitate an eMarketplace approach, financial services firms working with technology vendors need to craft a generic 'bank in a box' offering in order to provide a basic set of capabilities for the marketplace. A solution set will then be duplicated for each geographical area, providing multiple markets for financial services that are bounded by language and currency (and also the Euro if required) (see Figure 16.4).

This bank in a box framework is best facilitated by a collection of service providers organized in a joint technology infrastructure. The more generic the structure, the more flexible the offering and less integration required.

The ASP phenomenon in the United States is moving slowly towards Europe, resulting in a highly fragmented and emerging marketplace. Working with an ASP is not a question of or/or, but rather of and/and. It is not necessary to access all the financial product applications offered by an ASP. They can function perfectly in combination with applications that are run locally at the physical or proxy location of the financial institution. Some vendors may offer more than one type of service. For example: Fiserv offers customers the option of an application-based ASP as well as the technology infrastructure to support their product.[4]

A preliminary view of the European ASP market reveals that the new entrants vary in quality and delivery capability, providing a vast array of services. Unfortunately, there is no clear market leader for Eastern European financial services. Still, the power of Internet technologies allows an eFinance Interchange to be hosted in Western Europe, the United Kingdom or even the United States. However, the centralized customer support would present a logistical problem to overcome. Some of the ASPs may partner with other vendors or Internet portals to provide comprehensive service offerings along a specific transaction path such as mortgage services. An ASP could set up agreements with Internet portals to combine Internet financial resources with value-added content information on a co-branded website.

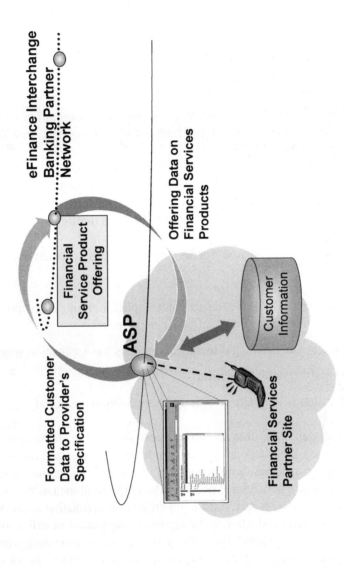

eFinance Interchange
Banking Partner
Network

Financial Service Product
Offering

Formatted Customer
Data to Provider's
Specification

ASP

Offering Data on
Financial Services
Products

Customer
Information

Financial Services
Partner Site

Figure 16.4 The ASP-enabled bank in a box

Regardless of the underlying structure of the ASP relationship, financial services firms electing to participate in this new co-opetition environment will need to concentrate on four things:

- Managing financial services product applications on locally owned servers;

- Maintaining continual communications with the ASP;

- Delegating responsibility for the operation and security of the applications to the ASP;

- Translating any of the financial services provider's integration requirements in terms of applications and functionality the ASP has to offer.

Consequently, the decision to use an ASP presents a level of risk to the financial services firm due to the untested level of implied and expressed trust in the ASP's ability to deliver to the new client base, and the chance that a percentage of the client base may be alienated during the conversion process if a failure occurs.

The decision to use an ASP for a certain application depends on four criteria:

- How complex is the financial product application and corresponding data passing through to financial services partners?

- How much maintenance and management does the application require?

- How complex is implementation?

- To what extent is integration with other applications required?

However, one can claim that the more effort involved in delivering retail services, the more advantageous an ASP can be to lower cost and risk. Financial services applications demand quite a lot of an organization, and the participation in this particular type of marketplace combined with an ASP allows a firm to concentrate resources on critical differentiation areas. What is advantageous is the reduction in the amount of significant modifications to be made in the infrastructure. This, in its turn, can reduce time during implementation and minimize or eliminate interruptions in service. In addition, well-trained specialists are needed in-house for the management of these, adding and removing the connections to various exchange mechanisms with the financial services partners. Developing the connective mechanisms will be the responsibility of a systems' integrator or be provided by the ASP.

The perceived benefits of the ASP to financial institutions include:

■ Lowering the cost associated with the purchase of applications;

■ Reduction in hardware costs;

■ Faster implementations in target geographic areas;

■ Software maintenance is the responsibility of the ASP;

■ The latest software releases will be maintained;

■ In-house management can be reduced to a minimum;

■ ASP absorbs peaks in usage and eliminates capacity problems;

■ Support for the financial services partners is from ASP specialists.

Taking these aims into consideration, the following requirements, which ideally would be met completely by the ASP, should be the baseline for developing a relationship. The ASP should ideally:

■ Have implementation experience in the target geography or at least in Europe, in order to reduce the amount of learning and to leverage as much knowledge, software, and hardware from previous implementations as possible.

■ Have a presence in the target geography with dedicated resources on the ground. Again, this will translate into knowledge of the markets and will ensure a concentration of time and effort.

■ Be able to bring to bear language capabilities in order to operate effectively in the markets.

■ Present a solution supporting multi-currency processing including the Euro.

■ Offer a wide range of standard products such as savings and current accounts, including ATM, debit cards and insurance.

■ Provide the capability of customizing these products to match an institution's brand image.

■ Offer multi-channel and device access, including PC/Internet, mobile phone, and fixed-line call centre support with intelligent voice response.

■ Bring to bear as much of the end-to-end solution as possible, and have partnerships in place to fill any gaps. Ideally, this should include the core processing system, or engine, upon which the end-to-end solution will be based and into which partners' solutions would be interfaced.

■ Have systems integration capabilities and proven experience. Although there will be little in the way of legacy systems to deal with, the ASP will necessarily have to integrate solutions not only directly from its own business, but also from other vendors and third parties. This may require a partnership between an ASP and a systems' integrator.

■ Be agreeable to different contractual arrangements in addition to a straight client–vendor relationship. In particular, the ASP should be open to risk-and-reward pricing and/or joint ventures.

■ Be able to support an eFinance Interchange Model for Internet banking, including aggregation of financial services products from other banks.

■ Demonstrate the capability to scale product offerings to meet rising transaction volumes.

■ Permit flexibility to allow participating firms to modify the products as new banking products evolve.

Key Things to Consider

The concept of the eFinance Interchange Model is viable technologically with several avenues for its ultimate accomplishment. To provide the greatest level of flexibility and long-term integration capabilities between joint ventures instituted by future financial services partners and potential technology providers necessitates the establishment of a suite of core competencies.

The requirement of owning the customer relationship presents the typical ASP with an additional feature or function that is not in the standard suite of offerings. Customer ownership is a rising issue within the financial services industry. A combination of the use of technology and partnering may offer two ways to accomplish a controlled customer experience: the ASP can use technology simply to transfer the customer seamlessly to the participating financial services firm, or the ASP can partner with a firm that specializes in CRM services and provide an interconnecting mechanism between the customer and the target financial services provider.

Eventually the interconnected, co-operative marketplace will mature and the need for members to enter and exit over time will drive the establishment of exchange rules. This may be especially true as consumers weed out good providers from less desirable ones through their selection process. In order to support the eFinance Interchange Model, a systems integrator or a system integration capability provided by the ASP will be necessary to maintain total infrastructure and the corresponding connections to the participating financial services firms.

Bringing the capability of an Internet bank in a box into the light of day as a complete package with an associated information exchange portal integrating data to and from financial services partners is a technological reality today. Organizations such as Kindle Banking Systems, Fiserv, FNS and System Access have demonstrated that the maturity of the core processing systems has advanced enough to support an eMarketplace with or without ASP intervention.

Using mature core banking technologies in conjunction with an ASP, or simply establishing a traditional banking service in an eMarketplace, is critically dependent on a core system that is flexible enough to accept connections with multiple software systems. The added requirement of multi-systems integration is fuelling the necessity of using a packaged solution to participate in an eMarketplace.

Utilizing packaged solutions is providing an added boost to overall productivity, given that it allows the rapid introduction of new financial services to the eMarketplace. A reasonable time to develop the technology is approximately 90 to 180 days; however, organizations should strive to reduce this to 30 days. As a complete unit, it can subsequently be cloned and specifically modified to reflect the local currency and language, thus being adjusted for each geographic location.

From a technological point of view, a co-operative marketplace for financial services is ultimately achievable. The technologies exist to perform the desired functions and provide the necessary features that would make the eFinance Interchange Model a viable marketplace for financial services companies to offer their services in Eastern Europe.

Although the technology for the development of an eFinance interchange environment for financial services exists, it is clear that there are many non-technology issues hampering the establishment of such a dynamic marketplace. The value proposition to the consumer is very compelling, and so is the ability to select the best of the best financial services products, link them together to support one's lifestyle, and seek out the best rates and lowest cost providers. This opportunity may be short lived before more sophisticated new market entrants develop capabilities that will fill this market niche.

CHAPTER 17

Developing a Twenty-first-century Middle Eastern Financial Services Agenda

Financial services firms operating in the Middle East face many of the same challenges as their western counterparts. In the quest for globalization, it is frequently the indigenous cultural values that are overlooked when designing financial services product offerings. New market entrants, large global institutions and a highly fragmented marketplace are the canvas of competition in which financial services organizations must paint the picture that differentiates their valued-added service offerings to their customers.

The opportunity for Middle Eastern financial services firms is to transform the traditional banking relationships into a network of Islamic-based eEconomy-driven services that acts as a lynchpin to broker services throughout the Middle East, while acting as a financial hub connecting Eastern Europe, Africa and Southern Asia. Middle Eastern banking concerns are in a unique position to lead the reinvention of financial services because of the collaborative nature of regional long-term relationships at the microeconomic business activity level.

The microeconomic business climate in countries such as the United Arab Emirates is predicated on a time-honoured tradition of building a relationship between parties, based on an implied trust and confidence that delivery expectations are met. This attitude of trust and developing an understanding between partners is the foundation for a collaborative organizational structure and the establishment of a molecular co-opetition marketplace, which operates by leveraging partnerships in a co-operative model.

The opportunities and challenges for regional financial services organizations in the Middle East share a striking resemblance with the geographically distinct regions in Europe. Competition in these regional markets has to be addressed on three fronts: large global organizations, new market entrants and small local firms. Technology is considered the key to competitive differentiation, and will continue to create an array of conditions that provide low-cost entry for new market entrants in the financial services sector.

As discussed previously, in order to compete in the new global eEconomy, it is crucial to create a regional agenda that positions cultural interests into a global perspective and reveals the importance of the issues of brand, technology, customer preference and way of life to overall Middle Eastern banking objectives. A simple framework for thinking can be employed to establish relevance and perspective: think global (combined infrastructures); act regional (targeted products); look local (service offerings).

Think Global

Large global financial services firms are interpreting globalization as identical to 'standardization' or providing a suite of generic financial products that are designed to reduce the overall cost of operations. New entrants to existing markets and newly forming marketplaces clearly have a competitive advantage because of their ability to adapt rapidly to market conditions and develop offerings to service niche market opportunities. The competitive advantage for small local banking operations is brand recognition and a greater propensity to provide a higher degree of customer service.

Act Regional

Like many geographies of the world, the preservation of the regional cultural values existing in the Middle East is foremost in the minds of financial services firms. This is expressed in their concern to establish brands, services and product offerings that reflect the beliefs of the region and provide a suite of services that incorporates the needs of many ethnic groups within the population. Creating a regional white labelled aggregation service that performs back office processing, trading and clearing services for local financial institutions enables smaller operations to outsource basic banking services and focus on strategic initiatives such as branding, customer service and introducing new services. Smaller operations can make a clear value choice on issues such as branding, driven by the attitudes of the local customer base. In that sense, an institution may elect to retain its local branding and simply participate in the network by outsourcing back office operations. Likewise, it may decide to co-brand with a larger institution for a wider market appeal and broker services via the aggregated marketplace. Consequently, a small institution may elect to co-brand in a particular geography and remain locally branded in others, and simply make use of the shared infrastructure.

Look Local

Accordingly, the marketplace for financial services at the local level is fragmented, and customers frequently do not have a single point of contact to compare financial services offerings from providers in a simple, easy to navigate environment or portal. This creates an opportunity for financial services companies to reinvent banking and target consumers who are shopping for services that meet the needs of their lifestyles, beliefs, cultural preferences and financial sophistication. Surprisingly, brand, company and product identity is now an integral part of how technology is crafted into new product offerings. The lesson learned over the last ten years is that not all cultures adopt financial services delivery technology in the same way. Local technology is adopted according to a number of factors including youth trends, religion, cultural preferences and other aspects that are indigenous to a specific geography. These cultural idiosyncrasies are essential ingredients in developing a value proposition by market segment. Developing a local/regional value proposition for financial services in the Middle Eastern theatre thus requires taking many local factors into account and striking a balance between cost of delivery and total potential value of the market segment serviced.

The Opportunity for Middle Eastern Co-opetition

Financial services, technology, consumer behaviour, market segmentation and other cultural factors create the conditions for a seedbed of co-opetition employing a Middle Eastern version of the eFinance Interchange Model, as described in Chapter 16. This model is a theoretical marketplace in which financial services organizations can provide suites of services (primarily retail banking services) to customers throughout Islamic countries. An interchange marketplace is an environment that allows previously competing financial services providers to establish a market presence for their products and services in a level playing field. Regions such as the Middle East present a set of conditions to exploit new technology to effectively surpass other areas of the world by providing a higher class of services via co-developed deployment infrastructure. In short, market conditions exist within the region for co-operative ventures between financial institutions that aim to develop symbiotic relationships of shared service offerings, infrastructure and products that concentrate on the needs of customers in that particular region.

So as to embrace the challenges and opportunities in the Middle Eastern regions and develop a regional financial services agenda, it is imperative that organizations encompass a clear value proposition as their market differentiator. In order to establish a value proposition, one should consider employing concepts presented in Treacy and Wiersema's The *Discipline of Market Leaders*,[1] which underscores the need for companies to discipline themselves to select one key area (or value discipline) where they alone can provide unique value to targeted customers, and then direct their energy and resources to consistently excel in their chosen discipline.

The three distinct value disciplines described are, as we have seen above, product leadership, operational excellence and customer intimacy. Focusing on the Islamic niche Halal[2] eMarketplace, MuslimsConnect.com's value proposition addresses the needs of the seller and buyer of goods.

Value proposition to the seller:

- Digital Halal certification at supplier level (MuslimsTrust) in addition to your physical certificate provided by your Halal certifier. This provides the trust necessary for your product to be recognized and trusted worldwide.

- Cost savings from using the portal as a communication medium. All Requests for Quotation, Quotations, Purchase Orders and other related trade documents will be created out of the portal and transmitted via the portal thus negating the need for fax, mail or telephone as a means of communication. This reduces administrative cost significantly.

- Preparation of documents via the portal enhances the accuracy of the documents. This enables easy negotiation with the bankers for the purpose of documentary credit (L/C).

- Ability to link your back-end accounting and information systems to the portal to enable online updating of your e-catalogue.

- Ability to link to your logistics partner or assign MuslimsConnect.com to provide you a quotation for logistics services.

- Integration of the Supply chain with the Suppliers network leads to better inventory management and more accurate forecast of future stock requirements.

- Access to information and application of new technology in the food industry with a focus on the Halal sector.

Value proposition to the buyer:

- Faster access to a broader range of products and services.

- Full confidence that products purchased are verified Halal.

- Ability to specify exact requirements of products with respect to levels of Halal verification, product quality, packaging etc allows for greater customisation of products to Buyers specification.

- The ability to conduct business in a public marketplace while maintaining pre-negotiated pricing and service arrangements with key suppliers.

- New and richer information to better support business decisions.

- Streamlined and simplified searching, invoicing, logistics and tracking processes.

- Improved integration with internal business practices.

- The opportunity for lower overall transaction cost.

- Access to information and application of new technology in the food industry with a focus on the Halal sector.

- A well-managed inventory management system for their business.[3]

Mirroring the Halal market, in today's competitive environment financial services organizations find themselves oscillating between the three operating states: product leadership, customer intimacy and operational excellence, having to continually introduce new services, optimize cost and increase market share, while developing a greater customer focus. In the halal market example, focusing on a niche market allows services to centre on clear value propositions for the buyer, seller and market aggregator. Seeing that specialization is one avenue to a defined value proposition, to achieve and sustain a profit margin as business conditions change requires moving through the value disciplines. The excellent company will be the one with the ability to focus on one market segment and develop an organization that first introduces new product innovation, shifting its focus to better service the customer by refining its product offerings (that is, improving customer service), and finally shifting again to streamline operating cost to remain competitive. Assessing the depth of your organization's capabilities and the level of awareness within each discipline is a key factor in knowing your readiness to participate in the new competitive landscape.

CHAPTER 18

Diaspora Financial Services for Mobile Populations

Technology is removing the barriers of geography from the financial services industry. Yet, product offerings to the retail consumer and small business market still reflect the traditional limits of single community membership. During the Middle Ages, Florentine banks established an extensive branch network throughout the known world, not to attract new customers, but to facilitate the business transactions of Italian merchants. The value proposition for operating a local branch presence in the merchant economy of fourteenth-century Europe was simply to reduce the time and cost of negotiating terms with local suppliers and buyers, thereby allowing vessels to presell cargo and merely dock and unload goods without having to take the goods to the market. Like the merchant branch network and its underlying value proposition, today's society is experiencing migrating populations that require a similar service. To illustrate: approximately 50,000 people of Brazilian heritage live and work in the area of greater Boston, Massachusetts, with strong family ties and social links to their native country. Like all communities connected by nationality and culture, many individuals are the umbilical cord for financial support to relations in both continents. The multi-nation, individual connection is in reality a definition of the global family and, at first glance, defines a highly specialized need for financial services. Upon closer examination, it is the basis of a new class of financial services products that allow an individual to obtain financial services in regional economies which span geopolitical boundaries.

One value proposition is the simple transfer of funds to and from corresponding accounts located in each country without the need to negotiate the value of the currencies. This can be accomplished either by allowing multicurrency deposits in each account or by establishing a daily rate at which the currency is transferable. In this sense, there is a second value proposition to investors who are looking for currency diversification in their portfolio and are able to utilize higher interest rates which may exist in a distant economy. A third value proposition is the one offered to small investors or traders seeking portfolio diversity in a local market, requiring brokerage and cash accounts that can be managed remotely to reduce the number of times that currencies need to be exchanged. Lastly, a fourth value proposition is applicable to any or all of the scenarios previously described: simply to provide cash management services to maximize the return on funds in both locations and during the transition periods.

One such organization that is practising the basic implementation of this concept is General Bank in East Los Angeles. Contrary to the popular image of early twentieth-century immigrants arriving penniless to seek their fortunes, today's immigrants arrive with money and a need for financial services. Arriving in California, immigrants from Korea and Taiwan are met with a financial institution that speaks their native language and is able to help in financing export–import business ventures and provide returns of two per cent on average assets. The value proposition presented by General Bank mirrors that of medieval Florentine banks, where the majority of customers run import–export businesses in both countries, allowing the bank to track the credit history of an immigrant to pre-approve loans. General Bank's value proposition is predicated on an organizational belief that immigrants arriving in the United States are new to doing business in the country, and not to running a business per se.

Another value proposition offered at General Bank is foreign currency advice to customers. Due to the bank's access to information in both countries, General Bank is in a privileged position to provide a perspective that is unavailable elsewhere. These corporate behaviours send a clear message to customers: that the financial services firm is acting in their best interest, thus promoting the value of customer loyalty, which will be a fundamental aspect of the relationship between banks and customers in the next two decades.

Finally, one could argue that diaspora banking is a new gateway to a global liquidity offering in which a financial institution can help customers to maximize the use and value of their global assets. With real-time technology links, account and asset balances in one country or time zone could be deployed and used elsewhere as intraday collateral, rather than remaining idle overnight. As the world markets continue to integrate into a trading and banking environment that runs twenty-four hours a day, seven days a week, the above scenario will move progressively from a possibility to a necessity. In conclusion, as world citizens become more technologically connected, the need for services that span geopolitical boundaries and link families and business associations will increase. Aggregation and consolidation services will enable families to engage new types of wealth management and transfer services.

CHAPTER 19

Globalization: One Size Does Not Fit All

As seen in Chapters 10–18, one aspect of globalization is the technology applied by financial services and its relationship to capabilities within global markets, and its adaptability to local market conditions and local cultures. A traveller to any airport can easily view the impact of globalization, with the endless parade of fast-food and merchandise outlets of multinational corporations eager to turn the travel experience into a continuous buying experience. The elements of globalization can be explored by examining the spectrum of available financial services technologies, that is, how micropayments will be transacted.

The Spectrum of Technology

At the vanguard of globalization is the retail transaction, commanding the highest profile interaction to the average consumer. Reviewing the technologies that will allow global transactions to happen seamlessly across nations, they fall into several categories; delivery technologies, interchange mechanisms, infrastructure and back office systems.

Financial services institutions are applying these technologies in different areas to support the new and sometimes floundering set of emerging business models. The focus has really been in the area of delivery technologies, with a flirtation in the area of smart card and encryption technologies. Now financial services organizations are starting to look at the other side, the core processing systems and are asking the question: Do I need to have a robust infrastructure to support these transactions?

Each of these technologies presents a variety of challenges, starting with the volatility of delivery technologies, due to acceleration of consumer adaptation and acceptance by different social groups. For example: laptop technology is far more fashionable in Europe than in the United States. In fact, within Europe, the Nordic countries have embraced it far more than the Southern European countries.

As we saw, smart card technologies were not embraced in the United States with the same level of consumer and merchant acceptance as in Europe, especially in North Western Europe, where they reached a higher penetration. Evaluating technologies, no single technology can be purchased that will guarantee differentiation in the marketplace and assure success. Financial services organizations need to develop a robust infrastructure, allowing the rapid assimilation of new technology to be crafted into a capability and ultimately a product offering. This is best explored on two fronts: experimentation and delivery. The closer to the core banking systems, the more stable the technology due to the smaller range of available systems and the smaller number of applied users. Therefore, building the infrastructure is the real key to achieving agility across the spectrum of globalized technology.

Retail Transactions, Payments and Micropayments

Payments are the very basic, fundamental keys of what a financial institution is about. There is the old story about banking that states that anybody can make a loan, but only a bank can make a payment, that is, a settlement. Financial services organizations are looking at the factors surrounding globalization and are asking: Is it time to replace core systems? An increased focus on payment systems is driven by the emergence of eMarketplaces, consumer demand and eCommerce over the Internet, made possible by changing technologies. At the heart of a globalized technology agenda is the need for a predictable infrastructure. Predictable infrastructure is a robust, scalable, reliable platform in which to launch financial products to a global marketplace with only an incremental cost. Considering most delivery technologies are a temporary state, subject to ever-increasing changes, financial services technology organizations need to develop the skills to adapt technology rapidly into a predictable infrastructure to complement the technology selection process.

The Holy Grail of Standardization

To achieve a greater level of organizational efficiency, technology organizations desperately endeavour to standardize on models and brands of technology, in order to minimize the maintenance and cost of ownership which add incremental operating cost as the number of vendors increases. Unfortunately, the technology industry is driven by the innovation of new devices and software, targeted at improving the utilization and application of technology to specific business problems. It could be argued that as organizations strive for standardization, they limit their ability to adapt to new business conditions and may incur additional costs when they standardize, because of the higher cost of switching technologies as conditions change. For example, a large multinational organization with 50,000 desktop and laptop computer users, having the capacity in the technology department to upgrade 1,000 users per month, will satisfy the entire upgrade request in 50 months just to maintain parity. At that rate, when combined with the rate of new technology introduction, software upgrades, and other user-demanded features, the actual probability of achieving standardization is virtually zero, not to mention that user satisfaction approval ratings would be low. When considering banking product offerings, these factors, combined with the varying regional preferences for technologies, exacerbate the standardization dilemma.

In the early commercialization of electricity, large business concerns employed electricians and maintained an electrical department to ensure that the firm was electrically capable. As electrical generating, transmission and distribution technologies became commoditized over the succeeding one hundred years, the need for average corporations to employ a staff of specialists in electrical power diminished. Let us go back to Edison's early value proposition to consumers: as electrical power use became commonplace, the focus of business switched from simply achieving electrical parity with competitors (a prerequisite of competition) to using a vast array of technologies that plugged into an electrical infrastructure to explore new avenues to service customers. Still, after one hundred years of electrical maturity and a compelling value proposition for cost savings, the end user technology has yet to reach a single standardized mechanism, as any world traveller notes as he or she carries an array of electrical adaptors in their luggage. However, the electrical appliances all work under a common infrastructure of 50–60 hertz and 110–220 volts, even though the plugging mechanism is different.

The essential thing to consider is that having a standardized infrastructure is more valuable and more attainable than a standardized end user device for delivering banking and commerce service offerings. Providing a suite of technologies for customers to simply select and utilize via a common infrastructure is the underlying value of technology.

Geography and Culture

Poised at the dawn of the twenty-first century, the factors of geography, culture and nationalism are still influential issues that cannot be ignored when developing financial services product offerings. Consumers and small businesses acquire, plan, spend, save and invest their income following a basic formula of savings and spending. What differs culturally is how each group accomplishes these financial goals, driven by motivating factors that are also influenced by religion, historical societal traits such as home ownership, ethnic traits such as family-focused income consolidation, and other traditional financial habits, which present a variety of challenges in retail and commercial banking.

Global Co-opetition

Global competition affects each financial institution in two ways: either the firm wishes to expand into various global markets or a global institution has suddenly appeared as a new competitor. What is clear is that global competition can no longer be ignored, and any firm offering financial services must develop a strategy to either compete or collaborate with other firms to provide value to all market segments. Even niche market players must continually evaluate their value to customers, as non-traditional financial services firms offer services that will replace or significantly alter what customers view as valuable.

Brokered Trust and Shared Risk

Co-opetition and collaboration do not necessarily translate into a diluted brand image or shortfall in capability to supply all things to all customers. However, it does mean that firms can enhance their brand by offering a brokered trust between product offerings. For example: a firm that is known as a good source of financial advice can co-brand integrated insurance offerings with a well-established insurance organization as a partner. Furthermore, in the area of eCommerce, the Internet and various delivery technologies, the investments and risks often associated with the implementation of new offerings to market sub-segments can be mitigated and shared between partners.

In summary, all financial services firm will experience globalization either as an active participant or as a competitive threat. European financial firms are presented with a unique opportunity to leverage the lessons learned from the first evolution of Internet technologies and develop product offerings that reflect the lifestyles and needs of customers spanning the diversity of the European continent. In the new global electronic marketplace, this development will be a benchmark for institutions competing to engage customers with products and services that supplement their lifestyles, transforming traditional banking services from a reactive consumer activity to a proactive consumer experience. Regardless of the end delivery devises and the continuous innovations that will be introduced by the computer industry, the essential ingredient to a strategic technology policy is to invest in a robust predictable infrastructure so that the lines of business can focus on developing offerings that demonstrate a clear value proposition to customers. Contrary to popular sentiment, globalization (or at least the process and technologies associated with the phenomenon) is an opportunity for financial services firms to extend not only their products and services, but to expose other geographically delimited societies to the rich diversity of cultures. The rethinking of how financial services are constructed opens avenues of investment to private investors and makes capital easier to acquire for business looking for capital markets to finance business operations.

PART IV

The Future of Payment Systems

At the heart of financial services are payments, the simple act of an intermediary providing mechanisms for individuals and business to pay for goods and services. A convergence of social, economic and technological issues places payment systems at the threshold of a quantum change. Glyn Davies puts into perspective the elements that will drive a fundamental rethinking of the exchange of value and society's relationship with money:

> Yet despite the antiquity and ubiquity of money its proper management and control have eluded the rulers of most modern states partly because they have ignored the wide-ranging lessons of the past or have taken too blinkered and narrow a view of money. Economists, and especially monetarists, tend to overestimate the purely economic, narrow and technical functions of money and have placed insufficient emphasis on its wider social, institutional and psychological aspects.[1]

However, a new understanding is only part of the equation to adding value as a payment intermediary. Assessing the convergent forces of technology, telecommunications, computer infrastructure and a host of delivery mechanisms is the key to competing in the new landscape of financial services. The continued evolution of technology, social adoption or 'appetite', and organizations' ability to absorb change represent the next wave of challenges for financial services firms operating to a global agenda. This section presents a variety of technological trends facing financial services firms and provides an insight into interpreting these market forces into a comprehensive set of strategies. The section looks at the question of what financial services firms should be doing to prepare for the future.

Competing in the integrated future state of co-opetition, eMarketplace banks will involve focusing companies' attention on developing value propositions that establish their actual value to customers in the realm of cyberspace and electronic competition. The challenge is to structure business models that are viable enterprises; learning from the dot-com experience, while not imitating easily copied product offerings displayed by new market entrants. Electronic marketplaces and, more importantly, services that enable electronic commerce present traditional financial services firms with new opportunities to leverage their knowledge of banking products, and partner with technology firms, supermarkets and any other organization that provides a clear channel to a targeted market segment. The rush of new market entrants into the financial services marketplace demonstrates that individual, traditional banking products can be duplicated with a relatively small cost to market, therefore resulting in a continually commoditized market for banking services and making it increasingly difficult to establish market differentiation between banks and their competitors. For instance, faced with high and rising costs and battered by the lower cost alternatives of home banking via PCs, telephone-based banking, supermarket banking, and automated kiosks, the conventional bank finds itself at an economic and cultural crossroad. How to develop a value proposition that addresses the new level of customer needs without fundamentally changing how the bank operates? Competitors are reinterpreting the character of the bank and the roles that bank personnel play in a variety of ways to make them leaner and more technologically adept.

The transformation of traditional banking was started in the United States, but is rapidly occurring through Europe and not surprisingly in Asia and the Middle East, offering services from telephone banking, mobile banking, Internet banking and a host of retail services that bear a striking resemblance to traditional retail banking activity; simply pouring old wine into new bottles. It is important to note that these Internet offerings mimic functions that are carried out in the branch, allowing customers to be more self-service oriented, with transactions that permit them to maintain current and savings accounts, perform credit card transactions, make balance enquiries, transfer funds, and pay bills. Organizations such as Charles Schwab, e-Trade and other Internet pioneers demonstrated that customers were indeed able to perform trading activities, and found that the investor required tools and information that facilitated investment decisions in order to reduce interaction with brokers.

Whilst new market entrants demonstrated that customers and investors indeed have an appetite for these products, financial services firms have been working furiously to provide this new level of customer service. Meanwhile, other more misunderstood technologies, such as smart cards, valagents[2] and eMoney, stand silently on the horizon waiting for their potential to be realized or applied.

The ability for the world to pay its bills and exchange value between trading partners, consumers, governments and markets is the foundation of all international economies. Technology promises to streamline the process of payments both foreign and domestic, providing a reduction in both cost and time in the facilitation of global business. The Internet has presented opportunities for businesses large and small to reach global audiences and increase their market reach. Consumers and business now have the capability to access a worldwide basket of products and services that allows them to bring the fruits of many nations and cultures literally to their doorstep. Unfortunately, the financial services organizations touting a global network of banking operations are falling short of being the one-stop shop in the facilitation of this global phenomenon.

Governments across the globe are racing to enact legislation to tax the activities of business on the Internet without realizing the implications on the embryonic state of the underlying business activity.[3] Unfortunately, the media hype and market research projections that surrounded the introduction to eBusiness placed business expectations of trade and commerce transaction so high that governments could not afford to ignore such a large potential revenue source. Now, at the dawn of the twenty-first century, the marketing hype is waning, and corporations are beginning to engage in eCommerce as a long-term viable medium of exchange. However, the political process has started, and at the moment it is only a question of when Internet commerce will be taxed and at what rate. Surprisingly, a side benefit to the economic downturn in the technology sector during 2001 is that traditional corporations and newly formed firms have stopped believing in the hype surrounding the high-tech market and started to embrace the root problem by developing a value proposition to customers and creating returns to investors. Despite a swing back to basic value creation, government intervention, or government interdiction, has the potential to hinder the physical implementation of technological advancement.

Government agencies worldwide are now recognizing the benefits of electronic currency in its many forms as having the potential to significantly reduce the cost associated with cash handling, cheque processing and other small-value payment mechanisms, while presenting a value proposition to customers of convenience and speed. The next few years of eCommerce will test the boundaries of government regulation and intervention in eMarketplaces, as the issue of risks, such as loss, fraud, insolvency, piracy concerns, money laundering, tax evasion, counterfeiting, and consumer protection, brings regulation of cyber-currency and public policy into the limelight.

In this sense, electronic currency presents another paradox for eMarketplaces, financial services firms and governments. Any organization that acts as an issuer of electronic currency is in effect acting as a minting source. This fact, coupled with the need to certify the value and origination of the electronic currency, may lead to a new level of specialized supervisory guidelines for certificating authorities and eMoney issuers. Theoretically, frequent flyer miles could be issued as certificated tokens of value that take on the same characteristics of cash, and could be transferred to other airlines, merchants and vendors, seemingly acting in the same way as a cash-based transaction. In this instance, the value of the frequent flyer miles is backed by the full faith and credit of the airline company and its ability to honour the value of the transaction. Technically, this could be interpreted as the airline minting its own money and it could be possible to pay your cable-TV bill with accumulated frequent flyer miles or credit card bonus points. This avenue of eCommerce activity presents a complex scenario for financial services firms implementing bill presentment and payment technologies. This fact, coupled with nation-backed multi-currencies, opens a new line of thought on the possible payment scenarios that are all within the realm of today's technology.

Regardless of which eMoney technology evolves into the standard and what value is represented from which issuing source, governments will have to establish national policies in order to protect consumers and business, while minimizing any impediments to international commerce and global competition. Nevertheless, financial services organizations must use a combination of payment, eMoney and traditional banking technologies to enable eCommerce and still make a profit.

Developing a value proposition for eMoney and payment technologies must not alienate customers; instead, it must demonstrate that these technologies are a stepping stone in the new economy, being an integral part of a future state in which society values and uses money differently from today. Putting these technologies into the context of a total customer relationship between a financial institution and the customer can be expressed as: an ATM is a substitute for a bank teller; a debit card is a card that acts like a cheque, a credit card is a prenegotiated loan in your pocket; and a smart card or stored-value card is an electronic substitute for cash.

During the course of the next fifty years, the relationship between individuals and money will change. Not only will the form or medium of exchange be altered, but the underlying value proposition will undoubtedly be redefined. At present, the system of money as represented by world currencies is backed by the full faith and credit of the issuing government, which establishes the relative rate in which the currency is valued against other currencies. As money migrates to a digital world, new representations of money are backed once again by the full faith and credit of the issuers, in this case global corporations. Frequent flyer miles, hotel points, bonus points and other loyalty schemes are all early demonstrations of linked rates of exchange between value partners. By today's definition, money and currency provide the base rate in which to establish the relative values of the future cyber-currencies.

Regardless of how money will evolve, and in which form it migrates to, making payments in whatever form will continue to be an area of great opportunity in which financial services firms can add value. Today, there are technologies that are capable of reinventing how payments are made and settled on a local and international scale. A host of new market entrants, including utility companies, cable TV, telecoms, retail stores and even financial services firms, are all hoping that online bill presentment and bill aggregation hold the keys to new sources of fee income. Providing consumers with the ability to pay bills with a single mouse-click from an aggregated statement is a value proposition that has a limited lifespan, being valuable at the onset and becoming less valuable over time since now any company can deliver it. Online bill presentation and payments has market appeal, but not a sustainable long-term value proposition; it should be considered a feature of a larger product offering, not an offering in and of itself.

The financial services industry and other aspiring aggregation firms are labouring under the premise that whoever presents the bill owns the customer relationship and this will tie consumers and small businesses closer to their brands. Equally, the industry is assuming that consumers enjoy paying bills and cannot wait to spend time on a PC clicking their way to a lower bank balance. To compound this dilemma, industry analysts continue to project the number of consumers who will be regularly paying bills online with ever-higher transaction volumes, fuelling the race to provide this service. One should examine the reason why consumers want to be able to see all their accounts on one page, and pay all their bills with one click. Consumer behaviour is based on the same motivation as that of any business which has a balance sheet and income statement – in order to monitor the overall health of the firm. In this case, it is to measure the wealth of the individual and monitor cash flow. If we see a consumer and his/her relationship with their individual finances as the same as the role of a CEO to a company, it would be pertinent to ask: Would the CEO be happy to take on the role of the accounts payable clerk? What consumers need is the same information that a CEO requires, with the details available on demand, and provided automatically by a third party. Bill presentment and account aggregation are merely steps towards the longer term value proposition of individual wealth and cash management services, which are similar to services offered to business. Corporate CEOs have learned that management by exception has an inherent value, because it removes the labour associated with chasing volumes of details and permits concentrated attention on areas outside the standard process. Paying bills and managing cash are all components of how a consumer conducts his or her lifestyle. The value proposition is twofold: to reduce the amount of time a consumer has to spend on these activities, and to educate the consumer on more effective ways of operating within a chosen lifestyle.

The biggest challenge for financial services organizations is not merely assembling the right collection of technologies to perform these services; it is how to develop a brand that engages the consumer to adopt them as the preferred access channel to the new world of financial services. Payment systems are one of the most visible connections between consumers and financial institutions. The act of paying bills will undergo a transformation now that the technologies exist to rethink the process of payments and the relationship between money and consumers. Financial services firms risk losing customers and potentially becoming a casualty of disintermediation if they solely provide bill presentment and payment capabilities, simply because it will become a commoditized offering which new market entrants can offer at a lower price point.

CHAPTER 20

An Evolution to the Exchange of Value

As we have seen so far, consumers, businesses, banks and governments are waking up in the new century with the consciousness that the very nature of how value will be exchanged between two or more parties have changed forever. Declining margins, a ceaseless appetite for customer-initiated services and a continual parade of new market entrants have today's financial services organizations wondering how to add value to a sometimes chaotic business climate. The problem behind this major swing in how financial services organizations create and demonstrate value is an ever-expanding range of technologies, designed to put the customer at the centre of controlling the value exchange.

Financial institutions are confident that they represent a brokered trust or third-party relationship, acting as an intermediary during the exchange of value. Trust is not to be confused with security; it is underwriting the credibility of the transaction in addition to guaranteeing its fidelity. Until the Internet was accepted as a viable entity for business, the icons of trust were typically brick-and-mortar buildings with glistening marble columns and bank vaults with massive brushed metal doors. Moving into the twenty-first century, the Internet disintermediation effect is allowing trading partners, consumers, merchants and business-to-business trading partners to question the relative value that financial services organizations offer to broker these transactions.

In ten years time, today's payments systems will seem arcane, possibly technologically elegant systems that reflect nineteenth-century methods of banking. The migration to the future state of payment systems will occur in three steps:

1. A shift from the concept of payment to the instantaneous exchange of value.

2. A move to anticipatory transactions focused on customer centricity.

3. Adaptations in the way global transactions transcend geopolitical boundaries.

Facilitating this migration is technology, heralded as the great enabler of new economy business processes. Its continued evolution will present new challenges regarding how services are designed and delivered. Systems that labour to produce aged accounts receivable and payable will be the tombstones found in companies that have not prepared for the shift to value exchange.

The exchange of value between parties follows a relationship life cycle that requires a comprehensive suite of services facilitating contemporary lifestyles and business relationships. This, coupled with scalable fees for transaction fulfilment systems, will evidence the need for financial services organizations to demonstrate a clear value proposition in each stage of the life cycle in the evolution of a trading relationship.

Relationship: First Encounter

Throughout history, trading partners have relied on local intermediaries to underwrite the risk of doing business with a previously unknown person or business. In the eleventh century, Italian merchants in Amalfi transformed their tiny fishing village into one of the richest trading ports by underwriting the risk of the exchange, sharing the risk and backing the transaction to provide a sense of security in the exchange of goods. Little has changed over the centuries in the primary role of the broker, who adds value by providing a service that answers the following questions:

- 'Who is my new trading partner, and is he who he says he is?'
- 'Is my new trading partner trustworthy?'
- 'Are they good for the payment, and if they don't pay, who will?'
- 'Will they deliver according to our agreed terms of trade and, if not, what are my options?'
- 'Will I have a way out if things go wrong?'

Now technology is facilitating this role by giving consumers and business a new expectation in trust. To some extent, credit card transactions have become the de facto standard for consumers in foreign and domestic exchanges of value, understanding that the credit card company will settle any disputes between parties. Companies such as eBay and other value exchange market-makers generate environments that demonstrate how technology will usurp the perceived trust that financial institutions enjoy today. Since the use of an intermediary such as a bank is based on an implied and expressed trust, as discussed in Part I, a new market entrant only needs to demonstrate the consistent reliable execution of a service to build that trust over time. Therefore, it can be ascertained that trust is not a one-time purchase, but a compound relationship that is built over time, developed by demonstrating predictable results, enhanced through a common identity or brand, and requiring investments by both parties.

Relationship: Honeymoon Period

In a business-to-business relationship, both parties issue transactions to develop an understanding of the limits or boundaries in the exchange of value. Next, they monitor the exchange of value during this stage of the relationship. This in turn builds a greater level of trust with each exchange of value. The value of the intermediary lies in the speedy resolution of problems and misunderstandings during the exchange of value.

Similarly, in a consumer-to-bank relationship, one party (the consumer) initiates a transaction and the other party (the bank) executes it. The relationship is built initially by the ease with which the basic banking service is established, for example opening the account, learning how to use the account, and who to call when a problem occurs. The old adage 'you never get a second chance at a first impression' is directly applicable here, since the actions taken during this period will be the legacy for the relationship.

Relationship: Normal Course of Business

As the transaction frequency in exchange of value increases, so does the level of trust between parties, thus decreasing the need for a trusted intermediary. Financial services organizations can only provide value in the swift execution of transactions between parties and the exchanging of information between parties in the form of data exchanges. In order to put this issue into perspective, one should consider that when cyber-currencies are indeed adopted by society, a consumer will simply be able to transfer a stored value amount to a merchant directly, without the aid of a financial intermediary like today, when a consumer makes a cash purchase. The interface with the consumer rests solely with the merchant, and the financial services firm is only included in the transaction as a final depository for the merchant's accounts receivable. Every transaction, regardless of its frequency or amount, must be perceived as having value added to it by the financial intermediary, or it will be a target for niche market players to provide the same service. During the normal course of business, added value does not equate with added fees; it is really additional worth, which can take the form of increased settlement speed, higher quality call centre coverage, reduced fees on bulk transactions and other transaction-based offerings designed to supplement the transaction.

Relationship: Change in Business Environment

Invariably, the business environment changes and one or both of the parties find it imperative to adjust the nature of the relationship and the composition of the exchange of value. The quick adaptation of the terms of value exchange is the value proposition for the intermediary; technology is able to make it even faster. Reducing the interruption to the normal course of business is one of the keys to adding value.

How will financial services organizations participate in the new value exchange? By consistently demonstrating value with quality transactions, using payment systems that adapt rapidly to changes and are price sensitive to the needs of an organization as its trading relationship matures and changes. In some cases, providing services such as security and certification (that are hard to find between trading partners) is another avenue of added value.

Financial services organizations across the globe have launched pilot projects to anticipate this change in their value proposition. WAP[1] delivery of retail banking in Scandinavia, Internet banking with biometric controls in North America, and smart card implementations in Europe and Asia all represent technology-hedging strategies to gain a competitive edge in bringing new services to the market. Regrettably, payment systems and their associated fees have not moved in proportion to customer expectations. This is primarily due to technology advances replacing the perception of trust in an exchange of value. Put simply, financial services companies are adopting more technology, without realizing that it increases costs due to its temporary nature; meanwhile, customers still expect better deals in the new competitive market. From the customers' point of view, the cost of performing a transaction at a branch is visible because one can witness the physical aspects of the bank and rationalize the cost of tellers, machines and the banking infrastructure. Likewise, as consumers have been continually reminded by the technology industry that the overall cost of technology is dropping, they are quicker to question the cost of transactions that are purely technological in nature. Consumers are questioning the fees associated with digital transactions, such as the cost incurred with an electronic transfer of funds. The actual transaction is similar to sending an eMail, which does not carry a transaction cost. So why should bank transactions be so costly?

Future payment systems will be designed in a customer-centric fashion, allowing the payment initiator options on how, when and where payments will be made. Systems will employ the intelligent agent technology to be anticipatory, and digital currency technology to integrate into a protocol of international value exchange. Digital certificates, encryption technology, intelligent agents, biometrics, WAP and a host of new exchange mechanisms are gaining credibility on and off the Internet, as well as offering some degree of trust.

Financial services organizations need to take clear, deliberate steps in evaluating how they add value to each component in the exchange of value between parties, and develop business systems that anticipate the evolution of the value exchange. The evolution of payment systems is leading the technology wave of new business challenges, consisting of three essential factors that financial services organizations need to keep in the forefront of their strategic planning: technology, social adoption and international regulation.

Seemingly, it is not possible to pick the one technology that will embrace the new generation of value exchanges between consumers and merchants. It is more likely that end consumer technologies will continue to be driven by market demand and will be transitory in nature. More importantly: Is technology the answer or simply a question? The implementation of payment technologies must add value to the existing array of financial product offerings within the organization; if not, the payment function must be considered for outsourcing to a viable partner, perhaps a new market entrant.

CHAPTER 21

Anticipatory Technologies and Customer Centricity

Customers and trading partners will determine which technologies your organization will implement to facilitate the exchange of value, or they will find someone else who will 'do it their way'. The Internet has acted as a catalyst for the evolution to anticipatory technologies and customer centricity. The opportunity for financial services firms is to develop product offerings that are proactive to customers' needs and not reactive as they are today. For example, consumers come to the bank for a debt consolidation loan when they are already experiencing credit trouble. Proactive banking provides consumers with tools that will guide them to avoid such actions. Technology can be employed to permit a customer to tailor financial services products to fit his or her lifestyle, and companies can advise him or her on impending actions and offer solution sets to meet life events. A customer's behaviour can be analysed against other customers in similar circumstances in order to develop an anticipatory view of actions to come. The behaviour aspect of transactions is also true between trading partners, and can provide valuable insight to identify opportunities that will allow trading partners to minimize cost. Technology's evolutionary transformation has three emerging aspects: redefinition, redesignation and redeployment, all of which influence how technology will migrate to add value in exchanges between trading partners or between consumers and merchants.

Redefinition

The first emerging aspect of technology transformation is a redefinition of technology by consumers and trading partners to exchange value. It is said that, in the last quarter of the twentieth century the road to hell was paved with good intentions and mountains of technology. The number of technologies that rose and fell with little regard for their underlying value can be best illustrated by this example: when PDAs (personal digital assistants) were introduced, TV commercials used to highlight their technological capabilities and interoperability; now, however, the commercials feature their availability in designer colours and rarely mention the technology components. Understandably, technologies that are in direct use by consumers will continually change and adapt as the market dictates. However, the functions they provide contribute to the overall value proposition and must be an integral part in the delivery of retail and Internet financial services.

The ever-changing state of technology creates a continual flow of electronic devices designed to improve the relationship between people and complex tasks. Vendors do not simply create technology to earn revenue. Each has a vision of a product with a distinct application to a business, scientific or predetermined task. In many cases, the final application of a technology is a by-product of the intended implementation or the reapplication of a technology to a secondary target.

Many technologies are applied to a problem simply because they are available at the time the problem is defined. For example, we have WAP technologies for banking and integrated appliances. Do I really want my toaster to know my current account balance? What is clear is that technologies that are designated as personal become applicable to social, demographic, cultural, or geographic preferences. Faced with a vast array of delivery technologies aimed at every market segment of customer, financial services organizations are racing to differentiate themselves in the market by implementing a vast assortment of technologies.

Redesignation

The second transformational aspect of technology is a redesignation driven by the increasing demand for customer centricity in servicing the exchange of value. This is not simply allowing the customer to fill out a form on a website for a credit card; it is rethinking plastic/magnetic cards. Global citizens today carry an array of value representation cards; credit, debit, frequent flyer, loyalty programmes and smart cards. Looking at these technologies from a customer-centric point of view begs the question: Could I have just one card that I control and determine what value exchange representation I want to use today? A consumer should have the ability to go to a merchant displaying a VISA logo and direct both the card and merchant to execute the transaction using his or her HSBC Visa account, and tomorrow use the same card as a Citibank Diners Club card. Conversely, how the receiver of value wishes to receive the exchange will influence who they want as trading partners.

Technology is enabling a variety of new market entrants to bring competitive offerings to the financial services marketplace with a relatively low cost of entry. As energy companies, telecommunications companies and financial services organizations strive for bill presentment technologies, they often underestimate the migration of these functions as stepping stones to anticipatory, proactive service offerings.

Anticipatory presentment technologies allow the value exchange partner to preset tolerances of a value exchange. For example: a consumer's bill for many services is often within a very small bandwidth of variability. The consumer should be able to preselect a range of payment tolerances for his or her utility bills and target funds for fulfilment, receiving a message only when the impending transaction is going to cross the upper tolerance limit. Unlike a standing order or the principle of direct debit, the consumer's total allocation for bills should automatically adjust to regulate the payments within tolerances. For example, £1000 is earmarked for bill payments this month with a total tolerance of £100, setting the customer's expectation that the total amount attributed to bill payment is £1100. Individual payees are identified and tolerances (for example approximately ten per cent, not to exceed £50 and so on) are established for each type of bill to be presented by the payees. As the bills are presented, the bank pays them and informs the customer of the total activity, not the individual activity. Corrections and adjustments to each individual bill are handled by the system and anomalies are reported at the individual bill level only when a payment goes beyond the prescribed limits. Customers will be presented with the final aggregated output and will have the ability to investigate the details on demand. The information that the customer needs to know is that all the bills were paid and there is £142 remaining to be brought forward towards next month's bills.

This is a shift in payments from a reactive to a proactive payment mentality, managing home finances by exception processing. It is not beyond the current technology to initiate anticipatory intelligent agents for financial services that act on a trading partner's behalf and broker an exchange of value. These financial services robots, finbots or valagents (value exchange agents), execute or act on one's behalf with an original certification (discussed in more detail in Chapter 24).

Paradoxically, financial services organizations are announcing their reputation of trust, while rapidly trying to implement technologies that replace the perception of trust with a digital representation of trust. Digital signatures, digital certificates, encryption and biometric technologies are being integrated into the mainstream for underwriting the fidelity of a transaction. These technologies offer a migratory path to customer centricity and increase the need for clear market differentiation of services in the value exchange.

Redeployment

The third transformational aspect is a redeployment of technology to facilitate the shift to customer centricity, which leverages technology as the lynchpin in facilitating customer relationship management (CRM) processes. Technology can rapidly bridge the gap between customer and product or service, testing the efficiency of the underlying business process design. Several financial services organizations have implemented CRM technology solutions, only to find little or no improvement in customer satisfaction levels. This was attributed to two factors: firstly, a sub-optimal process design which copied antiquated organizational procedures, and secondly, a lack of investment in employees to develop people skills required for the resolution of customer problems. Technology thus magnifies a poorly designed process or inadequately trained customer service staff by quickly exposing customers to long queues and product back orders. Many companies, having moved quickly to the Internet, discover that customers have little patience for poorly designed customer service processes and missed deliveries.

The most difficult area to justify investment in is the training of personnel beyond that of learning the new CRM software. The ability to resolve customers' disputes and take corrective actions requires the development of skills that are more than merely reading pre-scripted responses found in the software application. Internet technology combined with CRM software does present the opportunity to migrate many computer-literate customers into a self-service mode for a large percentage of service interactions. However, customers are quickly frustrated by multi-layered navigation and vague problem descriptions. The most successful implementations of self-service technologies design the user interaction capability most often by interviewing customers and developing the mechanisms of interaction from the customers' point of view.

Moving into Action

Financial services organizations need to adopt a customer-centric view-point and move into action by placing technology into a business perspective using a simple model. What are the steps in the value exchange process between trading partners and/or banking customers? How does our service offering add value to the exchange? Can we use technology to improve performance, increase customer satisfaction, lower operating cost or expand the range of products?

A strategic framework for thinking about the application of technologies to these emerging transformations is oversimplified in the following model: think global (combined infrastructures); act regional (targeted applications); and look local (delivery technologies). The key learning from the past thirty years of technology implementation is that success is not about picking the right technology; it is about selecting a suite of technological capabilities that deliver value consistently and can be migrated to the next wave of capabilities.

The core competencies that financial services organizations need to develop are the rapid commercialization of technology to business value, and the management of this new capability as a temporary asset, moving to a customer-centric design model when developing service offerings, and assessing the intrinsic value added to a transaction at each juncture of the business process.

Globalization, Social Adoption, International Regulation and the Evolution to Bankruptcy

The term 'globalization' is peppered throughout countless corporate annual reports as the next big expansion in growth strategies with little regard to the implications of long-term social, political, economic and cultural effects on operating profitability, risks and market volatility. Social adoption of technology and the reaction by domestic and international governments is often not well thought out in eCommerce strategy development. Taxation levied on any mechanism that provides an exchange of value is the final step in the socialization of the underlying technology. Put simply, when global governments begin levying taxes on the Internet, they legitimize its role as an international mechanism for trade and exchange and move to regulate the flow of goods and services through this exchange channel.

History records the effects of such short-sightedness. In the early fourteenth century, the market conditions for global (that is, the known and explored world) expansion were suitable for the emergence of three Florentine super-companies, Bardi, Peruzzi and Acciaiuoli.[1] These companies had very complex organizational structures and sophisticated double-entry accounting technology, branch networks and subsidiary companies. They efficiently provided an impressive array of international commerce services from banking, currency exchange, letters of credit, insurance, manufacturing and distribution services, as well as providing the financial infrastructure for the papacy, rivalling contemporary, multinational financial institutions.

Today's objectives replicate the medieval global expansion plans, incorporating an ever-growing network of connected relationships fuelled by an acquisition strategy designed to grow a wider selection of goods and services to existing and emerging markets. Armed with superior accounting expertise, corporate branding complete with logos and an enthusiasm for applying technology to all aspects of the business targeted at reducing cost, the medieval super-companies mushroomed into vast organizations within twenty-five years, only to collapse and fail within thirty months.

The eagerness for expansion tied with the socio-economic conditions surrounding the sudden collapse of the medieval super-companies echoes strange similarities to the twenty-first-century marketplace. The factors that contributed to the medieval bankruptcies were: excessive loans to governments to finance wars (high-risk ventures); a reversal in the gold to silver ratio (two-currency monetary system); and a sudden change in international trade, resulting in a price squeeze (loss of fee income) which rapidly reduced margins.

Basically, medieval banks expanded, or extended themselves, beyond their core competencies and built bureaucracies that imploded when a combination of adverse conditions occurred. They simply lost sight of their core banking competency, managing the gap between deposits and loans, and relied heavily on fee income. In essence, these medieval super-companies, employing more people than most medieval governments, were victims of their own greed. They could not survive the changes in business climate that disrupted their ability to sustain a vast bureaucratic infrastructure.

Focus on Core Competencies

Will today's financial services organizations reach a point of implosion if a particular suite of conditions emerges? It is tempting to say that the sophisticated markets of today do not resemble the socio-economic structure of medieval Europe, and therefore these events cannot happen in today's financial institutions. However, organizations often move to incorporate new service offerings before they have perfected core service-oriented products, and have enjoyed this luxury primarily because of the intense capital investment needed to compete in the market. It is clear that the Internet has changed the landscape of competition for payment systems and will continue to commoditize the marketplace.

Like their medieval counterparts, contemporary governments will move to erect digital tollbooths to apply tax structures on the sale of goods and services that move across geopolitical boundaries (government reliance on fee income) for two reasons: first, as a source of revenue for the tax coffers; second, to encourage or restrict trade thereby regulating commerce by acting as a balancing mechanism. Financial services organizations could easily find themselves providing services to newly labelled global citizens facing a range of local, state and federal tax policies. The picture gets even more complex when considering the concept of digital currency and digital token technologies.

With a digital representation of physical value or currency, any individual or business can become a certificating authority and theoretically mint money in cyberspace, which payment systems may be required to recognize. It is not inconceivable that exchanges could bypass these tollbooths by simply minting their own pseudo-cyber-money and act as bartering agents between companies, thereby mitigating taxes and regulations. It is necessary to remember that the representation of value (digital or otherwise) is backed by the full faith and credit of the issuer, whoever that may be. It is not beyond the realm of possibilities that the future of digital money is the end of the government monopoly on currency. After all, are people buying more savings bonds (government-backed value) or shares (corporate-backed value)?

Looking at eBusiness through traditional lenses (transaction fees, percentages of profits), one often overlooks opportunities to provide new services. For example: the Internet has spawned many new exchanges for services in the consulting market. Traditionally, a small consulting company's ability to make profits has been hampered by having to provide an accounting infrastructure that performed basic services such as accounts receivable and payable. New service exchanges such as Services.com[2] and Changepoint[3] offer an environment of prescreened service acquirers who specify the technology projects and prequalified service providers who bid on the projects. In the fulfilment of these projects, a clear value exchange proposition exists between acquirer and provider.

Financial institutions have reviewed this service model and calculated the fee income that could be generated by each transaction. In doing that, they have overlooked the basic concept which dictates that, if the acquirer and provider each had accounts in the same bank, managing the cash float between the two parties is more lucrative than the fee income estimates of the original business model. The value proposition to the acquirer is that the exchange environment ensures that all members meet a predetermined level of quality, and the value to the provider is a reduction in accounts receivable from 45 to 60 days to less than 10. The additional value added that is made available by the financial institution is in eliminating the need for a contract on successive projects and providing cash management services. The value to the financial institution is that they hold the cash during the complete life cycle of transactions.

Branding and Value Propositions

Looking at the new dynamic capitalism with a fresh perspective on how payment systems work and will work in the future gives financial services organizations a renewed lease of life, by designing value-added processes with highly leveraged technology and talented, well-trained people. Payment systems will continue to evolve at an ever-increasing rate, focused on how value will be exchanged between parties, and how the financial institution providing this exchange will add value to the transaction.

Moreover, providing a payment system that has no clear competitive advantage may be fatal, because the cost of the technology is low enough to encourage many new market entrants, thereby sparking a fee income price war. Consequently, brand identity and a clear value proposition are paramount in payment systems of the future. Social acceptance of the applied function of technology will continue to drive how financial institutions will craft an offering and, in some cases, will provide an opportunity to redesign the basic process of payments to an anticipatory model.

There are six steps in developing a payment systems agenda:

1. Identify how your organization provides added value in the payment process.

2. Align services and brand to a clear and distinct value proposition.

3. Excel at optimizing the payment process into a streamlined function with superior customer service.

4. Monitor market trends and develop a core competency that rapidly applies technology, thereby streamlining the payment process.

5. Look for new services in value exchanges between parties.

6. Anticipate dynamic changes in social, legislative and technological forces, and develop a method of scenario planning to manage payment systems' risk.

The Components of Technology

The financial services industry's fear of disintermediation paints traditional banks as the incumbent provider offering the option of paying bills from a consumer's checking account (US) or current account (UK). Many financial institutions were late to engage the new wave of technologies, and now they are providing only a limited set of capabilities. This fact coupled with incumbency puts some traditional banks at a clear disadvantage to the new market entrants labelled as aggregators such as Transpoint (linked with Microsoft) and Intuit (linked with AOL),[4] whose underlying value proposition is convenience and the ability to bring together bills from a variety of sources to provide a consolidated view of accounts for a consumer. Market indications from numerous research firms have identified that consumers want to have a single site where they can get a consolidated view of bills and payments. However, the same research indicates that corporations who are seen as the billers do not share the same enthusiasm towards traditional banks providing this type of service, and are more inclined to partner with a new market aggregator.

At the root of this debate on market aggregation is technology and the approach to providing the service, which is evolving into two distinct operating models. The first approach is simply rerouting, where the consumer's address is given to the aggregator, who then receives the bills on the consumer's behalf, scans the bill or receives it electronically, posts the bill to a consumer account under password protection, and makes it available on the Internet for the consumer to review and authorize payment, when the funds are finally withdrawn from a preselected bank account. The second approach is to act like a power of attorney, in which the aggregator employs a technology called screen-scraping which uses the consumer's user name and password to view information at the billing websites, replicates the billing information and posts it to the same type of account as the previous approach, and then follows a similar settlement process. In some cases, less sophisticated aggregators provide a combination of the basic services of both approaches and only provide a link to each biller's website, creating an illusion of aggregation; however, over the long term, consumers realize that the element of convenience in the value proposition is lost.

The technology to provide this type of aggregation is not the root of the value proposition; it is a mechanism to fulfil one component. The more viable value-added service would be for financial services firms to adapt to a new business model and become a financial portal for consumers to perform a wide array of banking, insurance, retail and other life event-based activities, in which bill consolidation is an integral part. This type of capability is not found on websites today, primarily because most financial institutions are using the latest technology merely to replicate traditional banking applications. Many of these organizations embrace new banking products simply to maintain competitive parity.

The basic financial services firms have three potential options to provide this type of service: acquire the technology and do it themselves; outsource the technology aspect of the service while centralizing the customer service aspect; or partner with a new market aggregator and focus on brand cohesion. The selection of option or combination of options rests solely on the financial services firm's appetite for risk and investment, and its success will be in its ability to bring the product rapidly to market with the intention of evolving into a market portal.

As a result, social acceptance of technology has provided the environment, technology itself has provided the means, and now financial services organizations can seize the opportunity to rethink how to engage customers with payments systems that assist their lifestyles, and meet the complex needs of governments in a connected economy. Traditional banks can avoid the fate of their medieval counterparts by creating a value proposition based on a reaffirmation of trust, and the establishment of a financial portal offering a more cost effective product than their competitors, developing a strong branded presence, and delivering superior customer service.

CHAPTER 23

Privacy: Big Brother Meets the Marketing Mavens

Merriam-Webster's Dictionary defines the term 'privacy' as:

the quality or condition of being secluded from the presence or view of others; the state of being free from unsanctioned intrusion; a person's right to privacy.

It is almost impossible to discuss privacy and security on the Internet without considering the moral and ethical implications that have been suddenly thrust on society during the last ten years. Governments, businesses, international courts and individuals are beginning to realize what a connected society entails and the new levels of responsibility it places on both corporate and private citizens.

The Fourth and Fifth Amendments to the US Constitution were once thought to be assured protective devices. Today's rapidly evolving computer technologies and sophisticated databases are challenging the boundaries of the legislation and confronting consumers' right to privacy. At the heart of the issue is information, traditionally regarded by businesses as their painstakingly acquired and often expensive-to-maintain property, a crucially important and valued asset in the quest for increasing sales. This is made evident in the eleven bills introduced to the United States 106th Congress on privacy of information. The following example underscores the gist of the attitude towards the privacy issue.

HR 5571 Electronic Privacy Protection Act (Holt) combats 'Spyware' by requiring the FTC to issue regulations mandating that companies distributing software that transmits information over the Internet back to the manufacturer, to disclose such activity and obtain user consent.[1]

HR 5430 Consumer Online Privacy and Disclosure Act (Green) prohibits online profiling that attaches personally identifiable information to a users' Web surfing habits, and calls for an FTC rulemaking regarding privacy policies and 'opt-out' protection.[2]

S 3180 Spyware Control and Privacy Protection Act of 2000 (Edwards) controls 'Spyware,' computer programs that collect information about their users and transmit it back to the software company. The bill requires that manufacturers notify consumers when a product includes this capability, what types of information could be collected, and how to disable it. The bill also makes it illegal for programs to transmit users' information back to software manufacturers unless the user expressly enables that capability, and grants users access to any such information that is collected. Exceptions are made for validating authorized software users, providing technical support or legal monitoring of computer activity by employers.[3]

S 2928 Consumer Internet Privacy Enhancement Act (McCain) requires web sites to provide 'clear, conspicuous, and easily understood notice' of their information practices, as well as obvious opt-out mechanisms; prevents collection of personal information unless users have the opportunity to opt out of that information's disclosure and use beyond the primary purpose.[4]

S 2606 Telecommunications and Electronic Commerce Privacy Act (Hollings) requires notice and opt-in for collection and disclosure of personally identifiable information. Requires access and security. Gives FTC enforcement authority. Creates private right of action.[5]

At the heart of the legislative aspect are five basic requirements for companies operating a website or online services:

(i) to provide notice on its Web site, in a clear and conspicuous manner, of the identity of the operator, what personal information is collected by the operator, how the operator uses such information, and what information may be shared with other companies; and

(ii) to provide a meaningful and simple online process for individuals to consent to or limit the disclosure of personal information for purposes unrelated to those for which such information was obtained or described in the notice under clause (i);

(iii) a description of the specific types of personal information collected by that operator that was sold or transferred to an external company; and

(iv) notwithstanding any other provision of law, a means that is reasonable under the circumstances for the individual to obtain the personal information described in paragraph (i) from such individual; and

(v) require the operator of such Web site or online service to establish and maintain reasonable procedures to protect the confidentiality, security, and integrity of personal information it collects or maintains.[6]

The United States 107th Congress has carried on this pursuit of privacy by introducing the following bills during the 2001 sessions:

- Online Privacy Protection Act of 2001[H.R.89.IH]

- Consumer Online Privacy and Disclosure Act [H.R.347.IH]

- Unsolicited Commercial Electronic Mail Act of 2001[H.R.95.IH]

- Unsolicited Commercial Electronic Mail Act of 2001 [H.R.718.RH]

- CAN SPAM Act of 2001[S.630.IS]

- Who Is E-Mailing Our Kids Act [H.R.1846.IH]

- Cell Phone Service Disclosure Act of 2001[H.R.1531.IH]

- Privacy Commission Act [H.R.583.IH]

- Financial Privacy and National Security Enhancement Act [H.R.3068.IH]

- Citizens' Privacy Commission Act of 2001 [S.851.IS]

- Location Privacy Protection Act of 2001 [S.1164.IS]

- Social Security Number Privacy and Identity Theft Prevention Act of 2001 [S.1014.IS]

- Social Security Number Privacy and Identity Theft Prevention Act of 2001 [H.R.2036.IH]

- Student Privacy Protection Act [S.290.IS]

- National Consumer Privacy Act [H.R.2730.IH]

- Consumer Privacy Protection Act [H.R.2135.IH]

- Personal Information Privacy Act of 2001 [H.R.1478.IH]

- Export–Import Bank Reauthorization Act of 2001 [H.R.2871.IH][7]

Developing a Customer Focus

Financial services companies across the globe are rapidly appreciating that customer intimacy, customer centricity and consumer focus are indeed key competitive objectives that can be realized by leveraging technology. However, this type of customer-focused business also carries an implied level of trust when information and personal data are concerned. In the realm of customer trust and privacy, perception is, in many cases, more telling than reality. Consumers' fear of making credit card purchases over the Internet is slowly waning as confidence in the security technology continues to improve. This behaviour is not unpredictable. As the frequency of transactions increases and incidents of fraud are maintained at minimal levels, the relative perception of safety increases. Similar to the introduction of credit cards over twenty years ago, familiarity breeds contentment. For example: consumers give little thought to supplying a plastic card representing a line of credit to an underpaid, often discontented, food service worker who disappears from their view for five minutes, returning to ask for their signature. Consumers do this because they are used to the process and have confidence in it, if not consciously, but by familiarity. Consequently, research organizations are beginning to educate the public in the true nature and volume of fraud on the Internet, which is small, compared to other forms of transactions, and, not surprisingly, found in very specific market categories:

'Only 3% of UK credit card fraud relates to the internet, according to experts, yet consumers are still concerned about buying online. Last year there were 5.9 bn of credit, debit and store card transactions, worth £292.6 bn', said the Association for Payment Clearing Services. Fraudulent transactions were worth £293 m, up 55% on 1999. Over 90% of internet fraud relates to adult sites. 'Criminals set up bogus sites knowing that those giving their details were likely to be too embarrassed to report it', said Paula Widdowson of Card Protection Plan, which covers 6 m cardholders in the UK. Regarding other cyber crimes involving eMail, she added: 'Anyone giving their credit card details in an eMail, or to a person who has phoned, is ridiculous'.[8]

Credit cards represent a mature implicit trust between the issuer and the consumer that is backed by an agreement in the relationship between the parties. This trust is predicated on maintaining a level of privacy and security that is often discounted by consumers when searching for cards with lower interest rates. New market entrants can offer packaged financial services that appear as substantial as those offered by large institutions and can discount fees to lure away customers. Unless they consistently take care of their customers' privacy and security needs, financial services companies will continue to lose their customers to competitors perceived to be more trustworthy.

Establishing a Competitive Advantage

Privacy is a competitive asset that is often overlooked and rarely exploited as a viable marketing tool. Creating services that allow consumers to select levels of information that can and cannot be shared between merchants and other financial relationships is unexplored territory for financial services companies. Providing a consumer home base for data that is directed by the consumer is a value-added service rarely incorporated into today's product offerings.

While investments to enforce security can be substantial, safeguarding privacy may yield returns relatively quickly through the implementation of simple policy initiatives. Whether financial services organizations have already invested in customer security technology or are still only considering it, a clear definition of the perceived desired state and a plan to achieve results are both critical.

It is clear that customer knowledge will be a competitive weapon in the information age. Financial services organizations need to quickly establish distinct levels of trust, proactively educating their customers about security and privacy issues. Moreover, they need to clearly state how customer data will be used within the firm and with connected value chain partners.

Financial services institutions are trying desperately to move to a model of customer intimacy and customer centricity, focusing on the needs of different demographic market segments of the population to target financial services products. There are four distinct levels of information security that arise from the application of convergent technologies: inclusion, seclusion, concealment and refuge.

Level one is *inclusion*, where a customer elects to make public information about him or herself. For example: if you go to a website, you may be asked to give your name, address or other piece of personal data in exchange for some type of free trinket. You may not even really consider the ramifications of what you are doing. Even though a number of websites state their company policy on how the data is to be treated and used, often consumers simply skip over the deliberately lengthy disclaimer written in small type.

The second level is *seclusion*, in which the information exchanged with retailers and suppliers centres on your product preference. A good example is that while making a purchase at Amazon.com the website informs you that other people who have bought that book also purchased another book. This is information association and data aggregation, which derives information about the consumer and presents the data back to the consumer for verification. This is accomplished by profiling the purchasing behaviour of groups of individuals. Although this level of information offers a seemingly non-intrusive analysis of large amounts of data, it presents an additional layer of privacy by suppressing the other purchasers' names and addresses. These now anonymous purchasers are aggregated into a composite customer behaviour. At first glance it appears that the consumer is secluded in some level. However, the ownership of data that is derived about a consumer is not necessarily protected under the current set of privacy laws.

The third level of security is *concealment*. Information is exchanged between trusted sources such as banks and government departments, using a collection of technologies that allow you to retain a certain amount of privacy and/or anonymity during the execution of the transaction. Consumers may elect to execute a transaction under the generic label of a financial institution during the transfer of monies from one account to another.

Finally, the fourth level is *refuge*. This is a secure place that basically guarantees, or gives the impression of a guarantee, that data is being recorded and is considered secure or safe. For example, medical records, biometric information and digital signatures have been considered inaccessible by third parties.

In summary, privacy can be described as having four distinct levels of interaction:

- *Inclusion*. This is information that the customer elects to make public about himself or herself (a homepage, an ad response, or newsgroup posting);

- *Seclusion*. Information to exchange with retailers, suppliers, private networks (name, address, eMail, and product preferences);

- *Concealment*. Information to be exchanged between trusted sources (bank balances, tax records and digital certificates);

- *Refuge*. A secure place to store information about you and your current status (medical records, biometric data and digital signatures).

Each level of interaction requires a different approach to security to contend with the complexity of the issues surrounding the collection, retention and dissemination of data transacted at each level. This presents businesses with a dilemma concerning the moral and ethical values within the business community as well as within society today. At each level, information becomes more personal and contains details about the characteristics of your behaviours and habits. The twenty-first-century technological paradox is that the more you use the Internet to acquire information, the more information is generated about you, and the less control you have over it.

Today, the technology exists which makes possible the following scenario: the results of a genetic test carried out at birth indicate that you have a higher than average probability of having a particular health problem: these could be sent to medical specialists around the world to craft a proactive programme that would help you to maintain a meaningful lifestyle. Conversely, the same data could be sent to insurance companies around the globe, who might perceive you as a potentially high-cost patient and possibly blacklist you from medical or life insurance. The same data could also be supplied to future employers who may weigh that information against you when selecting job candidates.

Today, information about a consumer is in the possession of the collector, who has visible signs of ownership, which transfer to the consumer over time, or at least under consumer-driven direction. The challenges faced by the healthcare industry have dramatic implications for firms providing financial services. US healthcare legislation requires that healthcare institutions, doctors, hospitals and healthcare insurance providers obtain the consent of patients to retain, process, or use collected personal information as well as health information. Surprisingly, in the USA the patient has no control over the information, and if a doctor or a health insurer requests information about a patient from another doctor, the doctor can send the entire healthcare record and the receiving doctor or insurance firm has to sift through the information to find the specific piece of data they need in order to process a claim. Legislation will require that the patient must authorize or give consent so that the specific requested information can be transmitted, partially or entirely. Under new legislation, doctors can only provide the specific data requested, unless a patient pre-grants authority to make available all information to the requesting parties. This raised level of information privacy has enormous implications on the privacy, security and access to customer data as the flow of information continues to accelerate between financial services organizations. As customer demand for account aggregation increases, the custody and fair handling of the information will need to be explicitly addressed in order to ensure safe passage of information to and from financial services marketplaces, trading partners and other third parties.

Financial services institutions must demonstrate proactively that they are addressing the issues of data transfer and information privacy and that the decision to share all types of information is clearly controlled by customers or governments. The key thought to remember is that there is a movement from institutions owning the data to the individual owning the data, and there is a growing distinction between data ownership rights and authorization rights. Regardless of the legislative process, financial services institutions must work hard to assure consumers about the security of personal information, primarily to ensure the perception of trust and integrity which is paramount to branding.

The Value of Trust

Interacting in a connected society requires an exchange of data and information in order to transact with other people, businesses and governments. In order to engage in interactivity in cyberspace, there are four levels of trust, either implied or expressed between parties:

- *Negligible.* No trust or claims are to be trustworthy (newsgroups, eMail list, or some ISPs);

- *Implied.* Giving data to a party that implies privacy but does not expressly make a claim to the degree of privacy (Internet clubs or special interest groups, other ISPs, and some retailers);

- *Brokered.* A proactive statement of privacy that is represented by a fiduciary responsibility (banks, medical professions and insurance companies);

- *Guaranteed.* Privacy protected by expressed means (Internal Revenue Service, social security, military records).

Unfortunately, not all levels of trust are understood when initiating a transaction on the Internet. There are no warning labels other than the disclaimers and other legal expressions found on the bottom of many corporate homepages. The Internet is still in an embryonic state, and websites such as the possible Top100PrivacyAbusers.com or ReallyEvilRetailMarketers.org have not been established to allow consumers to check who is being entrusted with their data.

The new opportunity for financial institutions is to capitalize on their already established brand of trust and offer new services that are separated from a customer's existing banking relationship. It is not beyond the realm of possibilities to develop a secure environment where users register their information and then issue tokens to retailers and/or banks giving them access to preselected information. Placing the consumer clearly in control of the data allows him or her to determine what data is appropriate for exchange. For example: when changing your address, why fill out countless cards and electronic forms when you can just issue eMail tokens that inform the recipient that new data about you is available. The institutions' computer systems then could synchronize by using the token to unlock and download your new data and update records. Technically, institutions could build databases without any customer data, storing only tokens and accessing the data from a centralized source when needed.

Inclusion versus Intrusion

The pervasiveness of technology and the data it generates are increasing at an astounding rate. Under the guise of convenience, these technologies silently and meticulously collect data with the sole purpose of establishing information about you and your habits. It is ironic that Orwell's vision of the clandestine observation of citizens by a centralized governing authority is being implemented by willing individuals eager to employ technology.

Perhaps the most intrusive and pervasive privacy trespasser is the spam eMail message. Mailboxes burgeoning with messages on low rate mortgages, weight loss programmes, body-part enlargements and get-rich-quick-penny-stocks seem like harmless irritants. They are, in fact, a sterling example of how information about you is acquired and abused. Spammers use various mechanisms to acquire your eMail address and use it as digital currency by selling it over and over again to businesses eager to reach customers. So as to give consumers a perceived sense of business ethics, many spams now carry messages that they are a one-time message or you can be removed from the list by replying with remove, only to find the message rejected later by the postmaster.

Developing a Privacy Agenda

As the issue of privacy moves into the spotlight, financial services organizations will need to supply a clear and distinct form of assurance regarding information policies and distribution. If your financial institution told you upfront that they were going to supply your name and address to direct marketing campaigns, would you still open an account with them?

How can organizations develop an action agenda on privacy? Merely posting a corporate privacy statement on a company's website falls far short of providing a comprehensive mechanism to ensure a perceived or implied trust safeguarding information. Organizations need to inform their customers periodically of how their information is to be used and what other organizations have access to it. Educating customers on the issues of privacy, the use of their data, and how the institution actively protects its data increases a company's value proposition as the public becomes more aware of the privacy crisis. A proactive approach reinforces the level of trust in the relationship with a customer.

Developing a corporate privacy agenda should be constructed around principles, that is, designed intentions that clearly state to consumers how data will be treated and set expectations on the confidentiality of information:

- Principle 1   Collection
- Principle 2   Use and disclosure
- Principle 3   Data quality
- Principle 4   Data security
- Principle 5   Openness
- Principle 6   Access and correction
- Principle 7   Identifiers
- Principle 8   Anonymity
- Principle 9   Transborder data flows
- Principle 10   Sensitive information.

Global Concern, Personal Seclusion and the Corporate Paradox

The issue of privacy is not limited to the United States. A quick scan of the global community finds that the privacy issue and associated legislation is being introduced in most of the world's legislative bodies. The following represents the issues on the Australian privacy agenda:

- Children's privacy;
- Making a complaint under the privacy legislation;

- Personal information held by government contractors;

- Direct marketing;

- Privacy and the electronic environment;

- Employee records;

- Overseas organizations and transborder data flows;

- Privacy and the media;

- Privacy and health;

- Exemption for bodies registered under electoral laws and political representatives;

- Related corporate bodies;

- Small businesses;

- Privacy and genealogy;

- Developing privacy codes;

- Privacy and existing database.

Regardless of financial products and services provided to end consumers, privacy should be in the forefront of the planning agenda. Setting expectations and managing the relationship that is built on an implied or explicit trust with customers is essential to a comprehensive business strategy. Customer loyalty is built on a series of interactions that establishes a relationship of trust. Technology is only part of the equation providing a medium for exchange to fulfil transactions. Developing a corporate philosophy of trust that is enabled by a comprehensive customer service focus promoting the highest quality of privacy is the hallmark of quality in the new economy.

CHAPTER 24

Valagents: Digital Indentured Servants in the Age of eMoney

Financial services firms are seeking to migrate into the role of a trusted advisor for individuals and small business. A lesser known technology that has an enormous potential for the financial services industry is that of 'valagents'. Valagents or value exchange agents are intelligent agent technologies that provide a bridge between advice and action in financial services. Agent-based technology can be employed directly to the value proposition of a customer relationship by performing functions such as a consolidated portfolio view, portfolio rebalancing, asset allocation recommendations, risk mitigation and trade execution optimization.

Products such as IBM's Virtual Private Banker[1] and German-based Financialbot.com's finbot[2] have created mechanisms for financial services firms that present a new value proposition to their customers by designing software that extends the reach of an investor. Customer account data aggregation is just one natural application for advisors, bots or intelligent agents, positioning financial services firms, credit unions and any other market aggregator in a unique position to act as an intermediary for niche marketplaces, performing the role of a data integrator within the financial services community. However, in order to develop a general awareness of how this type of technology can be applied to a value proposition within financial services, it is necessary to have a basic understanding of the technologies and their direct application. It should be noted that, in the area of financial services, these technologies are in an embryonic state and multiple experiments are currently underway.

Technologies that symbolize or represent an individual and execute tasks on their behalf are generally referred to as agents, including bio-enhancement, intelligent agents, robots, and avatars. Intelligent agents are adaptive computer programs that function within software environments such as operating systems and database networks. They assist users with routine computer errands, being customized to accommodate individual user-habits. Avatars are three-dimensional representations of individuals in cyberspace that users may employ to represent themselves in both appearance and assignment.

As discussed in Chapter 3, currently avatars are inanimate objects, but in the near future they may be animated to further express the personality that their controllers wish to portray. These technologies give you the ability to represent yourself in the eEconomy, bringing to light a new question: Will the physical appearance and personality you select reflect you or someone you would like to be?

Technology is enabling a variety of new market entrants to bring competitive offerings to the marketplace of financial services with a relatively low cost of entry. As energy companies, telecommunications companies and financial services organizations strive for bill presentment technologies, they often misjudge the relocation of these functions as facilitators of anticipatory and proactive service offerings. Anticipatory presentment technologies allow the value exchange partner to preset tolerances of a value exchange.

For example, a consumer's bill for many services is often within a very small bandwidth of variability. The consumer should be able to preselect a range of payment tolerances for his or her utility bills and target funds for fulfilment, receiving a message only when the impending transaction is going to cross the upper tolerance limit. This is a shift in payments from a reactive to a proactive payment mentality, managing home finances by exception processing. It is not beyond the current technology to initiate anticipatory intelligent agents for financial services that act on a trading partner's behalf and broker an exchange of value. As discussed above, these financial services robots, finbots, or valagents execute or act on one's behalf with an original certification.

What's a Bot?

A bot is a software tool for interrogating data. Supplied with directions, it retrieves answers or values. The word is techno-slang for robot, which is derived from the Czech word *robota* meaning work. The idea of robots as humanoid machines was first introduced in Karel Capek's 1921 play *R.U.R.*, where the playwright conceived Rossum's Universal Robots.

On the Internet, information robots have taken on a host of functions and tasks that are invisible to the majority of users. Web servers are connected and employ robot-like software to perform the methodical searches needed to find information. For example, search engines send out robots that crawl from one server to another compiling the enormous lists of URL data, domain data and meta-tags to compile the indexes needed for each engine. Shopping bots assemble enormous databases of products sold at online stores and provide shoppers with condensed pricing and delivery information.

The term 'bot' is now interchangeable with agent, to indicate a module or object of software that is sent out to find information and report back. Some bots operate in a single place; for example, a bot in Microsoft Front Page automates work on a Web page.

The greatest in-house potential for valagents is data mining, the process of interrogating data sources to derive patterns in enormous amounts of data. Data mining often requires a series of searches, and bots can save labour as they persist in a search, learn based on defined parameters, and refine information as they execute their task. Intelligent bots make decisions based on past experiences, an important tool for data miners trying to perfect complex searches that delve into countless data points.

Valagents for financial services functions can be organized into two distinct categories: active outward searching bots which seek out elements of data and execute transactions based on preset formulas, and inward investigating data mining bots that search through volumes of data to capitalize and reclassify data.

Active Outward Searching Valagents

The following is a list of the most popular active outward valagents under experimentation:

■ The JAM Project in collaboration with the Financial Services Consortium (FSTC) including Chase, First Union and Citibank as well as Columbia University and Florida Tech. Using local classifier agents and meta-learning agents allows financial institutions to inspect, classify and label each incoming secured electronic transaction.[3]

■ AgentBuilder: Agents for Electronic Commerce is an application integration toolkit that enables one to create intelligent agents quickly and easily, consisting of three interacting agents: one buyer agent and two store agents.[4]

- Agentis: Pioneered by the Australian Artificial Intelligence Institute (AAII) and now available through Agentis International, it applies artificial intelligence to business process management and can be applied to self-service call centre operations, real-time simulation and monitoring, and online compliance and detection.[5]

- The New York-based Artificial Life Inc. has been developing agent technology that engages a user in natural language conversations, reducing the complexity of navigational schemas that often confuse users in many websites.

- ALife-PortfolioManager assists individual investors in selecting securities that match their investment objectives, presenting performance-related information in a visually simple format. Investors select sources of their choice to keep abreast of the market and are constantly updated with news. Ashton, the portfolio bot, educates the user and also serves as an alert system.[6]

- ALife-WealthManager is designed for goal-oriented financial planning; it educates a user in investment concepts and assists in calculations, identifying variables and statistical information such as average costs, which are essential to managing investments. Using natural language, a conversation allows the user to interrogate options with personified agents Kubera and Ashton about retirement planning or planning for your child's education.[7]

- Botizen: Provides customizable customer service agents that enable rapid service response to a website 24 hours a day, seven days a week using natural language two-way conversations.[8]

- NativeMinds features virtual representatives (vReps) that can answer any questions you have about NativeMinds and its virtual representative technology with facial expressions that match their responses. vReps such as Nicole provide a best-fit response in conversational language.[9]

The value of these expressive agents that carry on two-way conversations and exhibit facial expressions is that they can extend the culture of the organization to the customer. A corporate look-and-feel can be presented to a customer that simulates a purchase or, in the case of financial services, conveys confidence in the advisory.

One of the most comprehensive websites that demonstrates the potential of agent technology is France's Agentland.com, where agents have been aggregated and made available for individuals to employ them in various activities such as shopping and active searching.

Inward Investigating Data Mining Valagents

■ MOMspider: Multi-owner Maintenance spider is a web-roaming robot that specializes in the maintenance of distributed hypertext info struc tures (that is, wide-area webs) developed by Roy Fielding as part of the Arcadia[10] and WebSoft[11] projects at the University of California. This software was designed for technology personnel to maintain website pages that are dispersed across many computer systems, and could be employed to aggregate financial information with a financial services company and across many firms.

■ Infogate: This technology provides organizations and individuals with a unique desktop presence and urgent messaging platform. The combination of content aggregation service and proprietary delivery technology enables an individual to receive up-to-the-minute personalized information on their personal computer and direct messages to their wireless devices.[12]

These broadcast-based agents can be used by financial services firms to enhance the brand image of a product offering or co-band products with complementary product providers and affiliated companies. The key component of this technology that is applicable to financial services firms is the sophisticated 'find-me-follow-me' concept, which allows users to elect when and where they want to receive personalized news and information alerts. This type of personalization could be used by investors to supplement and plan life events that can be triggered by dynamic information. For example: a customer could build a scenario that says 'alert me when there is a drop in interest rates that makes it worthwhile to remortgage my house and advise me of the financing options available and recommend which option best fits my current overall financial objectives'.

New Value Propositions

Some of the most promising valagent offerings are: IBM's Virtual Agent Technology, which is designed with the customer at the centre of the transaction; ALife-BannerBot, which could be adapted to use its natural language processing engine to lead customers to the right combination of investment and insurance products to fit their lifestyle; and NativeMinds, which could be used for virtual customer service representatives in retail products. Under IBM's Virtual Agent Technology, one application that financial services firms can readily capitalize on is the Virtual Private Banker offering, which plays the role of a trusted third party and acts as an advocate on behalf of the investor. Put simply, an investor employing this particular valagent can identify his or her investment goals and tolerance for risk, in which case the virtual agent then searches for the investment, insurance, loans and other financial instruments, identifies and recommends the best candidates, negotiates the best terms on the investors' behalf and executes the transactions.

The potential value propositions for valagents rests in applications that support mass customization, therefore enabling financial services providers and customers to co-design individualized financial products, from custom-building a portfolio based on investor preferences to custom-fitting financial products to a lifestyle. To supplement this, other valagent technology will be used to enhance customer support, delivering high-quality pre-sale, post-sale and customer education services. Financial services customers and employees who are part of the mobile workforce will also benefit from the valagent technology's ability to make financial services more simple and convenient.

In the technology maturity curve, valagent technology is still in its infancy. The underlying value proposition, although compelling, is not yet proven. However, like all previous technologies, its widespread dissemination will be directly proportional to its ability to promote customers' awareness in the marketplace and the rate of social adoption. In this sense, these technologies present several potential value propositions that are viable to certain market sub-segments:

■ The ability to remember past user behaviour and associate next behaviours or suggest similar actions to the user (for example Amazon.com informing you of other customers' purchases that you may like).

■ The ability to extend the customer's activities beyond their Web browsing and initiate transactions that take place when they are not online.

■ The ability to sift through information, aggregate it (such as market data, investment advice, company news, fee structures) and rank it, based on a user's criteria.

The overall value of these technologies to financial services firms is twofold: firstly, they place the customer in control of financial transactions and amplify the capability of self-service, which appeals to several market sub-segments; and secondly, they provide the firm with the ability to enhance the overall customer service experience. Any firm that embarks on the valagent journey must be aware of the fact that they are only a tool that must be integrated into a broader customer offering, requiring either a sophisticated end user with specific financial goals and awareness, or a training programme to educate customers in the new product, which in its turn would also mean changing their personal financial behaviour.

To summarize, the valagent experience can best be expressed by this simple rule: the perceived value for money is directly proportional to the customers' desire to proactively set up and execute a financial plan; poor planners who are impulse shoppers will be reluctant to pay fees for this type of service. Value is only perceived if the users believe that their own time is valuable and the valagent is saving them time.

PART V

eMarketplaces: The New Frontier for Services

The economic downturn of 2001 has given many financial services a renewed sense of complacency in the competitive arena, with a scaling back of Internet-based product offerings and a reduction in the acquisition of infrastructure technologies. These market conditions create an opportunity for financial services firms to re-engage the marketplace and lead the industry into the next evolutionary phase of eCommerce development. The emergence and development of eMarketplaces is an area overlooked by financial services firms because of the early stage of business maturity of today's eMarketplaces. However, the demand for global connectedness is creating various areas of opportunities to which traditional banks or new banks operating in a traditional fashion are unable to adapt quickly. These new eMarketplaces provide a host of new value-added services that will redefine the nature of financial services and present fertile ground for experimentation, product development, brand recognition and relationship-building between customers, partners and niche market players. This section introduces the need for financial services firms to develop a clear value proposition and craft new services that offer value-added transactions in the new areas of revenue opportunities. Financial services firms are asked to consider the question of redefining not only what they sell and how they sell it, but to contemplate creating and adding value by restructuring the organization and moving away from traditional hierarchical structures.

CHAPTER 25

Introducing New Financial Products and Services

Revolutions, by their nature, create new and unanticipated opportunities, challenges and risks for those caught up in them. We all find ourselves in the midst of a technological revolution propelled by digital processing. All around us, in ways and forms we cannot fully appreciate, new digitally-based economic arrangements are changing how people work together and alone, communicate and relate, consume and relax. These changes have been rapid and widespread, and often do not fit the established categories for understanding economic developments. As a result, early efforts to take the measure of these changes have often seemed to be inventories of what is not yet known.[1]

Introduction

What are eMarketplaces and how can financial services firms take advantage of the new business opportunities they present to the consumer and business-to-business markets? In Chapter 7, we saw that eMarketplaces represent a collection of converging technologies which are now moving from an embryonic state to the next level of maturity. Technology has played a key role in reshaping the delivery of banking services and the underlying processes that have supported traditional financial services product offerings. The evolution of technology has created the conditions that result in a variety of new opportunities for financial institutions to increase shareholder value by expanding revenues with new product and service offerings that reduce cost by employing technology to optimize business processes and streamline operations.

Many of these opportunities can be realized by providing new products and services in the emerging eMarketplaces. Unlike traditional commercial and retail banking product offerings, the new eMarketplaces demand services that transcend typical lines of business within a financial services organization and require the establishment of new relationships between parties, sometimes with organizations that have been previously viewed as competitors.

What is the eMarketplace Phenomenon?

The eMarketplace phenomenon is a result of the continued convergence between communications technologies and computing technologies used primarily to complete the information cycle or to enable the transference of data within a corporate framework and the business processes which exchange transactions between external entities. The classical definition of a marketplace is: the world of commercial activity where goods and services are bought and sold. The distinguishing feature of an eMarketplace is its ability to facilitate the exchange of commercial activity co-existing in both the digital and physical marketplaces.

The advantage is that eMarketplaces create an environment in which buyers and sellers come together in significantly more efficient ways than have been possible before. Businesses can use digital technology to augment their existing supply channels, creating new opportunities for financial services providers.

Early Internet pundits heralded its immediate benefit to consumers as being the effect of disintermediation on buyers and sellers. Nevertheless, few businesses were prepared to embrace the technology and redesigned core business processes to integrate an automated digital customer order fulfilment process and associated customer service systems. Consumers, faced with no clear avenue or pathway to interact directly with suppliers, turned to emerging intermediaries who simply provided a mechanism for locating goods and services and later facilitated the ordering process by providing a channel to the supplier. These evolving markets will undergo many transformations over the next few years, with a continuing focus on higher levels of customer service and increased customer data aggregation.

Alternatively, eMarketplaces empower demand chains by connecting distributors with their suppliers, dealers and consumers in an eCommerce network. Distributors who take their traditional buying, selling and special order processes to the Internet benefit from creating a virtual supply chain that allows all trading partners to profit from the eMarketplace.

An eMarketplace gives market participants the opportunity to:

- Increase revenue by expanding sales;

- Reduce selling costs by streamlining the fulfilment process;

- Improve customer service by employing CRM technology or outsourcing the customer service function;

- Accelerate the sales process by reducing process steps in the ordering process;

- Streamline supplier reordering;

- Strengthen partner relationships.

Innovative financial services firms have begun to realize the potential of eMarketplaces, not only for the purchase of products, but for the establishment of markets that are dedicated solely to financial services. One lesson learned from the dot-com experience is that a value proposition cannot be predicated on future earnings that are based on extremely large transaction volumes, for the following reason: if the level of fee-generating transactions does not rise fast enough to the levels needed to sustain the business model, the long-term viability is quickly eroded. That said, there are a number of other lessons learned from the dot-com experience and early eMarketplaces that should influence the strategic planning process within the financial firm, such as how consumers behave, how products need to be structured and the types of products that can be purchased using Internet technologies. These are products you know, products you have to experience once before using the Internet to repurchase them, and products that you might not buy on the Internet, but their purchase will be facilitated by information gained on the Internet (see Figure 25.1). Each type of product has an optimum corresponding level of customer engagement: interactivity, intimacy and immersion.

Product Categories

The first product category comprises products and services with which you are familiar; in this case, you go to the Internet simply to make the purchase or place a future order, for example: office supplies, books, CDs and other everyday products. Retailers such as Amazon.com have found that, in this product category, product-linking presents the consumer with

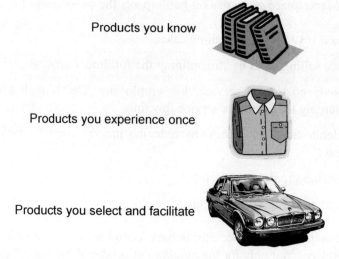

Products you know

Products you experience once

Products you select and facilitate

Figure 25.1 Product categories

additional choices for cross-selling. For financial services, this can be a powerful cross-selling tool, where a customer can be advised that other customers in the same income, lifestyle and/or financial position have just recently purchased a home and a certain insurance coverage on the property, contents and liability, establishing a profitable connection between buyers through their common interests or purposes.

The second category of products are those which need to be experienced once, either by developing a tactile relationship, or, in the case of services, as an experiential event to educate and familiarize oneself with the product. For example: purchasing a new dress or shirt in store requires a number of steps in order to complete the buying experience: firstly you identify the look that is appealing; then you feel the material; then you try it on and see if you like it, if the value for money is adequate, and if it will shrink, or stain, depending on the fabric. It is in fact a complicated process that is taken for granted because everyone is familiar with doing it. On the Internet, on the other hand, the only step that is fulfilled in a first purchase is step 1, that is, identifying the product. Indeed, when one sees a picture of what one wants, like buying from a paper catalogue, all the other steps in this process are suppressed. If the customer buys online, he or she will assume that the information on the website is accurate (size, dimensions, type of material and washing instructions) and that once the purchased items arrive, he or she will have the opportunity to try it on and keep it if the product meets his or her expectations, or return it at no cost if it doesn't. The customer is less interested in the buying experience the second time round, and will simply place the order on the Internet for a new colour or additional pieces.

For financial services firms, each time a customer enters into a new type of interaction with the firm (such as opening an account, applying for a mortgage, refinancing, loans and insurance), they assess the overall experience with their basic perceptions of how the institution adds value. A series of good experiences builds loyalty and trust. It could be argued that certain customer market sub-segments have not moved away from traditional banking relationships simply because they are still inconvenient, and the processes associated with opening and closing accounts are laborious enough to discourage changing unless they reach a high level of dissatisfaction.

The third type of product category requires a longer consumer-education process and typically characterizes higher priced items in which visual examination and tactile experience of the product are essential to the purchase, but the decision to purchase can be augmented by information, and the transaction of the purchase can be accompanied by the need for other services. For example: the purchase of a new automobile does not require physical inspection, but it is often the buyer's preference to sit in the car, hear the door close, look in the mirror and turn on the stereo. The Internet can be used to find the car of choice, narrow down the options and locate a dealer or person wanting to sell the vehicle. Using the Internet, car registration with the local Department of Motor Vehicles Registration Authority can also facilitate additional transactions that support the purchase, car insurance policies can be written, and financing can be prearranged. Firms such as CarMax and Autobytel were pioneers in this process.

Product Types and Customer Experience

These three product types relate directly to the customer's experience in transacting with the providing organization and are composed of a variety of customer-driven fulfilment preferences. There is an uncanny similarity between a consumer's retail shopping experience and the activities of financial services customers, which can be linked to a variety of financial services products. For instance: in the first product type, customers are familiar with current and savings accounts and will interact rapidly to establish an account at a branch or on the Internet because it is something they know. In the second product type, customers often need to be educated about more complicated financial products such as a mortgage, brokerage account, small business loan, ISA, or mutual fund, but once over the initial learning curve, they are able to make rapid decisions on acquiring additional loans, funds, or accounts. The third and more complex product type is analogous to share trading, derivatives, commodities, annuities, linked insurance products, in which the customer can elect to perform the transaction but, in many cases, empowers the financial institution to act on his or her behalf. Obviously, as the complexity of the product increases, the need to educate the customer rises, and the underlying technologies to deliver these products can be vastly different.

Organizations in the retail industry have developed click-and-mortar strategies that can provide insight into customer behaviour for retail bank services. Retail customers adopt technology at a rate slightly ahead of banking technologies, and their buying habits are more impulsive for low-cost items and planned for higher price durable goods. Consumer and small business transactions take place within three types of environment: the interactive, the intimate and the immersed. Each environment offers the backdrop for the customer experience by providing details on the item to be purchased, communicating pricing, displaying shipping options and in many cases describing the way in which the product can be used or applied. The environment is divided into two distinct domains: cyberspace, the techno-jargon term for the Internet and World Wide Web, and terraspace, the techno-jargon term for the physical world.

However, what is most important to learn from the retail markets is that the behaviour of consumers within both domains is surprisingly similar to how the transaction is executed and dissimilar to the way in which the interaction occurs. Customer behaviour can be broken down into three increasing levels of engagement with the selling and fulfilment process within a firm: it starts as simple interactions or interactivity, intensifying to higher degree of customization or intimacy, and finally evolving to complex customer relationships or immersion (see Figure 25.2). These three levels of behaviour represent a challenge for financial services firms because they are in conflict with the objectives of standardization of services to a generic one-size-fits-all strategy.

Customer Experience: Interactivity

The first level of engaging a customer is interactivity, that is, the simple act of transacting with the firm. This level is best represented as a dialogue or exchange between a community, customer or an employee that results in a transaction of value. For example: going to a website and purchasing a book

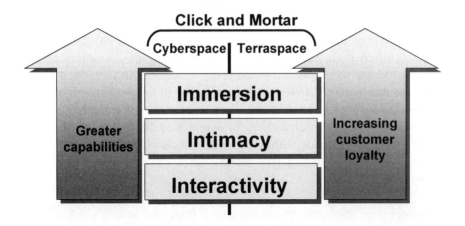

Figure 25.2 Click-and-mortar strategy

or opening a savings account is the simplest form of interactivity. This level often represents the highest volume of customer interactions, in which customers are very sensitive to fees charged because of the perception of a commodity. It can be said that when all financial institutions offer this level of service (for example, cheques, savings, loans, brokerage, credit cards, insurance), the market will eliminate all the fees to remain competitive.

Customer Experience: Intimacy

The second level of engagement is intimacy, which places the customer at the centre of a total process of customized solutions, or a collection of optional products allowing the grouping together of components to form a customized solution set. This level is often represented by a community or affinity group that acts as a consolidation body and associates transactions. For example: on the USAir website, a frequent flyer can select a preferred travel destination; this location will be monitored, and, when the prices change to the customer's advantage, he or she will be informed via eMail of the reductions or special offers.[2]

Customer Experience: Immersion

The third level, which is most difficult to achieve, is called immersion. Here, the customer is the process and the firm provides a total environment to supplement a lifestyle with anticipatory services. Few retail firms have achieved this level of customer behaviour, and many dot-com firms, such as Peapod.com and Streamline.com that tried to apply this to the mass market, often realized too late that the majority of customers are not willing to bear the expense of that level of service. In fact, each market segment may have a different definition of the immersion experience.

The Discovery Channel Stores offer an example of extending a click-and-mortar strategy to customers by integrating the television programming into an experience within the store. Julian Markham points out that the combination of interactive technologies links to a wider customer experience:

> Shoppers are responding by expecting more from store designs which incorporate innovative and original technology. Customers' increasing experience and knowledge, therefore, will drive how a store's features are implemented. The 'new breed' of customer is likely to be looking for presentation which is more attention-grabbing, and the entertainment-based retailers are turning into more than mere stockists of products in the traditional sense. Instead they are moving to be attractive locations which, in themselves, entertain.[3]

The implications for financial services firms is that the retail banking experience will be transformed into more than a place to deposit money, withdraw cash and open or close accounts; it will become a financial learning centre that educates individuals on how to tailor financial products to a lifestyle. As discussed in Part IV, there is a rising trend for individuals to use a branch even more, as well as an Internet banking offering.

This new role for financial services branch operations is in stark contrast to the current trend to close branches as a method of cost reduction. In the United Kingdom, NatWest, one of Britain's largest banks, was among the first to embrace the preservation of the branch network. Financial services firms need to rapidly develop comprehensive click-and-mortar strategies or face disintermediation in a competitive war of customer attrition, with new market entrants and other niche market players slowly eroding market share. A click-and-mortar strategy should engage the research findings that indicate a stronger demand for in-branch services by retail and small business customers regardless of their technical know-how, and undertake to build product offerings that include consultation time with the customer. Whereas it has been the express goal of financial services firms to reduce the overall cost of operations by reducing the number of branches in operation, it could also be considered contrary to their implied goals of becoming trusted financial advisors. Considering that many customers prefer face-to-face meetings when planning life events and discussing large financial transactions, technology can be used to minimize the total time spent with a customer by passing information to and from the customer prior to a face-to-face activity. Much of this process can be facilitated by Internet technologies and the process can be streamlined as the customer becomes educated in the products and their delivery mechanisms. It remains to be seen if the current trends in social adoption of technology continue, or if individuals will reach a saturation point in which delivery technologies will lose their appeal.

Technology and market segments

As discussed in Chapter 19, many financial services firms subscribed to the belief that a generic technology solution could be applied across the total customer base, and are currently facing disappointment as the anticipated benefits fall short of their expectations. In developing a click-and-mortar strategy, the application of technology should be focused on which technology provides the greatest value to a specific product and interaction type. The key lesson learned is that, in many cases, generic technology solutions often provide mediocre results. One can take the previously mentioned product types, rank and index them against the interaction types to form a matrix of value and technology which can be applied towards specific market segments (see Figure 25.3).

Content, Context and Infrastructure

As a consequence of the increased levels of interactivity between the customer and the financial services institutions, product offerings must develop the mechanisms for engaging customers. This is proving to be a daunting task in the development of products and mechanisms to service every market sector and every customer segment. Financial services firms are finding that partnering with a collection of delivery firms that can provide access channels to consumers is a cost effective strategy from a technological viewpoint, but more complex business issues arise over branding and customer ownership. Partnering with existing eMarketplaces is a fast route to a consumer market, in many cases not entirely the desired customer base, but the technological portal provides an avenue in which to guide existing and potential clients. The opportunities for financial services companies reside in one or all of the following avenues of infor-

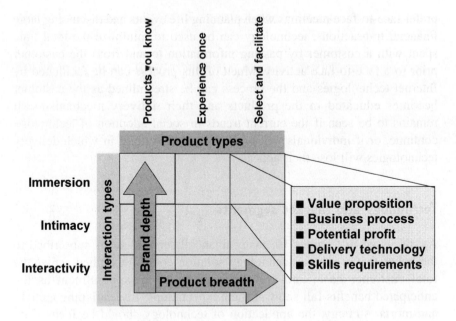

Figure 25.3 Product and interaction types

mation exchange between the participants in eMarketplaces: by providing or facilitating content (what is offered), context (how is it offered) and infrastructure (what enables the transaction to occur).

For financial services operations, content is the key asset of the business. It includes: services such as credit, interest on savings and advice; financial data such as account details; and, significantly, customer information. Successfully managing content calls for qualities such as creativity, speed of development and, perhaps most importantly, a sense of trust.

Context is a less familiar concept to financial services organizations. Defined as the overall customer experience in any particular situation, context combines elements of both content and infrastructure, embracing qualities such as levels of service and support, the look and feel of a particular interface, pricing, branding, and a host of other largely subjective qualities as experienced by a particular customer in a particular environment. Managing context calls for continual attention to the dynamic nature of changing customer needs and behaviours, differentiation from competitors, and interfacing with new eMarketplace partners to create a compelling packaged service offering. Traditionally, financial institutions are not as well versed at managing context.

Infrastructure corresponds to the technology of the eMarketplace provider and the financial services institutions' computers and networks, the back office operations, and the physical aspects of technology, encapsulated in the bricks and mortar of the headquarters and branches. Managing infrastructure is all about maximizing reliability and minimizing cost in an area in which financial services firms have a long tradition of competence.

These elements of an eMarketplace, content, infrastructure and context, are comparatively similar to their brick-and-mortar counterparts of product, delivery and market respectively. Content includes not just the products themselves but also the information associated with these products and the customers who use them. Infrastructure includes not just delivery channels but also the whole complex of information systems and processes, which enable a transaction to be processed reliably and efficiently. By default, context should equate to market, but clearly the concept is much more complex than that, embracing not just a particular segment of consumers, but how individual consumers feel and behave in a variety of different circumstances.

Viewing the financial services value proposition, in terms of how their services will add value in an eMarketplace, reveals several aspects that are not immediately apparent. First, in order to be successful, financial institutions must manage all three value-generating components (content, context and infrastructure) in an eMarketplace, employing three distinct sets of associated skills. Financial services organizations need to optimize their core competencies of managing content and infrastructure and develop the necessary skills to manage context.

Managing context is certainly the most important part of providing a sustainable value proposition to an eMarketplace, primarily because whoever controls the context controls the relationship with the customer, and this is the key to most companies conducting business in the new eEconomy. In previous generations, financial institutions were very good at customer relationships, but, for a variety of reasons (such as lack of attention to changing customer needs, overemphasis on cost cutting, economies of scale, shareholder value, and insufficient attention to the core asset of trust), their relationship skills have been severely eroded.

Three types of non-financial companies are very good at managing context – retailers, technology companies and strongly branded consumer companies. Not surprisingly, these types of organization are successfully challenging the boundaries of the exclusive channel to customers enjoyed by the traditional financial industry. These new market entrants make possible the disintermediation of the retail consumer, business-to-business markets and financial services. The implication of disintermediation is the alienation of customer loyalty, allowing consumers to migrate to skilful context players. Financial institutions could be distanced from their customer base and reduced to the status of providers of commoditized financial service product offerings, competing mainly on price.

In this early stage of development in the eMarketplace arena, the opportunities for new market entrants become especially apparent in the world of how the Internet is facilitating electronic commerce. In the current market, the companies currently making money are primarily context specialists. Companies that act as a conduit of content, such as AOL, Amazon, ISPs,[4] ASPs and other providers, own no content and no infrastructure, but through a combination of technology and attention to their customers (or members) have managed to create unique and strongly branded contexts. The term 'portals' has been coined to describe these context specialists. Such companies are increasingly turning their attention to financial services. Within the financial services community, the establishment of multi-bank portals for specialized product offerings is in the early stages of development, as demonstrated by UK firms such as Atriax, Centradia, Currenex, FXall, and US firms such as State Street's Global Link and SunGuard's STN Treasury.

CHAPTER 26

How to Approach the eMarketplace Space

The evolution of the medieval marketplace was briefly discussed in Chapter 2, contextualizing how the Internet has followed somewhat predictable lines of maturity. The evolution of eMarketplaces and how to approach them interests us here because of the specific relevance to the development of competition and co-opetition in the new Internet-based landscape of financial services. Using history as a mechanism for comparison, one must say that medieval commerce did not just appear: it evolved as a direct product of the convergence of transportation and commercial technologies, in response to rising demand for a wider range of goods and services which transcended the traditional geographic boundaries of feudal communities. Basically, as medieval people became more aware of the products of the world and the infrastructure to get these goods to them improved, they matched their purchasing to the rising lifestyles and new levels of wealth. Reviewing the evolutionary path that medieval markets followed to their ultimate maturity as they transformed into the marketplaces of Renaissance Europe, one can see striking similarities in the contemporary developments of Internet commerce. As seen in Chapter 9, the ultimate death of the baby-boom generation over the next 20–30 years will be the second major transition of wealth between two generations since the Black Death. The tragedy of the Black Death led to the changing of the fundamental social contract between lords and vassals, as the diminished labour force found new wealth by commanding higher wages due to the labour shortage. An analysis of spending, merchant and banking activity during the post-Black Death period from 1350 to 1450 reveals that:

During that same period, there was rapid transfer of wealth from the older victims of plague and war to younger generations, who had an unsurprisingly pessimistic view of life expectancy. Many were accordingly determined to enjoy life to the fullest while they could and embarked on a spending spree of gargantuan proportions. The resulting surge in demand for luxury goods of all kinds – fine clothing, jewellery, exotic foods and spices – sharply boosted international commerce, especially long-distance trade with the East.[1]

This rise in spending on expensive clothes and luxurious ornaments by the lower orders of society (including peasants, artisans, merchants and urban wage earners) led to the sumptuary legislation in 1363[2] to regulate and limit personal expenditure (see Figure 26.1).

In today's economy, it is difficult, if not impossible, to predict whether the next generation of financial services' customers will adopt this same attitude towards money and finance, as the wealth-receiving generation of fourteenth-century Europe. It can, however, be argued that the same conditions and behaviours will be exhibited within certain market segments. For example: as seen above, today's social, economic and market conditions are similar to those found in the late Middle Ages. In addition, there will be a shift in generational wealth in the next twenty years, which parallels that of the medieval period to some extent, but with one key

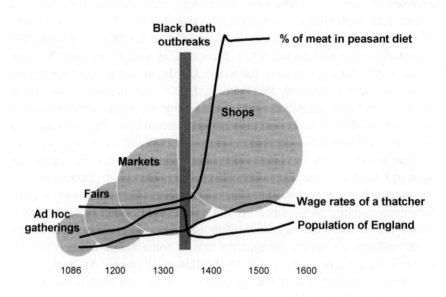

Figure 26.1 The market maturity curve

difference; the speed of departure will not be as abrupt or concentrated within whole family units as in the aftermath of the Black Death. This aspect may alter the direction of how eMarketplaces function. The value proposition for a potential generation of savers is distinctly different from that of a generation of spenders. It would be rash to believe that a sweeping generalization will apply to all customers of a generation. However, it is prudent to consider that a shift from savers to spenders will occur within a variety of market sub-segments. Simply, the next evolution of eMarketplaces will involve a fundamental rethinking of the products and services offered to consumers in non-changing financial situations and those whose financial situation may change drastically and very quickly. The shift in generational wealth may indeed have significant repercussions on customers' lifestyles, requiring a rethinking of the financial services offered in these channels.

Similar to the strategies employed by medieval merchant bankers, today's financial services organizations must develop an approach that contains two key aspects: an understanding of the market's maturity and its relevance to the customers it serves; and the establishment of a strategic approach that seamlessly engages both the traditional channels to market and those to the eMarketplace.

Market Maturity

The first aspect is to develop an awareness of the market's maturity and where value can be propositioned. Turning to Hunt and Murray once again for a medieval perspective, it can be surmised that the markets matured in five phases: from the early ad hoc formation; a period of formalization; an inward focus, to reduce cost by leveraging technology and new business partnerships; a boom caused by the transition of wealth; and finally a consolidation of intermediaries as the demand cycle waned. Therefore, one could argue that the same phased maturity of formation, formalization, inward focus, boom and consolidation awaits the eMarketplaces and the Internet as a medium of exchange for consumers and business, and that the current state of the markets is in the inward focus phase. The dot-com phenomenon was the formation and formalization phase. Now that business is refocused on creating a clear value proposition, the inward focus aspect of market maturity has begun.

As with all technological progress, there are three foreseeable phases through which eMarketplaces will evolve in the coming years, which represent the impact that using this technology to facilitate these markets will have on the industry. They are:

- *Inception phase:* where eMarketplaces are at the present; the technology behind the new business process is in its infancy and a substantial amount of investment is required so as to make the application widely available commercially;

- *Growth phase:* where the application of the technology to new business processes becomes more defined within the eMarketplace and becomes increasingly available to customers;

- *Maturity phase:* where participation in eMarketplaces is widespread, and institutions that do not offer such applications are likely to be at a competitive disadvantage.

In order to take advantage of the opportunities emerging in eMarketplaces, financial services organizations must develop a varied approach, which will move in lock step with the maturity of the market and the adoption of technology used within the marketplace. The opportunities exist for financial services firms in all three stages of eMarketplace maturity. The essential understanding is that as the eMarketplace matures, your approach to the marketplace must adapt to the changing conditions and your products must evolve to meet customer demand. In many cases, financial services products have the unique opportunity to lead the market because many services sought by consumers (such as wealth management by the newly affluent) are predictable and therefore can be anticipated.

The initial opportunities in each phase of the eMarketplace are, as seen in earlier in this chapter:

- *Inception phase:* partnering, experimentation, definition of an operating model, exploration of new channels (customer acquisition), branding, portal establishment, new product definition, bill presentment;

- *Growth phase:* refinement of the operation model, core banking services, rebranding of products and services with maturing partnerships, revenue/profit sharing model with channel partners, consolidation of retail services, wealth management, anticipatory payments;

- *Maturity phase:* drive down cost, optimize processes, customer relationship management, customer order fulfilment, comprehensive wealth-generating strategies.

What is clear is that opportunities that present themselves in the eMarketplaces require a continual adjustment to your approach to the market as it matures. Regardless of your approach, the primary elements needed are: a clear value proposition; the organizational competency to sense market changes; an information feedback loop; the ability to react quickly to the market; the mechanisms to retain customers; and the ability to manage a broad palette of relationships.

Channels and Segmentation

The second aspect of establishing a strategic approach that engages both the traditional channels to market and the eMarketplace seamlessly can be best described as a fundamental rethinking of the traditional banking channels and demographic profiles. The lure of disintermediation is to present a product that is customized specifically for the customers' needs. This perceived mass customization is a driving factor in only a few market segments and is precipitated by technologies' ability to enhance individualism. That is to say that the approach to the market must have a clear and distinctive value proposition for each market segment, regardless of the definition of the segmentation.

Various segments of customers for financial services are very knowledgeable, and, with the diversity of product offerings, delivery technologies and services available from traditional banks and, more importantly, new market entrants, these segments are becoming increasingly demanding. Moreover, with retailers, convenience store operators, utilities, petroleum distributors and other new market entrants introducing new linked product offerings and other non-traditional banking services, customers have a wide range of choices. The financial services industry is squarely focused on how to develop services that cater to these well-informed consumers.

To meet the competitive pressures of sophisticated financial services customers, firms need to differentiate themselves by developing a micro-segmentation and a dual-brand strategy, in order to target not only specific product offerings, but delivery technologies as well. Financial services organizations that are using the traditional market segments will find that they are competing head to head with other traditional banks. On the other hand, new market entrants discover unserviced niche markets because they reject the traditional lines of segmentation and draw on the attributes that drive customer behaviour. For example, traditional retail banking demographic segments have been: wealth market, upscale retired, upper affluent, lower affluent, mass market, mid-scale retired, lower market, downscale retired, primarily delineated by income or asset size. This assumes that everyone within a market segment has the same behaviour and requires the same banking services.

Typically, retail banking markets have been segmented using one of four methods. Firstly, geographical segmentation divides customers into different geographical units, for example states, regions, countries, focusing on geographical differences in the needs and wants of a customer base. For example, Californians may prefer individual share trading and people in the United Kingdom may prefer mutual funds. Secondly, demographic segmentation divides customers into groups based on characteristics such as age, family size, life cycle, occupation and sex, aligning customer needs to each variable which provides a convenient mechanism for measurement. Demographic segmentation is often used to establish sub-segments within other segmentation schemas. Thirdly, psychographic segmentation divides buyers into groups based on personality characteristics, socio-economic status, means, and lifestyle. For example, dividing the retail banking market into sports-fanatics, fast-trackers, leisure-seekers, work-oriented and family-oriented segments to develop a product offering that amplifies their interest, such as a sports branded credit card linked with a current account that carries a sports motif on the cheques. Finally, behaviour segmentation, which divides customers according to their product knowledge, usage, attitudes or responses, often focusing on benefits sought by buyers from the product class. For example: the retail lending market can be segmented based on benefits of linked product offerings each targeted to the needs of the specific sub-segment:

- Brand identity, such as Citibank's image of global full service;

- Special needs, for example self-employed, bad credit or recent college graduates;

- Service convenience, for example local relationships, 24-hour or special access;

- Price sensitivity, for example lowest rates, no fees or special pricing for consolidated services.

Micro-segmentation

Micro-segmentation is a process which seeks similar characteristics of customer behaviours independent of the market sector in which they are found. Characteristics shared across the major segments are bundled together into a product offering to meet the need of a specific niche or set of circumstances. For example: a financial services firm can examine the borrowing and credit activities of individuals seeking mortgages, automobile loans, credit cards and others across the various market segments to develop a common set of requirements for people seeking loans. In doing so, the firm can develop highly targeted lending products that have a value proposition to individuals that spans market segments, such as reorganizing your loans as the result of a divorce. In the retail market, the key drivers have been pricing and service, and customers fall into the four broad market segments described below:

- *Sophisticated professionals:* these are mainly professional people, such as small company executives, entrepreneurs, computer professionals, equity and bond traders, salespeople, mobile workers, insurance and estate agents. These customers are always on the move, and they view 24-hour-a-day access to financial services as essential to their business. They place a premium on the reliability of technology that keeps them in contact with their business and customers.

- *Quality of life customers:* they consider banking, insurance and other financial services essential to improving their quality of life. They are looking for financial products that reflect their own values, and offer choice and flexibility at an affordable price. These customers tend to shop for financial services that are encapsulated under one brand image or a family of brands that equate to quality.

- *Peace of mind customers:* they are apt to be more traditional in their approach to financial services, less mobile and place a higher value on consistent, reliable and convenient services that represent some level of stability in an ever-changing world. These customers are very sensitive to price and will tolerate a lower quality and poorer service delivery before considering switching financial institutions. Often they utilize only the very basic product offerings that do not require complex planning.

- *New young professional customers:* they are often overlooked by customer service agents, as requiring too much time, carrying low balances, and not possessing sufficient knowledge of financial services products to warrant the investment needed in educating them to use more sophisticated services. However, financial services firms that have previously shunned this group may want to reconsider their approach, primarily due to the fact that these new young professionals will be the recipients of the generational transfer of wealth over the next twenty years.

To measure the effectiveness of targeting market segments and their associated sub-segment attributes, financial services firms must establish specific goals of how they will achieve market leadership as the customer's preferred choice in each segment. Alternatively, since it takes a great deal of resources to achieve this in all segments, firms should prioritize and rank segments in the order of value delivered to customers. Lesser ranked segments present the firm with a choice of re-evaluating its value proposition to those segments, or simply partnering with firms that have a more compelling value proposition to those particular segments.

Dual-branding Financial Offerings

As one can observe from the aforementioned market maturity and segmentation discussion, it will be difficult for any product offering to appeal to such a contrasting collection of customer groups. Fortunately, the new generation of delivery technologies enables organizations to develop dual-branding strategies in which working from a suite of core services, macro- and micro-segment product offerings can be crafted without the need to duplicate computer systems. A dual-brand strategy is simply using the core systems, capabilities and organizational competencies to offer collections of services that come from either a central brand or stand as independent brands. For example, XYZ bank may continue to offer basic banking services coupled with an Internet version of these services to the peace of mind market segment under the XYZ bank brand, while repackaging the same basic services featuring the Internet as the primary mechanism for interaction under a more youth-oriented branding to target the new young professional market segment. In both cases, the core banking services are the same but the packaging is different. In fact, they may offer two completely different websites, both emanating from the central banking facility.

However, simply applying a multi-branded approach to various market sub-segments may not bring forth the anticipated results due to the varied level of customer maturity and product experience within each segment. Some sub-segments, like the sophisticated professionals, may have a propensity for using technology with little or no customer service support, while other groups may require a larger amount of initial assistance before transitioning to a new technology. That said, it becomes evident that even though all market segments and sub-segments share similar customer traits or habits, they must advance through a behavioural maturity curve which will make some offerings more palatable to one group over another.

Within each sub-segment, individuals can be categorized into customer behaviours such as innovator, early adopter, early majority, late majority and laggards, all of which indicate either their ability or inability to adapt to new products and embrace change. A non-exhaustive list of some of the characteristics of these customer behaviours segments follows:

■ *Innovators:* customers who are the first ones to embrace a new innovation or are willing to try new product offerings. It is perhaps the group representing the smallest volume. They are eager to experiment with new ideas, are often well educated and can afford the financial risks associated with adopting the new product or service. They are tolerant of incomplete or not fully formed offerings, if presented with a regular flow of information regarding progress of implementation. Typically, they are well informed about new products by other innovators and influenced by impersonal, scientific and other objective sources of information.

■ *Early adopters:* these customers typically are more socially active in their local communities or belong to organizations that have shared interests. Often these customers belong to or are children of a more educated social class; they have a greater diversity of interests and consult specialized sources such as magazines and the Internet about new products and innovations more than the average consumer. Regularly called on to recommend products to co-workers, family members and others, they play a decisive role as opinion leaders who sway other customer groups.

■ *Early majority:* this customer group regularly adopts a new product innovation immediately after the early adopters. Customers in this group are slightly more cautious than the previous two groups, taking longer to decide on the value of the new offerings. This group can be characterized as having a larger age-spread, and an above-average education, including in many cases post-graduate level work; they command a higher socio-economic status than the average member of society.

■ *Late majority:* this consumer group classically delays the adoption of a new product offering, chiefly because they are sceptical of its perceived value. Their reluctant decision to adopt a new product, technology or way of conducting business often follows a feeling of strong societal pressure or a sense of being left behind, and is influenced by the informal opinion of acquaintances versus media sources. One of the last groups to embrace the Internet as a communications media, they will be one of the last groups to use Internet banking, electronic bill payments and other new forms of financial services.

■ *Market laggards:* these are the customers most likely to adopt a new product offering when it is so mature that it is nearing the end of its value to all other market sectors and is ready to be superseded by either the next new product offering or a completely new innovation that will render the original offering obsolete. Often socially secluded and mistrustful of the benefits of product innovations, they are in many cases older customers of lower socio-economic rank.

This added complexity of customer behaviour presents both a dilemma and an opportunity for financial services firms offering products and services to these markets. The obvious problem is the greater need to develop product differentiation at a higher level of granularity for market sub-segments. The opportunity lies in the greater diversity of offerings to service niche markets with highly tailored products. The need for a dual strategy can be illustrated in Figure 26.2 in which each market sub-segment should be considered at the various levels of customer maturity.

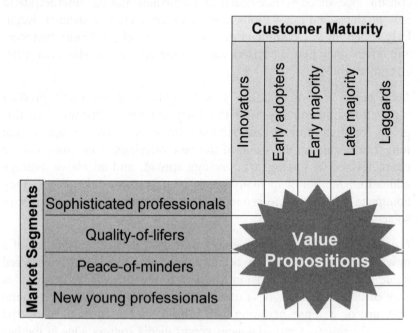

Figure 26.2 Value to segments and maturity

Noting the behavioural aspect of each sub-segment's level of maturity, new financial product offerings should be developed as introductory products and targeted to customers with complementary behaviours such as those found in innovators or early adopters. Therefore, one could argue that as the complexity of financial services product offerings increases, the need to target products to niche market sub-segments can be driven by a number of factors which include, but are not limited to, behaviour, economic classification, societal propensity and station in life. Regardless of the target market, it is clear that each financial services product offering needs to present not only a clear value proposition, but a targeted customer group which perceives its value. This matching of a value proposition to a customer is further complicated by the level of maturity found within a target customer group. Fortunately, this complexity does present the opportunity for financial services firms to design offerings that cut across traditional market segments and address customer behaviours to hedge which services are likely to generate sustained volumes based on past customer behaviours.

What can be observed in Figure 26.3 is that each end of the customer maturity spectrum presents an opportunity for premium services. To early adopters eager to participate in new offerings, the opportunity of access and convenience usually outweighs the higher cost associated with the new product.

In the case of the early and late majority, sensitivity to price and performance rises as the purchase price falls. Typically, as the product becomes

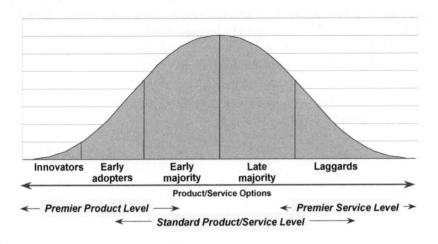

Figure 26.3 Technology adoption curve

commercialized and the volume rises, the price falls in response to competitive pressures. By the time the laggards begin to use the product, another opportunity for a higher priced service arises due to the associated higher cost of maintenance as a result of the latency. The point is that early adopters and laggards are more easily convinced that they should pay more for the use of a service, whereas the middle groups probably will prefer to pay lower or no fees associated with services. Understanding that different social groups also have different expectations in regard to services and fees is fundamental for financial services companies that are investing in new product offerings at the moment, generating not only value propositions to customers but also to shareholders.

The recognition that a value proposition must address the needs of a defined customer group or collection of consumer behaviours is only half the value equation. A product offering must be viable long term and operate profitably, or it will quickly rise in popularity, only to be quickly withdrawn as the firm realizes it can no longer sustain underwriting its value to the customer. A value proposition must extend through the entire life of the product from inception to withdrawal. During this life cycle, the value equation must be revisited to ensure that it still generates the proposed value to customers. When the product's value proposition is eroded by unforeseen changes in business activity, the decision to terminate a product offering based simply on its value proposition may be hazardous because of the effect of alienation within the customer base. Therefore, product offerings and their customer value propositions must be viewed by the firm in the context of the complete suite of product offerings, in order to assess their relative value. In some cases, a retiring product may be continued simply to provide customers with a transition path to a new product offering or to be used as a loss leader for the collection of offerings by the firm. However, as said above, a value proposition is not a one-sided equation focused on the customers; there is also an expected return for corporate shareholders. In the following chapters we will be examining how firms can guarantee shareholder value in the current business climate.

CHAPTER 27

The Evolution of eMarketplaces

Organizations that develop winning products or achieve optimum operating states often fail when market conditions change and their approach does not adapt to the new market condition. Realizing that all markets mature and undergo successive transformations is an important ingredient in developing an effective approach to an eMarketplace. Various industries, consumer groups and international partners will all mature with slower or faster rates of adoption in technology, process design, integration, taxation and other factors.

The emerging eMarketplaces are maturing from an initial market reaction of rapidly developing small marketplaces for countless market niches and products to more comprehensive markets that offer distinct channels to collections of product suppliers and service providers. Consumer or market exchanges bring together sellers who offer products and services targeted at traditional market segments with buyers who are seeking out the offerings via electronic means. These eMarketplaces digitally replicate previously established interchanges between consumers and manufacturers, emerging as an intermediary between the parties. The initial establishment of these digital value exchanges focused on spot sourcing of materials, allowing them to penetrate rapidly the services marketplace. The next evolutionary phase in these exchanges will be a focus on strategic sourcing and continual replenishment, evolving the exchanges into a digital value chain.

Digital Value Exchanges

Exchanges provide channels or portals between buyers and sellers, brokering the exchange of value between the parties. The exchanges have emerged as a mechanism to aggregate suppliers and concentrate buyers, often manifesting themselves as cyber-stores, online auctions, trading venues and purchasing communities. Put simply, these marketplaces assist geographically dispersed suppliers and buyers to locate goods and services rapidly in a facilitated environment. Focusing primarily on the spot sourcing markets, the exchanges are giving financial services organizations new entries in selling merchandise either directly or indirectly, such as ClearlyBusiness.com, which is 60 per cent owned by Freeserve and 40 per cent by Barclays Bank.

Digital Value Chains

Similar to exchanges, digital value chains are focused on strategic sourcing, targeting business-to-business pathways or conduits providing a mechanism for fulfilling a continual demand for goods and services to support a direct or indirect business process. Digital value chains mimic digital value exchanges, but are uniquely different, supporting the continual replenishment of a demand for goods or services. A primary characteristic of a value chain is the focus on a vertical industry or the support to a discrete industry market segment, such as specialty chemicals.

Today the level of business maturity within eMarketplaces is embryonic. However, eMarketplaces are developing along two distinct lines, that of a digital value chain and/or a digital value exchange, which mirror their terraspace counterparts in the physical world. As said previously, financial services organizations have three distinct opportunities to add value as eMarketplaces mature into viable channels to consumer and business markets: as a provider of services to eMarketplace suppliers to rebrand or resell; as a participant in eMarketplaces as a service or product offering, becoming or partnering to be an eMarketplace provider; and, finally, as an eMarketplace integrator, offering services that interconnect eMarketplaces such as cash management.

CHAPTER 28

Opportunities for Financial Institutions in eMarketplaces

Opportunities are often overlooked unless you rethink the value proposition presented by an eMarketplace to your customers on a regular basis and develop organizations or partnerships that leverage technology to rapidly capitalize on market trends.[1]

The new eMarketplace phenomenon provides financial services organizations with a broad range of new product and services opportunities to support the exchange of value between parties. Financial services organizations can develop core processes to support these marketplaces on a number of levels.

Level One: Market-maker

By collaborating with firms that provide technology, financial services institutions can participate in the development of eMarketplaces, acting as a market developer, market co-developer, or market participant. By engaging technology, organizations manage to provide the necessary infrastructure to ensure a stable and secure environment for the exchange of value between trading partners. Financial services organizations possess the skills and access to investment necessary to craft the agreements needed and to bring together technology providers with their own technology capabilities in order to service eMarketplaces. Technology providers are eager to partner with financial services organizations by sponsoring or taking a sponsorship role in many of the emerging marketplaces and thereby reducing the risk of the venture.

Possessing core competencies in technology, vendors are supporting various electronic exchanges that focus on business-to-business and business-to-consumer pathways. The business case to participants is to reduce the cost and time during the acquisition of technology for business and personal computing. Technology vendors are also electing to own or take an ownership role in several eMarketplaces, but are now more cautious in selecting partners as a direct result of losses associated with numerous dot-com start-ups.

As an example, Services.com provides a range of powerful new business-to-business capabilities for connecting and supporting the activities of professional services firms and their networks, as well as the buyers of professional services, through both public and private Internet trading communities (see Figure 28.1). In this marketplace, the value proposition is clear to both participants: service acquirers have an expectation of the quality of the providers because of the rating system, and providers receive a better-managed accounts receivable. The opportunity for financial services firms in this type of marketplace is to provide cash management services to all three parties, service provider, service acquirer and the market-maker.

For financial services, the role of a market-maker presents the most risk and the higher potential returns. The success of the eMarketplace is derived chiefly from the volume of business which passes through the eMarketplace, generated by the market and its participating member firms.

Connecting the Services Economy

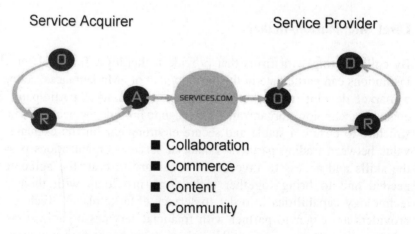

Figure 28.1 An intermediary of services

Put simply, low volume gives negative profits, and volume is proportional to the number of people accessing the market via the member firms. In Chapter 3, we noted Buckminster Fuller's observation of a commercialization time lag between the invention of a technology and its practical application. Fuller's idea can be illustrated by AusMarkets Ltd,[2] the highly publicized Australian eMarketplace for wholesale financial services, which is sponsored by ANZ, the Commonwealth Bank of Australia, the National Australia Bank and Westpac. This Australian financial market aggregator shut down after one year of planning after realizing that its opportunity to create a new market had ceased to present a viable value proposition to customers. What is clear is that playing the role of the market-maker is difficult because it takes a long-term vision backed by substantial investment resources to sustain the operation until volumes or margins can move the market to viability.

Level Two: Market Facilitator

Opportunities exist within established or emerging eMarketplaces to provide services for market participants. These services facilitate the exchanges between members in the marketplace. Offerings such as cash management and transaction brokering are services that supplement the exchange between members and in the business-to-business market could be expanded to provide outsourced accounts receivable and payable.

Additional opportunities exist to act as intra-market facilitators by providing services that interchange within a marketplace, linking support services. For example: providing trust services for trading partners, customer relationship management, call centre product support and other services to collections of members within an exchange.

Partnering with technology vendors to provide a secure environment for eMarkets creates the opportunity to supply introductory services to businesses that have little or no experience of participating in eMarketplaces. Coupling business start-up financial services with technology consultative services offers a low-risk alternative to organizations wanting to outsource the functions required to participate in market exchanges.

As an example, the next logical progression of the Services.com business model (discussed in Chapter 22) is either to franchise or to expand their offering to other geographic locations around the world. The opportunity for financial services companies resides in providing the financial infrastructure to facilitate these eMarketplaces. A host of services are required in the initial set up of the eMarketplace: brokering technology partners, financial services providers, and a wide range of products that complement service companies (for example pension plans, insurance) are all services that can be provided by niche players, resulting in a highly fragmented offering. The big opportunity is to make available to the eMarketplaces a suite of services that allows them to reduce the total number of relationships needed to run their eMarketplace.

Another example is BanxQuote.com, a company that acts as a customer-centric market facilitator, providing consumers with direct access paths to specific banking products by ranking them on preselected criteria, such as best mortgage rates and highest interest rates, acting primarily as a channel to the eMarketplace. The value added is purely saving time for the consumer who is shopping for the best deal in a banking product. It does not, however, provide a holistic approach to financial services offerings or allow a consumer to develop a financial plan that needs products that fulfil a set of requirements. It could be argued that the customer using this service is simply shopping for parts (for example mortgages, savings, current accounts) and not looking for a complete financial solution (for example wealth management).

Level Three: Market Integrator

The least explored area of opportunity is acting as a market integrator or extra-market intermediary providing services that interconnect market-places. Many multinational companies need to participate in several eMarketplaces; therefore they require services that span market and geographic boundaries. Foreign exchange, trust, cash management and other services that aggregate transaction-based activities can provide organizations with a consolidated view of their global market interchanges.

Still using Services.com as an example, in the final stage of their growth providing services portals around the globe, the opportunity for financial services companies is to link and integrate the associated financial services offerings into a seamless infrastructure exchange, providing global cash management, foreign currency exchange, international taxation and trade services, which would allow service companies to compete on a world-wide scale.

CHAPTER 29

Creating a Value Proposition

In the previous chapters, we focused on the value propositions for customers in the financial services industry. Here we would like to analyse the shareholder value. As seen in Figure 29.1, a value proposition is composed of a two-sided equation of value, a differentiated customer value and an incremental shareholder value. The delta between the two is the performance of the financial services firm and its ability to seize market opportunities. Half of the equation is defined as the utility of the product to a consumer, which determines the value of the product

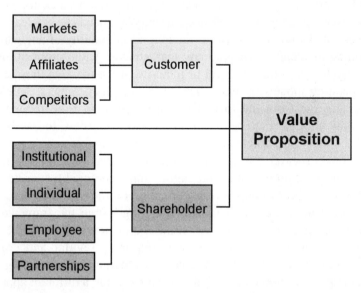

Figure 29.1 The two sides of the value equation

offering (customer value). This value is market-driven and often is not based on costs-plus accounting, but on market forces. The second component is shareholder value, described as the difference between the value of a firm's output realized in total revenues, attributed to selling the financial services product offerings, and the cost of the input of raw materials, components or services that the firm adds to its bought-in material to produce the output. In other words, the efforts of the organization must result in supplying a financial product offering that the market needs at a cost that delivers a reasonable return to those who invested in the organization.

Creating and, more importantly, adapting a value proposition has been the Achilles heel in many of the dot-com lifespans. A lesson learned from the dot-coms is that it may be easy to develop a value proposition that is based on acquiring short-term market share, but it is more difficult to create a value proposition that is viable in the long term. Many dot-com value propositions were based merely on heavily discounted pricing to win market share, while other aspects of value were ignored, in many cases, until it was too late to address them.

Operating Models of Market Maturity

It cannot be overemphasized that developing a value proposition that is based on providing a clear and distinct added value to a customer is vital in the establishment of any eMarketplace. What needs to be clear is that a differentiated value is critical for the long-term viability of any participant providing financial services to any marketplace. Value propositions must also take into account the level of maturity of the markets they serve and the operating models in which they interact with customers. As eMarketplaces emerge from the formalization phase of market maturity, three operating models can be observed. Firstly, markets to facilitate the purchase of basic goods and services operate under a business paradigm called the eProcurement model. Secondly, markets that develop to facilitate the acquisition of low-value, high-volume commodities or items have been labelled as operating in a dynamic commodity exchange model. Thirdly, an integrated marketplace operating within the framework of a vertical exchange model focuses on the acquisition of items to be used in conjunction with a production cycle requiring regular and consistent replenishment. All three of these emerging eMarketplace operating models are examples of digital value chains, each requiring a different approach to customer and shareholder value.

Shareholder Value

Understanding the operating model within an eMarketplace is crucial in developing a suite of products and services that add value in the exchange with consumers and, more importantly, with partnerships, alliances and associations in the eMarketplace. If the eMarketplace has a losing operating model, it will have a detrimental effect on your brand if they go out of business. The root of shareholder value is in the operating model adopted by the eMarketplace, the mechanisms used to measure the performance of the market relative to the investment made, and the management of the expectations of the market participants, affiliates and shareholders. Most eMarketplaces start as a mechanism to sell one or more products; if they succeed in attracting buyers, they evolve to a channel devoted to a market segment or collection of market sub-segments. For example: Amazon.com is no longer simply selling books; it is channel to market providing a mechanism for consumers to look for associated merchandise or products that are linked to facilitating a lifestyle.

From a shareholder's point of view, eMarketplaces are found to follow one of three operating models: seller-centric, buyer-centric and trading-community market, each adding value to the underlying transactions of exchange between member organizations and customers. What is important for firms that provide services to these eMarketplaces is that each operating model requires a different type of added value and may even require a change in the financial product offering or branding.

The first operating model is a *seller-centric market* which is focused on customer acquisition and revenue expansion, catalogues, promotions, pricing and order payment. This market comprises virtual showrooms with brochure information about the products and services for sale, and strives to replicate the traditional avenue of shopping by creating an environment that is similar in nature to brick-and-mortar retail outlets. A value proposition in seller-centric markets focuses on the use or application of a product to a specific buyer's need. In a seller-centric market, the challenge is to make the customers aware of the product, educate them on why they need the product and how to use the product.

The second operating model is a *buyer-centric market*, which focuses on reducing cost and increasing procurement efficiency by facilitating direct purchase, indirect purchase, shop schedule and production schedule enhancement. Put simply, this operating model labours to broker the consistent fulfilment of goods to various lines of production within a firm or group of firms. These markets typically form discount buying groups and provide auction services with a focus on low-cost or best-cost pricing. A value proposition in buyer-centric markets focuses on the efficiency of purchase and fulfilment of a product. In a buyer-centric market, the customers already know what they are looking for and the challenge is to fulfil the need with a quality product that is competitively priced and delivered on time.

The third operating model is that of *trading-community markets* which are focused on market expansion and purchasing efficiencies, targeting vertical or horizontal markets using business models that combine catalogues, auctions, RFP/RFQ (request for proposal/request for quote), exchange, and other mechanisms to integrate services to support continual replenishment. These markets are striving to provide a suite of full service capabilities such as invoicing, bill presentment, payments, financing, logistics and business services to both buyer and seller. A value proposition in trading-community markets focuses on the efficiency of the process, not the purchase and fulfilment of a product.

Creating a value proposition requires that any proposed service demonstrates a clear added value to the recipient of the service. Financial services firms can play a pivotal role in all three of the operating models used by eMarketplaces by providing services that increase the market's capacity, reduce the cost of transactions within the market, supplement their own customer service and enhance the business processes used in transactions between parties. For example: providing financing and credit checking services to members of a business-to-business exchange or to an individual member and its customers reduces the time required to broker an exchange.

Clearly, merely repositioning old product offerings to new markets is a short-lived value proposition that is rapidly copied and commoditized. Moreover, if your value proposition is concealed under a marketing veil of discounts and gimmicks, the participants in the exchange will be unable to differentiate your core offering from that of your competitors. This clarity of value added is critical in competing in an eMarketplace where many offerings will often appear similar in design.

For financial services firms offering services to these eMarketplaces, the core capability that must be developed is the ability to rapidly develop new products that are a direct result of demands from the customers and partners within the market. The core competencies that are essential for providing products and services to the eMarketplaces are the rapid product development cycle and, more importantly, the capability to sense the market, change and adapt products, coupled with an awareness that triggers the withdrawal of a product.

CHAPTER 30

Developing Centres of Competencies

Getting products and services to eMarketplaces is only half the challenge for financial services firms. Fulfilling the customer's needs is the lion's share of the activity. The essence of customer service is harnessing resources, outsourcing or partnering to deliver on the associated activities surrounding transactions such as origination, brokering, passing, aggregating, consolidating, managing and providing interchange between partners, competitors, merchants and customers. The agility and efficiency of these services and transactions are a direct reflection on the performance of the firm. Organizational competency is a combination of employee know-how and a robust technological infrastructure, as discussed in Chapter 2. Core competencies are almost impossible to define if the product and its value proposition are not clear and if the underlying business process is not designed with graduated process measurements. In summary, typical core competencies to support new financial services offerings fall into several categories:

- Sensing the market and customer trends

- Establishing a feedback loop

- Establishing a fast market reaction

- Managing customer relationships

- Managing partner relationships

- Managing technological context.

The competency of the firm is anchored in the employees' abilities. These are often known as human capital or knowledge assets, in many cases being poorly managed or not given reinvestment. If indeed people are the greatest asset of the twenty-first-century financial services institution, why are they not managed in the same manner that a fund manager invests in and manages equities or other assets?

People, the Leveraged Asset

If an institution wants to bring an offering to the market and the capability to develop and operate the offering does not exist in-house, an opportunity to partner with another provider and rebrand the offering becomes very compelling. Although the focus of this book is on the customer value proposition and the application of technology, it is important to mention that financial services firms will undoubtedly have to rely more on the competencies of people within the firm to ensure their competitive position. The increased complexity of partnerships, the advance of technology and the redefinition of business processes require people with ever-increasing skills. It can be argued that people are the underinvested resource in the future performance of the corporation. Motorola, for example, spends almost $100 million annually on education and training and calculates a return of $3 in sales for every education dollar spent.[1]

A quick review of corporate annual reports reveals that many organizations regard people as their greatest asset and feel compelled to include it as a key feature of their value proposition to customers and shareholders as expressed by the following firms:

- At Union Bank of California, our people are our greatest asset.

- At Solutia, our people are your greatest asset.

- At UBS we know that our people are our greatest asset so we offer them a professional, dynamic and multicultural environment in which they can thrive and take on responsibility.

- Service provision is at the core of our business and as a result people are our greatest asset (Lakewood IT Solutions, UK).

- At DMR Consulting we believe our people are our greatest asset (Ireland).

- At Missouri State Bank, we understand that people are our most important asset. We also know that we are only as successful as the outstanding people who work with us.

Maintaining competitive success greatly depends on the ability to motivate and retain highly skilled employees on a predictable basis. Changes in the business cycle often create a condition in which cost-cutting efforts and workforce reductions result in disrupting the ongoing operations and impair corporate efforts to motivate existing employees. Failing to retain highly skilled personnel limits the rate at which revenue is generated and new financial product offerings are developed. A lesson learned from the dot-com phenomenon is that with the right motivation, products, services and entire business processes can be rapidly brought to market by enthusiastic teams.

As people are the firm's greatest asset, financial services firms need to invest in a continual process of formal and informal education of personnel. Attending classes at a local college is not enough, individuals also need to be mentored, and taught the process of the business in order to develop a broad understanding of every facet of the offerings of the firm, as discussed in Chapter 1.

The financial services industry is undergoing a transformation as competition, customers and technology redefine the very nature of how traditional banking services add value to contemporary society. The business of financial services, and its associated processes, is changing to adapt to the new levels of business efficiency, customer focus and drive for value. It would be short-sighted not to recognize that people are an integral part of this process and need to be acclimatized to these new standards. Without delving into a philosophical debate on whether firms exist simply to make money for their shareholders or promote the wellbeing of their stakeholders, it should be acknowledged that both conditions exist in a symbiotic relationship, and that the previous approach to training individuals has continually fallen short of expectations.

The essential things for financial services firms to remember are:

- Downsizing is a final outcome, not a competitive strategy;

- Learning should be process-focused and continual;

- Collaboration is not a technology; it is a learned behaviour;

- The rise in computer literacy is undercapitalized on by corporations;

- Customer services personnel need to be empowered to resolve problems quickly;

- As the role of the branch network is redefined, personnel will require many new skills.

The important message here is that, although restructuring, redundancies and staff cuts frequently produce an immediate gain in financial measurements and occasionally moderate gains in productivity, the longer term consequence can be disappointing levels of customer service as experienced individuals depart with product knowledge. With a clearly defined value proposition, a financial services firm can ascertain the need to strengthen or build up one aspect of the business process while trimming or removing from another. Taking into consideration the implication for services that are sensitive to global cultures (as discussed in Chapter 19), geographically based business units, with a clear understanding of the firm's value proposition to customers, need a degree of autonomy to map their own strategic plans.

CHAPTER 31

Selecting the Right Partners and Managing Relationships

A key feature of eMarketplaces is that they can be relatively easily disaggregated into their component parts, enabling financial institutions to specialize on one component. Insurance companies are effectively product specialists, relying on a network of brokers and agents to distribute their product. Credit card companies are good examples of an infrastructure specialist. Financial services organizations need to take clear and deliberate steps in evaluating how they add value to each component in the exchange of value between parties and develop business systems that anticipate the evolution of the value exchange. Leading the technology wave of new business challenges is the evolution of payment systems consisting of three essential factors that financial services organizations need to keep in the forefront of their strategic planning: technology, social adoption and international regulation. Is it possible to pick the one technology that will embrace the new generation of value exchange customers? More importantly: Is technology the answer or simply a question?

One strategy open to financial services companies is to manage the complex relationships of a digital value exchange or digital value chain through strategic alliances. For example, financial services organizations are partnering with supermarkets to address context, and an increasing number of institutions are outsourcing their technology group and other infrastructure components to specialist processing companies.

Partnering with legacy independent software vendors, technology consulting organizations and technology infrastructure firms can provide significant advantages in a firm's ability rapidly to mobilize resources. However, relationships needed to be clearly defined and availability is often a point of contention with deals that are not the full outsourcing of a capability. Often large established vendors provide consistent resources but are not as flexible as smaller, more aggressive firms.

Competing in the new eEconomy demands a realignment of business processes that lead to relationship-centric business processes. These processes need to leverage the interchange of thoughts and ideas; they can do this by using powerful technologies to facilitate collaboration and knowledge. Technology solutions such as CRM systems fall short of delivering real business value unless they are coupled with a new outlook on how to serve the customer, accompanied by an education process that engages employees to be focused on customer-centric value creation. Often organizations underestimate the cost of CRM implementations and reduce or eliminate training programmes that cover more than the basic operating skills for the software.

The cornerstone to CRM is developing an approach to the customer that embraces a philosophy of service to the customer, solving the customer's problem by gaining an understanding of the elements of the problem and assembling a solution within the confines of profitability. In CRM, simple models bring the most clarity. Take, for example an extremely crowded, small coffee shop. There is a long queue of customers; two of the counter staff are absent due to illness; the length of the queue is increasing and the customers' attitude is deteriorating rapidly. A couple of tourists complain about the size of the muffin accompanying their coffee, and start a debate with the counter staff. They were completely caught off-guard when the cashier simply told them that the two muffins were 'on the house', handed them their change and moved on to the next customer in the queue. When the manager of the coffee shop was interviewed later, his technology-free solution was explained. The counter staff are empowered to resolve conflicts quickly and understand the nature of the business. Margins are small, so the shop relies on volume; therefore arguing with a customer or trying to negotiate their expectations with an explanation takes more time and results in fewer customers being served. They know that they cannot give free products to everyone everyday, but they realize that one or two muffins a day will not bankrupt the business. Having these guidelines and understanding the nature of the business, plus its optimized business process, streamline the process and eliminate the need to call the manager or involve any other staff. The net result of the exchange is clear: the customer's expectations are exceeded, the staff has a feeling of process ownership and empowerment, the need to generate volume to support the business is maintained and cost of the two free muffins is distributed across the volume of the daily sales.

Regardless of the technology solution, CRM or any process that interacts with customers must be leveraged with a clear operating philosophy of what customer centricity means to an organization and how every individual within the firm contributes to ensuring that the customers' expectations are met. The same set of conditions and values must be applied to partners in whom continual expectations need to be managed.

CHAPTER 32

Moving into Action

The biggest hurdle for financial services companies is to determine which are the opportunities to capitalize on and which are those to ignore. A mistake repeated many times by firms is to attempt to be all things to all people. The central lesson to be learned is first to define how the firm will add value and then to develop a vision and strategy to bring the firm's offerings to market. What is clear is an apparent shift in what financial services organizations need to deliver to each type of eMarketplace, and how they will participate as an aggregator of services or proceed slowly and become a commodity offering within the realm of content providers. The emerging eMarketplaces provide an enormous range of opportunities for financial services organizations to reach out into new areas of fee income and transaction-based revenues. These opportunities require a clear value proposition in a rapidly changing, competitive market to establish both market credibility and quality of service. Developing an action agenda for competing in an eMarketplace should contain the elements that span a host of business, technology and organizational issues. The fundamental elements in an action agenda should include:

- Know your value added and how it complements the market it serves;
- Create mechanisms for market sensing;
- Rebrand products to reflect your identity;
- Build capabilities for rapid market reaction;
- Develop competencies in CRM;

- Leverage technology to facilitate transactions;
- Get good at managing partner and affiliate relationships;
- Change offerings and approaches as the markets mature and evolve;
- Develop relationships with technology and services providers.

Developing a Twenty-first-century Agenda

To meet the competitive challenges of the new century of business, financial services firms must develop an action agenda that continually assesses its value proposition from the customers' and shareholders' viewpoints. Interpreting technological, behavioural and cultural trends requires direct observation of customer actions and comprehensive analysis to foster innovation and new business opportunities. Individuals in the financial services industry need to develop process knowledge and consider an ever-widening array of factors that are often overlooked while developing strategic initiatives. Disintermediation is the link between a competitive advantage and organizational shortcomings, creating opportunities for new market entrants while increasing the demands on corporate resources in traditional financial institutions. In any case, the landscape of financial services is being drastically altered as is the nature of how multiple generations of customers are defining the value of financial intermediaries.

What has been observed is that technology will continue to alter consumer interactions:

- A clear value proposition to your customers is not an option;

- Do not confuse customers with choices for choices' sake;

- Brand identity must be distinct and identifiable;

- Brokered services must show your value added;

- Mature markets are often areas of great change;

- And major changes in the market create many new opportunities, all of which indicates that the next ten years of financial services will be a stimulating place to work and innovate.

The new level of strategic alliances that will need to be forged to meet customer demands is what is distinctly different in the operations of financial services organizations. The development and utilization of core competencies of providers and within the firm demand a greater need for collaboration between firms, co-ordination between the centres of competencies and a more integrated approach to technology as a custodian of customer data and market intelligence. Financial services as a business will need to excel at business process optimization and use the Internet as a revenue generator, design facilitator, partnership broker and a low-cost distribution channel, in conjunction with traditional delivery mechanisms, and reinvigorate the branch network. Electronic communities offer new avenues to customers by allowing financial services firms to design value-added content and product functionality for reinforcing brands and strengthening customer relationships. The same technologies can take an inward focus and enable organizations to optimize core banking processes and adopt non-hierarchical structures, supplementing skill sets to focus on product innovation and delivery of higher levels of customer service. Employing these technologies as a part of a comprehensive global brand allows firms to design a common look and feel across global markets while preserving the individuality of culture within geographic and demographic customer groups.

Moreover, for financial services firms to become the first provider of choice with customers, innovation and experimentation with emerging technologies for continuous improvement must be maintained as a priority. New product offerings and new core banking and infrastructure capabilities must be brought to the market by in-house resources or via a network of partners and affiliated relationships. The goal of globally competitive financial institutions is to achieve service excellence by developing world-class customer service over all available channels. The new intensity of customer intimacy in the virtual and physical worlds can be achieved by intelligent market sub-segment analysis of market behaviours for forecasting customer requirements. The assessment of market conditions and customer demands will also require new levels of partnering with technology providers and other industry specialists to capitalize on technological innovations in a timely, cost effective manner.

Therefore, it can be said that financial service firms will undergo a renaissance as the role they play in society is redefined by forces such as technology, lifestyles and profits. One of the biggest challenges will be to rethink how branding is an integral part of the value proposition and how it can be applied across geographies. Since the Internet makes geography less important, customers will expect more electronic online services over a variety of yet-to-be-developed technologies. The perception of low-overhead, electronically driven financial services will usher in an extremely competitive environment in which a clear value proposition – not technology – is the market differentiator. As digital currencies and more electronic transactions occur via computer appliances, the need for cash and cash handling will be reduced, and will possibly be settled using new forms of currency and value exchange mechanisms. Therefore, financial institutions, new market entrants and traditional banks are vulnerable to price wars as customers opt for banking services on the basis of costs and interest rates. In order to combat gradually reducing margins in a slowly commoditized industry, financial services firms must develop a strong identity and create, market, partner and deliver services that are targeted to niche customer segments. The new value propositions must include not simply performing financial transactions, but the means to support changing lifestyles and set customer education in motion, encouraging a more proactive approach to financial responsibility. In conjunction with financial products, customer service and branch personnel will be redeployed as highly trained and trusted financial advisors who add value to the customers in all aspects of banking, insurance, investment and other services by assisting in the development of lifestyle what-if scenarios that tailor product offerings to customers' goals, aspirations and dreams.

NOTES

Part I

1. R. Buckminster Fuller, *Critical Path* (New York: St. Martin's Press, 1981).
2. The 'Internet effect' has been popularized and misunderstood as the process of merging different societies into one homogeneous culture. Contrary to this belief, in this book we operate with the idea that the nature of the Internet effect is to bring the diversity of cultures to the individual, and to engage society in an exchange of value and values. This will be our point particularly in Part III, in which we discuss the globalized economy.
3. F. R. Upton, Speech to The Lawyers' Club of New York (February 11, 1918). Special collections series: Francis Upton collection of unbound documents. Piscataway: Rutgers, the State University of New Jersey, MU 167; TAEM 95:952. Available at: http://edison.rutgers.edu/sno4.htm~mu18.

Part II

1. M. Hammer and J. Champy, *Reengineering the Corporation: A Manifesto for Business Revolution* (New York: HarperCollins, 1993) p. 85.
2. G. Davies, *A History of Money from Ancient Times to the Present Day* (Cardiff: University of Wales Press, 1996).
3. International Reciprocal Trade Association. Available at: http://www.irta.com/.
4. Euro Barter Business. Available at: http://www.ebb-online.com/.
5. BarterCard Ltd. Available at: http://www.bartercard.com.au/index.htm.
6. Contranet. Available at: http://www.contranet.ie/contranet/index.h tml.
7. BarteritOnline: BarterTalent. Available at: http://www.barteritonline.com/bartertalent.htm.
8. BarteritOnline: Equity Swaps. Available at:http://www.barteritonline.com/equity_swaps.htm.
9. C. England, 'Are Banks Special?' *Regulation*, 14.2 (1991). Available at: http://www.cato.org/pubs/regulation /reg14n2a.html.

10. The idea of the 'digital value chain' is adopted from the concept presented by Professor M. Porter in *Competitive Advantage: Creating and Sustaining Superior Performance* (Free Press, 1985).

Chapter 1

1. M. Quennell and C. H. B. Quennell, *A History of Everyday Things in England 1066 to 1499* (London: B. T. Batesford, 1931) p. ix.
2. M. Treacy and F. Wiersema, *The Discipline of Market Leaders* (Reading, Massachusetts: Perseus Books, 1997).

Chapter 2

1. E. Hunt and J. M. Murray, *A History of Business in Medieval Europe 1200–1550* (Cambridge: Cambridge University Press, 1999) p. 58.
2. WordNet 1.6, 1997 Princeton University.
3. The American Heritage Dictionary of the English Language. Houghton Mifflin Company, 2000.
4. See Note 3.
5. N. Machiavelli, *The Prince* (New York: Penguin Books, 1999) p. 58.
6. ASP means application service provider. These are firms that let, rent or lease computer applications on a set of host computer servers that act as a bridge between customers and the supplier by providing additional computer capacity. A large-scale example is US Internetworking in Annapolis, Maryland, USA.

Chapter 3

1. R. Buckminster Fuller, *Critical Path* (New York: St. Martin's Press, 1981) p. 148.
2. Avatars are an image representing a user in a multi-user virtual reality space (or VR-like, in the case of Palace).

Chapter 4

1. 'The Near Future of Public Utilities', posted to Humor Space. Available at: http://www.humorspace.com.
2. See Note 1.

3. R. Clifton and E. Maughan, *Twenty-five Visions: The Future of Brands* (Basingstoke: Macmillan – now Palgrave Macmillan, 2000) p.xiii.
4. See Note 1.
5. A. Ries and L. Ries, *The 11 Immutable Laws of Internet Branding* (London: HarperCollins Business, 2000) p. 7.
6. See Note 1.
7. Staff, 'System aimed at cutting red tape', *The Guardian Unlimited* (19 November 2001).
8. BanxQuote: A service of BanxCorp providing daily market quotes on deposits and loans from financial institutions in all 50 states, with state-by-state, regional and national composite benchmarks. It is available through a proprietary website and through a syndicate of co-branded websites in partnership with various media and financial organizations, including *The Wall Street Journal*, *The New York Times Digital*, UBS PaineWebber, *New York Daily News*, and *New Jersey Online. The Wall Street Journal* has published the company's data in print weekly since 1985.
9. Please see Part III for further discussion on the subject.

Chapter 5

1. IMRGlobal Corporation: Available at: http://www.imrglobal.com/insurance.html.
2. Fidelity Investments, Insurance.com Insurance Agency LLC. Available at: http://www.insurance.com, January 2002.
3. Internad Ltd. Available at: http://www.intern.com/.
4. G. Irwin, P. Lockmiller and L. Altman, 'Insurers: How to Win the Web Finance Wars', *Strategy and Business*. 24, Third Quarter (2001).
5. *Dictionary of Banking and Finance* (Middlesex: Peter Collin, 2000).

Chapter 6

1. *Dictionary of Banking and Finance* (Middlesex: Peter Collin, 2000).
2. EASDAQ re-emerged as the NASDAQ Europe.
3. Kenya Capital Markets Authority. Available at: http://www.CMA.UR.ke.
4. Egyptian Capital Markets Authority. Available at: http://www.lma.gov.eg.
5. The Center for Ethics, Capital Markets and Political Economy is available at: http://www.iath.virginia.edu/cecmpe.
6. International Monetary Fund, Dissemination Standards Bulletin Board. Available at: http://dsbb.imf.org.

Chapter 7

1. This chapter offers a perspective on the historical emergence of markets, marketplaces and eMarketplaces. For further information, please consult Chapter 27.
2. E. Hunt and J. M. Murray, *A History of Business in Medieval Europe 1200–1550* (Cambridge: Cambridge University Press, 1999) p. 23, hereafter Hunt and Murray.
3. Hunt and Murray, pp. 22–5.
4. Hunt and Murray, p. 26.
5. Open Financial Exchange. Available at: http://www.ofx.net.
6. Hunt and Murray, p. 26.

Chapter 9

1. W. Buffet has been associated with coining this phrase in reference to investors over-applying diversification in their portfolios, calling it diworseification. However, within the business strategy community it can be considered as being when a company attempts to reduce business risk by acquiring a collection of diverse firms or products, then attempting to apply resources to a wider rather than a narrower spread of activities, often losing sight of the original value proposition and business mission.
2. Hunt and Murray, p. 166.
3. Mankiw, Gregory and David Weil, 'The Baby Boom, the Baby Bust, and the housing Market', *Regional Science and Urban Economics* (1989) pp. 235–58.
4. Hunt and Murray, p. 162.
5. C. Christensen, *The Innovator's Dilemma: How Disruptive Technologies can Destroy Established Markets* (Cambridge, MA: Harvard University Press, 1997).
6. D. A. Norman, *The Invisible Computer: Why Products can Fail, The Personal Computer is so Complex, and Information Appliances are the Solution* (Cambridge: MIT Press, 1998) pp. 233–4.

Part III

1. N. Machiavelli, *Discourses on Livy* (Oxford: Oxford University Press, 1997) p. 105.
2. For a detailed assessment, please see Chapter 26.

Chapter 10

1. N. Saul, *Richard II* (London: Yale University Press, 1997) p. 237.
2. Saul, p. 238–9.
3. S. J. Park, 'The Future of Brands', Rita Clifton and Ester Maughan (org.), *Twenty Five Visions: The Future of Brands* (Basingstoke: Macmillan – now Palgrave Macmillan, 2000), p. 47.

Chapter 11

1. This point is discussed in detail in Chapter 16.

Chapter 12

1. Hewlett Packard Company. Newsroom – Press. Available at: http://www.hp.com/hpinfo/newsroom/p ress/17jul01c.htm.
2. Parametric Technology Corporation. News and Press release. Available at: http://www.ptc.com/company/news/press/releases/19991026cpc.htm.
3. AsianNet Trade InfoCenter. Available at: http://tradeinfo.asiannet.com.
4. Asia-Pacific Economic Cooperation. Available at: http://www.apecsec.org.sg.
5. Hunt and Murray, p. 193.

Chapter 13

1. AusMarkets Ltd. Available at: http://www.ausmarkets.com.au, January, 2002.
2. BankWest, Agribusiness. Available at: http://www.bankwest.com.au/agribusiness/.

Chapter 14

1. *Oxford Advanced Dictionary* (Oxford: Oxford University Press, 1991).
2. N. Machiavelli, *Discourses on Livy* (Oxford: Oxford University Press, 1997) p. 79.
3. J. A. Goddard, P. Molyneux and J. O. Wilson, *European Banking: Efficiency, Technology and Growth* (Chichester: John Wiley & Sons, 2001) p. 162, hereafter Goddard.
4. Goddard, p. 152.

Chapter 15

1. F. Wiersema, *Customer Intimacy: Pick Your Partners, Shape Your Culture, Win Together* (London: HarperCollins Business, 1997) p. 29.
2. Bluetooth Special Interest Group. Available: http://www.bluetooth.com. Bluetooth is a technology communications protocol designed for wireless data transmission at the relatively low speed of 768k bps (bits per second) over a short distance (10 metres or less).
3. Euronet Worldwide. Available at: http://www.arksys.com/index.htm.

Chapter 16

1. ABN Amro. Available at: http://www.mortgage.com, January, 2002.
2. Intuit Inc. Quicken Loans. Available at: http://quickenloans.quicken.com.
3. W. Shakespeare, *Romeo and Juliet* (Mitcham, Victoria: Penguin Books, 1959).
4. Fiserv Inc. Available at: http://www.fiserv.com.

Chapter 17

1. M. Treacy and F. Wiersema, *The Discipline of Market Leaders* (Reading, MA: Perseus Books, 1997).
2. Halal is defined as: 'Permitted, allowed, authorised, approved, sanctioned, lawful, legal, legitimate or licit.' When used in relation to food or drink in any form whatsoever it means that it is permitted and fit for consumption by Muslims.
3. MuslimsConnect.com Pte Ltd. Available at: http://www.muslimsconnect.com.

Part IV

1. G. Davies, *A History of Money from Ancient Times to the Present Day* (Cardiff: University of Wales Press, 1996) p. xvii.
2. Valagents are value exchange agents: computer software that acts on behalf of a user executing predetermined instructions based on manipulating a set of value parameters. This is discussed in greater detail in Chapter 24.
3. The United States 107th Congress has introduced several bills on the issues of Internet taxation: Internet Tax Moratorium Equity Act [S.1542.IS], New Economy Tax Fairness Act or NET FAIR Act [S.664.IS], Internet Tax Fairness Act of 2001[H.R.2526.IH], Internet Tax Moratorium and Equity Act [S.1567.IS].

Chapter 20

1. WAP stands for wireless application protocol, and is a set of specifications for developing web-like applications that run over wireless networks. The WAP technology is similar to Internet technology, optimized for small, narrowband client devices (such as mobile phones) and limited over-the-air bandwidth.

Chapter 22

1. Hunt and Murray, p. 102.
2. Evolve Software, Inc. Available at: http://www.services.com.
3. Changepoint Corporation. Available at: http://www.changepoint.com.
4. Intuit is rapidly becoming a trusted brand that instils the same confidence that consumers have in traditional banks. With the introduction of QuickBooks, small businesses will also discover this and may provide a lower cost alternative to traditional fee structures in business banking.

Chapter 23

1. US House 106th Congress, 2nd Session, HR 5571: Electronic Privacy Protection Act. ONLINE. Thomas Database. Available at: http://thomas.loc.gov/cgi-bin/query/z?c106HR05571.
2. US House 106th Congress, 2nd Session, HR 5430: Consumer Online Privacy and Disclosure Act. ONLINE. Thomas Database. Available at: http://thomas.loc.gov/cgi-bin/query/z?c106:HR.5430.
3. US Senate 106th Congress, 2nd Session, S 3180: Spyware Control and Privacy Protection Act of 2000. ONLINE. Thomas Database. Available at: http://thomas.loc.gov/cgi-bin/query/z?c106:S.3180.
4. US Senate 106th Congress, 2nd Session, S 2928: Consumer Internet Privacy Enhancement Act. ONLINE. Thomas Database. Available at: http://thomas.loc.gov/cgi-bin/query/z?c106:S.2928.
5. US Senate 106th Congress, 2nd Session, S 2606: Telecommunications and Electronic Commerce Privacy Act. ONLINE. Thomas Database. Available at: http://thomas.loc.gov/cgi-bin/query/z?c106:S.2606.
6. US House 106th Congress, 2nd Session, HR 5430: Consumer Online Privacy and Disclosure Act. ONLINE. Thomas Database. Available at: http://thomas.loc.gov/cgi-bin/query/z?c106:HR.5430.
7. US Senate and US House 107th Congress, ONLINE. Thomas Database. Available at: http://thomas.loc.gov.
8. M. Keating, 'Net accounts for only 3 per cent of card fraud', *The Guardian Unlimited* (23 June, 2001).

Chapter 24

1. Virtual Private Banker is a concept of IBM's Financial Services. Available at: http://www.ibm.com/industries/financialservices.
2. Financialbot.com AG is a subsidiary of the Incam AG group, a stock market information service which specializes in the asset management of shares and investment fund deposits as well as the marketing of investment products.
3. Stolfo, Salvatore J. JAM Project. Columbia University: Available at: http://www.cs.columbia.edu/~sal/JAM/PROJECT.
4. AgentBuilder, Reticular Systems, Inc. Available at: http://www. agentbuilder.com.
5. Agentis. Available: http://www.agentisinternational.com/.
6. PortfolioManager, Artificial Life, Inc. Available at: http://www.artificial-life. com/products/portfoliomgr.asp.
7. WealthManager, Artificial Life, Inc. Available at: http://www.artificial-life.com/product s/wealthmgr.asp.
8. Botizen, VQ Interactive Sdn Bhd. Available at: http://www.botizen.com/ product.html.
9. vRep, NativeMinds. Available at: http://www.nativeminds.com.
10. The Arcadia Project, Department of Information and Computer Science, University of California, Irvine. Available at: http://www.ics.uci.edu/ Arcadia/atUCI.html.
11. WebSoft Project, Department of Information and Computer Science, University of California, Irvine. Available at: http://www1.ics.uci.edu/pub/websoft.
12. Infogate purchased Pointcast in 1999. Available at: http://www.infogate.com.

Chapter 25

1. R. Shapiro, US Under-Secretary of Commerce for Economic Affairs, US Department of Commerce. Available at http://www.ecommerce.qov/ede/ intro.html.
2. US Air Group. Available at: www.usair.com.
3. J. Markham, *The Future of Shopping* (Basingstoke: Macmillan – now Palgrave Macmillan, 1998) p. 119.
4. ISPs means Internet service providers. Typically, it refers to a firm that supplies the connection to the internet or 'last mile' of service to the customer. Examples are firms such as AOL, Compuserve and NTL.

Chapter 26

1. Hunt and Murray, pp. 147–8.

2. C. Dyer, *Standards of Living in the Later Middle Ages: Social Change in England c.1200–1520* (Cambridge: Cambridge University Press, 1989) p. 207.

Chapter 28

1. J. DiVanna, 'How to Create Real Value in Financial Services Using the Internet', NetMarkets Europe: *City Insiders Forum*. London (June 2001).
2. AusMarkets Ltd. Available at: http://www.ausmarkets.com.au.

Chapter 30

1. A. J. Viscio, and B. A. Pasternak, 'Toward a New Business Model', *Strategy and Business*, 3 (1996).

REFERENCES

D. Archibugi and B-A. Lundvall (eds) *The Globalizing Learning Economy* (Oxford: Oxford University Press, 2001).

R. Buckminster Fuller, *Critical Path* (New York: St. Martin's Press, 1981).

C. Christensen, *The Innovator's Dilemma: How Disruptive Technologies can Destroy Established Markets* (Cambridge, MA: Harvard University Press, 1997).

R. Clifton and E. Maughan, *Twenty-five Visions: The Future of Brands* (Basingstoke: Macmillan – now Palgrave Macmillan, 2000).

G. Davies, *A History of Money from Ancient Times to the Present Day* (Cardiff: University of Wales Press, 1996).

Dictionary of Banking and Finance (Middlesex: Peter Collin Publishing, 2000).

C. Dyer, *Standards of Living in the Later Middle Ages: Social Change in England c.1200–1520* (Cambridge: Cambridge University Press, 1989).

C. England, 'Are Banks Special?' *Regulation* 14.2 (1991).

H. Engler and J. Essinger (org.) *The Future of Banking* (London: Reuters, 2000).

J. A. Goddard, P. Molyneux and J.O. Wilson, *European Banking: Efficiency, Technology and Growth* (Chichester: John Wiley & Sons, 2001).

M. Hammer and J. Champy, *Reengineering the Corporation: A Manifesto for Business Revolution* (New York: HarperCollins, 1993).

E. Hunt and J. M. Murray, *A History of Business in Medieval Europe 1200–1550* (Cambridge: Cambridge University Press, 1999).

G. Irwin, P. Lockmiller and L. Altman, 'Insurers: How to Win the Web Finance Wars', *Strategy and Business*. 24, Third Quarter (2001).

M. de Kare-Silver, *e-Shock: the New Rules* (Basingstoke: Macmillan – now Palgrave Macmillan, 1998).

N. Machiavelli, *Discourses on Livy* (Oxford: Oxford University Press, 1997).

N. Machiavelli, *The Prince* (New York: Penguin Books, 1999).

G. Mankiw, and D. Weil, 'The Baby Boom, the Baby Bust, and the Housing Market', *Regional Science and Urban Economics* (1989).

J. Markham, *The Future of Shopping* (Basingstoke: Macmillan – now Palgrave Macmillan, 1998).

C. Mayer and X. Vives (eds) *Capital Markets and Financial Intermediation* (Cambridge: Cambridge University Press, 1993).

D. A. Norman, *The Invisible Computer: Why Products can Fail, The Personal Computer is so Complex, and Information Appliances are the Solution* (Cambridge: MIT Press, 1998).

S. J. Park, 'The Future of Brands', Rita Clifton and Ester Maughan (org.) *Twenty-five Visions: The Future of Brands* (Basingstoke: Macmillan – now Palgrave Macmillan, 2000).

M. Porter, *Competitive Advantage: Creating and Sustaining Superior Performance* (Free Press, 1985).

M. Quennell and C. H .B. Quennell, *A History of Everyday Things in England 1066 to 1499* (London: B.T. Batesford, 1931).

W. D. Raisch, *The eMarketplace Strategies for Success in B2B eCommerce* (New York: McGraw-Hill, 2001).

A. Ries and L. Ries, *The 11 Immutable Laws of Internet Branding* (London: Harper-Collins Business, 2000).

N. Saul, *Richard II* (London: Yale University Press, 1997).

W. Shakespeare, *Romeo and Juliet* (Mitcham, Victoria: Penguin, 1959).

Staff, 'System aimed at cutting red tape', *The Guardian Unlimited* (19 November 2001).

M. Treacy and F. Wiersema, *The Discipline of Market Leaders* (Reading, MA: Perseus Books, 1997).

J. Viscio, and B. A. Pasternak, 'Toward a New Business Model', *Strategy and Business* 3 (1996).

F. Wiersema, *Customer Intimacy: Pick Your Partners, Shape Your Culture, Win Together* (London: HarperCollins Business, 1997).

INDEX

A

ABN-Amro, 131–2
Acciaiuoli, *see* Middle Ages, super-
  companies
action agenda
  economical, 8
  eMarketplaces, 71, 73–4
  financial services, 6, 145, 158, 240–1
  growth, 86
  payment systems, 172, 176
  privacy, 187–8
  technology, 152
  value creation, 20–2
Africa, 101–5, 142
  branding, 101–5
AgentBuilder: Agents for Electronic
  Commerce, 192
Agentis International, 193
Agentland.com, 193
AIB, *see* Allied Irish Banks
ALife-BannerBot, 194
ALife-PortfolioManager, 193
ALife-WealthManager, 193
Allianz Investmentbank, 132
Allied Irish Banks, 132
Amalfi merchants, 99, 164
Amazon.com, 184, 195, 201, 210
Amphicar, 73
ANZ Banking Group, 114, 227
AOL, 177, 201
Application Service Provider, 32–3,
  134–41, 210
Arab banking, *see* Middle Eastern
  banking
Arcadia, 194
Artificial Life Inc., 193

Ashton, 193
Asia, 91, 106–13, 142, 158, 166
  AsianNet, 112
  financial services, 106–13
  insurance, 60
ASP, *see* Application Service Provider
AsianNet, 112
AsianNet Trade InfoCenter, 112
Asia-Pacific Economic Cooperation, 112
Asiatravel.com, 86
Asiatravelmart.com, 86
Atlantic Mortgage, 131
ATM, 89, 97, 122, 128, 139
Atriax, 210
AusMarkets Ltd., 114, 117, 227
Australia, 114–17
  AusMarkets Ltd. 114, 117, 227
  Australian Artificial Intelligence
    Institute, 193
  BankWest, 116–17
  BarterCard Trading Program, 11
  Commonwealth Bank of Australia,
    114, 227
  economy, 114–17
  National Australian Bank, 114, 227
  Westpac Banking Corporation, 114,
    227
Australian Artificial Intelligence
  Institute, 193
Austrian National Bank, 132
Autobytel, 203
avatars, 42, 191, *see also* valagents
AXA, 132

B

B2B, *see* business-to-business